the CIA

against Che

the CIA against Che

Adys Cupull / Froilán González

Capitán San Luis Printing House
Havana, Cuba, 2009

Translated by: **Germán Piniella Sardiñas**
Overhaul: **Jacinto Valdés-Dapena**
Cover design: **Eugenio Sagués Díaz**
Digital composition: **Zoe Cesar Cardoso/ Julio Cubría**

ISBN: 978-959-211-314-5

Editorial Capitán San Luis, Ave. 38 no. 4707 e/ 40 y 47, Playa, Havana, Cuba. Email: direccion@ecsanluis.rem.cu

Índice

The role of the CIA in Bolivia's repression / 71

The role of the CIA in Che's Murder / 107

International repercussions of Che's assassination / 135

CIA agents against Regis Debray and Ciro Roberto Bustos / 146

Che's Diary in Bolivia and the new CIA disinformation campaign / 160

Revelations of Bolivia's former Minister of the Interior Antonio Arguedas about the CIA's interference in his country's internal Affairs / 173

Contradictions at top government level and the Bolivian Armed Forces. Permanent interference of the United States / 201

The CIA's plan against Ovando's and Juan José Torres' government / 230

The CIA destabilizes Juan José Torres' government / 274

To Commanders Ernesto Che Guevara,
Inti and Coco Peredo and to the Bolivians, Peruvians and
Cubans of the Ñacahuasú Guerrilla.

To Tania, Imilla and Maya.

To Jenny Koeller and Elmo Catalán, whose lives were cut
short as the work that was dreamed and begun.

To Giangiacomo Feltrinelli.

To Benjo Cruz and the Teoponte guerrillas.
To Fathers Luis Espinal and Mauricio Lefebre, priests that
were murdered for practicing true Christianism in the service of
Bolivia's dispossessed.

To the young Bolivians massacred
in 10, Harrington St, La Paz.

To the miners, peasants, students, members of religious
orders, intellectuals, and all who have laid down their lives in the
attempt to achieve the happiness of the struggling, noble and
generous Bolivian people.

The CIA and the US embassy take action against the guerrilla movement in Bolivia

The National Liberation Army of Bolivia is born

On November 3, 1966, Commander Ernesto Che Guevara de la Serna arrived in La Paz, the capital city of Bolivia, with a passport issued in Montevideo in the name of Adolfo Mena González, a Uruguayan national. He was also carrying credentials signed and stamped by the head of the Office of the Presidency of Bolivia's National Information Department, Gonzalo López Muñoz, identifying the bearer as a special envoy of the Organization of American States (OAS) commissioned to perform a study and to gather information on the economic and social relations that prevailed in the Bolivian countryside.

Next day he met with Iván, codename for a member of the urban network whose true identity has not yet been revealed. Acting on Che's instructions, Iván had settled in Bolivia as a prosperous businessman, using the ID of a person who had agreed to stay underground so long as the mission lasted. Iván had been trained in surveillance and countersurveillance techniques, data collection and reporting methods, counterintelligence, visual surveillance, security measures, radio communications, coding and decoding, and invisible ink.

In La Paz, Iván started carrying out underground and compartmentalized activities and on November 4, 1966, he established secret contacts with Alberto Fernández Montes de Oca, codename *Pacho,* at El Prado Restaurant, located on El Prado Boulevard, half a block from the centric Copacabana Hotel. Through Pacho, Che scheduled a meeting with Iván for 8 p.m. at a safe house where he debriefed him regarding the work he had done so far and gave him new instructions.

On the night of the 5th, Che left for Ñacahuasú where he arrived late on the night of the 7th. Iván was to remain in La Paz pending the arrival of other comrades whom he had to take to safe houses. After that, other members of the urban network would take care of them, ensuring their protection and transportation to the guerrilla area. Each traveled along previously established routes using specific means of transportation with utmost secrecy.

The last guerrillas to arrive in La Paz were Jesús Suárez Gayol, codename *El Rubio,* (Blond) and Antonio Sánchez Díaz, codename *Marcos,* who were taken to Ñacahuasú by Iván himself. At the guerrilla camp, Che met with Iván, gave him new instructions and agreed to his request to marry a Bolivian girl he had fallen for. She was the daughter of a renowned politician, a member of the National Parliament and a close friend of President René Barrientos Ortuño, who was his business partner and a frequent visitor. The girl's father wanted Iván to establish links with the Bolivian president with the aim of developing an agricultural project in the department of Beni, an important area where Che was planning to open a guerrilla center. Ivan's relations with the family would allow him to make friends in military circles and visit various barracks.

The group of Cubans and most of the Bolivians finally got together on December 31. During that period, Che met with members of the urban support network: Rodolfo Saldaña, Loyola Guzmán, Julio Dagnino Pacheco, Sánchez, Iván, and Tamara Bunke Bider (*Tania.*) He also held a meeting with Juan Pablo Chang-Navarro, a Peruvian known as *El Chino* (the Chinaman); Moisés Guevara, leader of the miners, and Mario Monje, Secretary General of the Bolivian Communist Party (PCB).

Meanwhile, the members of the guerrilla group went on treks, explorations, and reconnaissance trips to get acquainted with the terrain. They set up and organized camps, built tunnels and conditioned caves, set up the radio equipment, opened an observatory, dug trenches, assigned operators to the different posts, studied Quechua and carried out defense drills. These preparations took up all their time until January 31, 1967.

On February 1st, they began exploring up to the Grande, Masicuri and Rosita Rivers and the Tatareada area with the purpose of familiarizing themselves with the terrain. This gave them a chance to get more rigorous training, and also to analyze the possibilities of organizing peasants into groups and of establishing contact with them.

During the period when Che and the guerrilla group went exploring, two members deserted. On March 11, Vicente Rocabado Terrazas and Pastor Barrera Quintana, two of the men who had arrived on February 14, abandoned the group. They went to the 4th Army Division, stationed at the town of Camiri and provided the Bolivian army and its intelligence services with detailed information, the first indication of Che's presence in Ñacahuasú along with Bolivian, Cuban and Peruvian guerrillas. They also mentioned Tania, Frenchman Regis Debray, Argentine Ciro Roberto Bustos and Peruvian Juan Pablo Chang-Navarro. They led the army, first by air and then by land, to the camps that had been set up. Some time later, it became known that Vicente Rocabado had worked for the secret police and for army intelligence.

Right after the army was tipped off by the deserters, President René Barrientos Ortuño immediately called on the US for assistance and coordinated with the intelligence services of Argentina, Brazil, Chile, Peru and Paraguay.

On March 17, guerrilla Salustio Choque Choque was taken prisoner while carrying a message. Several days later, the US military attaché in Bolivia, Colonel Milton Buls, CIA Station Chief John Tilton, officer Edward N. Fogler, and a Cuban-born agent known as Eduardo González, traveled to Camiri to question the two deserters and the prisoner.

Despite all the information in the hands of the army and the CIA, the first military clash took place on March 23 with catastrophic results for the Bolivian army: the guerrillas occupied the enemy 3 mortars with 64 shells, 2 bazookas, 16 Mauser rifles with 2,000 rounds, 3 Uzi submachine guns with 2 clips each, a .30 caliber machine gun with two ammunition belts and the operations plan;

in addition, the army sustained 7 dead and 14 were taken prisoner, among the latter, Major Hernán Plata Ríos and Captain Augusto Silva Bogado, commanders of the military units.

Alarmed by the guerrilla victory, Colonel Milton Buls traveled to the United States to request urgent assistance. The answer was immediate. Advisors, intelligence officers, Rangers-2 equipment, ammo and food rations were hastily dispatched while the Bolivian Army Chief of Staff, General Leon Kolle Cueto, set out on a tour to Brazil, Argentina and Paraguay to ask for aid of the local military commands.

On March 25, 1967, Che met with all his men and they all agreed to give their guerrilla the name of National Liberation Army of Bolivia.

The government immediately unleashed an all-out campaign of repression, which resulted initially in the detention of Ernesto Guzmán, Moisés Arenas, Lidio Carrillo, Antonio Cejas, Mariano Huerta, Humberto Ramírez and other citizens who were considered suspects.

A disinformation campaign is orchestrated

A communiqué released by the Bolivian army on March 27, aimed at manipulating the events of the 23rd, portrayed the actions as follows:

"While units of the Armed Forces were performing a survey of a section of the Vallegrande-Lagunillas road in the Ñacahuasú-Lagunillas sector, soldiers working on the road under Sub-Lieutenant Rubén Amézaga Faure, were the object of a surprise attack by a group of unknown individuals bearing automatic weapons. Sub-Lieutenant Amézaga, 6 soldiers, and Epifanio Vargas, a civilian guide who worked for YPFB (Yacimientos Petrolíferos Fiscales Bolivianos, the government's oil company), were wounded and then cowardly shot dead.

"This preposterous and merciless action, perpetrated while members of the Armed Forces were working to turn into a reality the long-cherished dream of linking the central and southern regions of the country, is further compounded by the pain and the mourning the relatives of the soldiers, workers and peasants are now suffering.

"The timely alert of the survivors helped counteract the attack through the rapid deployment of the troops of the 4th Army Division, with the support of Air Force planes. The aggressors were forced to flee, leaving behind several casualties and some prisoners. In their flight, they abandoned cases containing clothing, various items, pamphlets on guerrilla warfare and Castro-communist propaganda of Cuban origin, as well as a recorder, a portable high-frequency radio and a vehicle (jeep).

"The prisoners, people from the area and the surviving soldiers informed that the attackers were a large group of individuals of different nationalities, among them Cuban, Peruvian, Chinese, Argentine, European and also Bolivian communists. They also said that they were armed with modern automatic weapons and bazookas, unlike those used by our army.

"The Commander in Chief of the National Armed Forces, in fulfillment of the mission enshrined in the political Constitution of the State and of the duty to safeguard national sovereignty and the peaceful existence of the people, has ordered the drastic and immediate eradication of this pocket of insurgency described as a Castro-communist guerrilla.

"The National Armed Forces, in making these events known to the Bolivian people, call upon their sense of patriotism and their lofty democratic and Christian convictions, and request their cooperation in wiping out these international communist groups, wherever they may appear, as the residents of Monteagudo and Muyupampa are already doing."

As of that moment, the Bolivian government unleashed an all-out disinformation campaign, issuing official releases with little, if any, connection with reality. The first army communiqué contained several misrepresentations, regarding the fact that:

• The military were not building roads in the area where the clash had taken place;

• The prisoners had been given humane and respectful treatment;

• The prisoners were set free in safe places, so that they could be picked up easily;

• None had been shot.

• The wounded had received medical attention;

• The guerrillas remained in their positions;

• The Bolivian army had inflicted no casualties nor had they taken any prisoners;

• They had not seized any items or documents;

• The townspeople of Muyupampa and Monteagudo were too distant from the scene of the combat to be able to inform the army.

The anti-guerrilla press campaign saturated all radio stations. In order to make the truth known, Che prepared Communiqué No. 1.

"To the Bolivian people: in the face of reactionary lies, the revolutionary truth.

"Communiqué No. 1

"The group of usurping gorillas, after murdering workers and preparing the conditions for a total handover of our wealth to US imperialism, mocked the people through an electoral farce. When the hour of truth comes and the people take up arms, responding to armed usurpation with armed struggle, they are bent on continuing with their fabrications.

"In the early hours of March 23, forces of the 4th Division, stationed in Camiri, some 35 strong under Major Hernán Plata Ríos, penetrated guerrilla territory along the banks of the Ñacahuasú river. The whole group fell into an ambush prepared by our forces. As a result of this action, our forces seized 25 weapons of all types, including three 60-mm mortars with their corresponding shells, abundant ammo and equipment. Enemy casualties included 7 dead — among them a lieutenant— and 14 prisoners, 5 of them wounded in the clash and later attended to by our health assistants who afforded them the best care our means would allow.

"All prisoners were set free once they were given an explanation of the ideals of our movement.

"The list of enemy casualties is the following: Dead: Pedro Romero, Rubén Amézaga, Juan Alvarado, Cecilio Márquez, Amador Almazán, Santiago Gallardo and the informer and army guide whose second name was Vargas.

"Prisoners: Major Hernán Plata Ríos, Captain Augusto Silva, Privates Edgar Torrico Panoso, Lido Machicado Toledo, Gabriel Durán Escobar, Armando Martínez, Eduardo Ribera and Guido Terceros. The last five were wounded.

"On making known our first action of war, we are laying down what will be the norm of our Army: the revolutionary truth. Our deeds proved the veracity of our words. We regret the innocent blood that was spilt by the fallen soldiers, but it is not with mortars and machine guns that peaceful roads are built, as the puppets in gold-tasseled uniforms affirm, in an

18

effort to fabricate the legend purporting us to be a bunch of murderers. There was not — nor will there ever be — a single peasant that can complain about our treatment or the way we get supplies, save those who, betraying their class, agree to serve as guides or informers.

"Hostilities have begun. In future communiqués we will clearly spell out our revolutionary position. Today we are calling on workers, peasants, intellectuals, on all who believe that the time has come to respond to violence with violence and to rescue a country that has been carved up and sold, slice by slice, to Yankee monopolies, and to raise the living standards of our people, who grow increasingly hungry with each passing day.

National Liberation Army of Bolivia".

On May 1st, International Workers' Day, when the town of Cochabamba was getting ready for the traditional parade, Communiqué No.1 issued by the National Liberation Army of Bolivia was published in the *Prensa Libre* daily.

International news agencies rapidly reproduced the news and mining radio stations re-broadcast it throughout the country. In a fury, Barrientos ordered the Mayor of Cochabamba, Eduardo Soriano Badani, to arrest the editor of the paper, Carlos Beccar, who was placed in solitary confinement, questioned, tried and sentenced to five years in prison. The government was forced to set him free because of pressure by the solidarity of groups of Bolivian journalists and intellectuals, who were joined by other sectors of the country. Pressure was also exerted through demonstrations of the University Federation of Cochabamba, headed by its executive secretary, Alfonso Ferrufino, son of the city's prosecutor, Filiberto Ferrufino, who, at his son's request, filed a writ of habeas *corpus,* stating that the law enshrines and protects press sources.

In response, Barrientos enacted the State Security Bill, which provided that the entire national territory be placed under a state of exception, legally allowing the repressive forces to act freely under the mantle of said bill.

Americans send weapons, food rations and CIA agents

Lieutenant Colonel Redmond E. Weber, commanding officer of the US Army 7th Special Forces Group, reached the town of Santa Cruz on March 27, 1967, accompanied by Major Ralph W. Shelton. On the following day, a US plane landed in the city carrying 15 instructors specialized in anti-guerrilla warfare in Vietnam. On March 28, 1967, Che wrote in his diary that "radio stations are still saturated with news about the guerrillas. We are surrounded by 2,000 men in a radius of 120 kilometers, the siege is growing tighter and, in addition, we are being bombed with napalm [[...]]". The news was denied by the Americans through the State Department, which noted that such an assertion was totally unfounded; however, soon afterwards, the Commander of the Bolivian Air Force, Jorge Belmonte Ardiles, declared that "AT-6 Air Force planes have started to use napalm" with the aim of getting the same excellent results the US Air Force had achieved in Vietnam.

On March 30, several Mustang airplanes stepped up the bombings that had begun on March 24 over the entire area where the guerrillas operated. Barrientos´ statements and the aid requests addressed to neighboring countries gave rise to a wave of comments.

The Chilean morning paper *El Mercurio,* printed in great detail on April 2 a statement by Víctor Paz Estenssoro, the former Bolivian president exiled in Lima: "There is no justification for the international hullabaloo that is going on, or for the shameful request for military assistance. What is actually happening is that in my country there is growing discontent [[...]] The inability of the regime to solve the most pressing problems, the constant persecution of the opposition parties, the system of forced labor, the periodic massacres, the handing over of our national wealth and the sustained increase in the cost of living have made for a state of latent insurrection.".

By April 4, military missions sent as "observers" by the governments of Argentina, Brazil and Paraguay had already arrived in Bolivia. On that day, Argentine journalist Héctor Ricardo García, a correspondent for his country's weekly *Crónica,* reported that on Saturday April 1, a huge C-130 US cargo plane from

Panama had landed at the Santa Cruz military airport carrying military materiel and food rations for the troops involved in anti-guerrilla actions. The cargo was stored until the following day, when they started shuttling it to Camiri on DC-3 planes. Several hours later, a DC-6 of the Argentine Air Force arrived with weapons and other materiel. This was the first of a series of shuttle flights between the Palomar Airport in Buenos Aires, and Santa Cruz, Bolivia. Majors De Lió and Lauría arrived on that plane, as well as the Argentine military and air attachés in Bolivia, Colonel Saúl García Truñón and Commodore Raúl Lartigue, who traveled from La Paz with the aim of establishing an office to coordinate assistance. In the meantime, US intelligence services had been sending several of their agents to Bolivia.

On April 10, there were two more clashes. The first, at 10:20 a.m., was a setback for the army: 3 of its members were killed, 1 was wounded and 7 soldiers were taken prisoners. In addition, the guerrillas seized 6 Garand rifles, 1 M-1 carbine and 4 Mauser rifles. The second clash occurred at 17:00 hours and resulted in the guerrillas seizing 1 Browning, 1 mortar, 15 hand grenades, 4 M-3s, 2 M-1s, 5 Mauser rifles and many other weapons. The army had 7 dead, 6 wounded and 13 of its members were taken prisoners, among them the column commander Major Rubén Sánchez Valdivia. The Bolivian government prohibited all papers from circulating and censored all radio stations.

On April 12, the press reported the arrival of 5 military experts from the US Command in the Panama Canal Zone. They had been sent to set up a jungle warfare and anti-guerrilla training center. The following day, 2 more planes arrived from the Panama Canal, both carrying supplies and weapons. Milton Buls flew in on one of them. He had been entrusted with setting up an office for coordination and advisory services. A press release estimated that some 100 US military were already in Santa Cruz and in the areas of guerrilla operations.

That same day, shortly after noon, the guerrillas started out for the Camiri-Sucre road with the purpose of getting Debray and Bustos out.

The United States, on its part, continued to provide immediate assistance: a Hercules C-130 plane of the US Air Force, fully loaded with weapons, equipment, food supplies and all kinds of military implements, landed in Santa Cruz on April 14 on a direct flight from Panama.

Two days later, a special envoy of the Buenos Aires paper *La Razón* reported that he had been able to detect in Santa Cruz, Camiri and Lagunillas, the presence of US experts well seasoned in actions in Vietnam who formed a hand-picked group whose mission was to serve as advisors to the Bolivian armed forces.

The US Ambassador to Bolivia reports to Washington

The clashes on March 23 and April 10 caused the army 18 dead, 9 wounded, 40 captured and abundant losses in terms of ammunition, food supplies and weapons. Bolivian intelligence service reports recognized the army's weaknesses in terms of operations on the ground as well as in their command. They noted that the morale of the troops was extremely low and comments made by officers, NCOs and soldiers, all former prisoners in the hands of the guerrilla, conveyed despondency and a sense of defeat and impotence that generated a generalized feeling of psychotic fear. Annihilating the guerrillas, they added, would not be easy, since they were well organized, disciplined, with fighting experience, and would receive support from domestic intellectuals, known as *movimientistas* — members of the Revolutionary Nationalist Movement Party in the opposition — teachers, peasants, students and miners, sectors animated by revolutionary effervescence. These reports reflected open distrust for the military with a professional and ethical behavior who questioned the active participation of the Americans, considering it an affront against the dignity of the military institution. Bewilderment and fear gripped Barrientos and his closest henchmen. Douglas Henderson, the Ambassador of the United States to La Paz, personally confirmed to President Lyndon B. Johnson that "communist guerrillas had become established in the Bolivian jungle". His concerns were not taken lightly.

Henderson was born in Massachusetts on October 15, 1914. He got a B. Sc. from the University of Boston in 1940 and two years later he embarked on a diplomatic career as vice consul in the city of Nogales, México, and later in Arica, Chile, and in

Cochabamba, Bolivia, a position he occupied from 1943 to 1947, when he returned home to perform other jobs. He was Assistant Economic Head of the Defense Division in the Department of State and economic advisor in Lima; in 1963 he was appointed ambassador to Bolivia.

From the very beginning his relations with Barrientos were strained, for he opposed the latter's scheme to stage a coup against President Víctor Paz Estenssoro. Henderson followed State Department policy, but at the US Embassy in Bolivia other powers brought pressure to bear —namely Air Force Attaché Edward Fox and the CIA Station, which prevailed.

Initial CIA actions against the Ñacahuasú guerrilla

Che's presence in Bolivia forced the CIA to put an end to the campaign it had launched against the top leaders of the Cuban Revolution regarding Che's disappearance.

In its slanderous campaign, the CIA resorted to its agents and collaborators. It paid journalists, blackmailed others and took advantage of the monopoly over the media to further its own ends: newspapers, magazines, TV newscasts and counterrevolutionary radio stations based in Miami made public a number of interviews with people who, for different reasons, had left the country, some paid off by the Agency and others induced by it. All, however, confirmed that Che had been murdered in Cuba.

Such profuseness of falsehoods on the topic managed to attract the ignorant, some unprofessional individuals and even confuse people of good will. While the campaign raged, the information monopoly silenced all news from Cuba.

The CIA covered up the presence of Che in Ñacahuasú until it managed to create the conditions to counteract the setback its espionage apparatus had suffered when it failed to detect Che's trip and his entry into the country, despite the enormous resources they had used to locate him. The guerrilla group had become established in front of their very noses. A new disinformation campaign had to be orchestrated to replace the old.

In April 1967, US intelligence agencies sent significant groups of officers and agents into La Paz and the guerrilla area, among them experts in disinformation and psychological warfare, while at the same time it took steps to isolate the guerrilla movement in the cities. To this end, they carried out mass arrests, implemented migration controls, performed raids against foreigners, and also set in motion a plan to dismantle urban support and establish prison camps.

The control by US intelligence service increased. On one hand, they hastily trained Bolivian officers, and on the other they took direct command of special operations. They sent other agents to Bolivia, some of them Cuban-born with false identities, whom they introduced into US institutions and firms as auditors and financial experts. Many of them were placed with the Military Intelligence Service and the Ministry of the Interior of Bolivia, among them José Hinojosa, Eduardo González, Miguel Nápoles Infante, Félix Ramos Medina, Julio Gabriel García, Aurelio Hernández, Luis Suárez and Mario González.

The CIA Station in La Paz was reinforced with Charles Langalis, Robert Stevens, William Culleghan, Hugo Murray, William Walter, John Mills, Burdell Merrel, John H. Corr, Stanley Shepard and others. John Tilton was Chief of station. Thomas Dickson, Timothy Towell and John Maisto were under the cover of the US Consulate in Cochabamba,

CIA agents Félix Ramos Medina and Eduardo González were sent to the military operations zones. Aurelio Hernández was put in charge of interrogations and records; Julio Gabriel García was appointed head of the technical department, located in the home of Mrs. Albertina del Castillo, at 2904 Gregorio Reynolds St., in La Paz, leased to a metallurgical engineer, Dimitri Metaxas Gales, and his wife, Mrs. Aghati Soulioti, with an alien registration card number 20385, issued in Sparta, Greece. The house rent was paid monthly by Max Jaldin, a Bolivian born CIA agent. CIA agent Miguel Nápoles Infante worked in press processing and counterintelligence tasks.

The CIA established strict control over the passenger lists of the various airlines, as well as over all foreigners registered in luxury and in less expensive hotels, hostels, rooming houses and inns known as *tambos* that catered mostly to people of scant resources. All suspects were detained and questioned. At the La Paz international airport and in the various border checkpoints, all travelers were questioned by CIA agents.

After the guerrilla events, Miguel Nápoles Infante remained in Bolivia at the service of the CIA. He bought an optical shop on 1156 Potosí St., telephone number 342855. He also married a Bolivian born in Beni by the name of Leonor Elena Calle, with whom he resided at 329 Bueno St., telephone number 366198. In 1988 he moved to the United States and at present lives at 2655 Carolina Avenue, apartment 1005, Miami Beach, Florida. He is known as *El Manco* (One-Arm) due to the fact that he lost an arm in a traffic accident in Cuba.

CIA officers and agents travel to Camiri

At Camiri, CIA officers questioned Majors Hernán Plata Ríos and Rubén Sánchez Valdivia, Captain Augusto Silva Bogado and others who had been taken prisoners by the guerrillas. They showed them a bulky album containing photos of the people who, according to the CIA, might be involved in the guerrilla movement. One of the interrogators was an advisor to Barrientos, Klaus Barbie, a former head of the Nazi-Fascist Gestapo in Lyon, France, responsible for numerous crimes and assassinations during the Nazi occupation, who had brutally tortured detainees linked to the antifascist resistance and sent thousands of French and Jews to mass extermination camps. He had personally tortured and murdered Jean Moulin, Charles de Gaulle's delegate in France under German occupation. Barbie was internationally known as the "Butcher of Lyon". Among his most unconscionable crimes was the extermination in the gas chamber of 44 Jewish children, aged four to sixteen.

In their book *A Criminal to the End: Klaus Barbie in Bolivia*, Bolivian journalist Gustavo Sánchez Salazar, and Elizabeth Reimann, a Czech-Chilean, wrote:

"When the war ended, US Intelligence Services were concerned over the political space occupied by the USSR. Without the least compunction, the Americans resorted to the services of German Gestapo officers; a new enemy had to be countered, 'communism'.

"Another recruit was Klaus Barbie, a war criminal and former SS captain. The murderer of Lyon had not been punished for his war crimes. Far from that, the victors rewarded him. In the spring of 1948 —after thousands of people were killed in an orgy of assassinations— courtesy of the United States Army's Counterintelligence Corps (CIC), Barbie was given a house in the Bavarian city of Augsburg, as well as food supplies, cigarettes and an expense allowance. His job: organizing spy networks for the Americans.

"In 1950 it became obvious that France was searching for Barbie to try him for his crimes against humanity. The CIC decided to give the Nazi criminal a new identity and send him with his family to a distant country where he could start a new life. Klaus Altmann Hansen, a mechanic born in Kronstadt —a non-existing town—, left Europe by the "Rat Route," organized by a Croatian Catholic priest.

"With his wife and two children, 'Altmann' arrived in La Paz, Bolivia, on April 23, 1951 [...]

"In 1964 General René Barrientos, a CIA man, seized power. He appointed Barbie advisor to the Army in the field of counterinsurgency. The German was assigned offices in the Civilian Intelligence Service and in the airport of La Paz [...]"

In 1983, the government of Hernán Siles Suazo deported him to France to be tried for his war crimes.

Another agent sent by the CIA to Camiri was one known as George Andrew Roth, who traveled to Bolivia from Santiago de Chile, where he was temporarily staying. On March 30, 1967, while in Buenos Aires, he contacted South America *Time-Life* correspondent Moisés García. They met two officials of the US Embassy in Argentina. Later Roth got together with the press attaché of the London embassy in that country.

On April 5, Roth arrived in Santa Cruz de la Sierra and met with a member of the US Peace Corps. The following day, he traveled to Camiri and registered at the London Hotel. He was given a safe conduct and a special permit by the head of the Bolivian intelligence services to visit the guerrilla camp, and accompanied the army on trips to various locations in the periphery of the guerrilla zone.

On April 10 he traveled to La Paz. There he held several meetings with CIA officers. The pictures taken by Roth were published in the local newspaper *El Diario*. Six days later he returned to Camiri on a new mission.

He then left for Lagunillas with two CBS-New York cameramen, Argentines Hugo López and Hermes Muñoz. Next day, a guide provided by the military led him to the guerrilla area. On April 19 he reached the place where the guerrillas were camping. His unexpected arrival spurred well-founded suspicion: on his passport his occupation as student had been crossed out and replaced by that of journalist. He said he was a professional photographer free-lancing for some foreign publications. He was carrying documents representing him as an instructor with the Peace Corps and a Puerto Rican visa. In his notebook, they found a questionnaire aimed at verifying whether Che was there under the name of Ramón, and if Tania and Regis Debray were also present. Another mission Roth was to accomplish was to drop chemical substances on the guerrillas' belongings so that trained German shepherd dogs that had been secretly taken to Camiri could trace them. The application of these chemicals was an innovation in the struggle against the revolutionaries on our continent and their use was therefore unknown.

The presence of the dogs was reported by some journalists. Mexican Luis Suárez wrote in *Siempre* magazine (No. 750, of 8 November 1967): "The discovery of this canine reserve by journalists caused great irritation among military intelligence members, since it implied revealing a secret [...]."

The guerrillas allowed Roth to leave the area on April 20. Regis Debray and Ciro Roberto Bustos decide to leave with him. On their arrival to the little town of Muyupampa, all three were arrested and taken to Camiri.

Advised by the CIA, the Bolivian Intelligence Services released a report announcing the death in combat of 7 guerrillas, including Debray, Bustos and Roth. The plan was to have Debray and Bustos given up for dead, then to torture them, make them talk, kill them and do away with the bodies. This was the scheme revealed by CIA agent Eduardo González to Bolivian military collaborators, but the plan misfired when Hugo Delgadillo, a correspondent for *Presencia,* who was in Muyupampa, published several pictures of the detainees.

Colonels Eladio Sánchez Suárez and Alberto Libera Cortez took part in the initial interrogations. They were joined by another two American experts, Theodore Kirsch and Joseph Keller, accompanied by CIA agent Eduardo González, who continued the questioning with Colonel Federico Arana Cerrudo, Chief of Army Intelligence, and Lieutenant Colonel Roberto *Toto* Quintanilla, Ministry of the Interior's Chief of Intelligence.

In May, Kirsch returned, accompanied this time by Lieutenant Colonel Joseph Price and by James Evett.

An American journalist, Lee Hall, stated that Regis Debray's mother had told him that "within 48 hours after his son's arrest, President Barrientos had a dossier on his desk provided by the CIA".

Following instructions from the CIA, Roth, Debray and Bustos were kept under arrest. Each day a male nurse would visit Roth under the pretext of giving him shots against a venereal disease he had contracted in a brothel in Santiago de Chile. His job was to gather all the information Roth had obtained from the detainees. He was also visited by Federico Arana, who gave him food and money, and by a priest from the US Embassy, Andrew Kennedy, who acted as chaplain of the Bolivian army and who was identified as a CIA agent.

On April 25, six days after Roth's visit to the guerrilla camp, there was another confrontation. This time German shepherds were used.

"Shortly after," Che wrote in his diary, "the vanguard appeared and, much to our surprise, it was made up of 3 German shepherds with their guide. The animals were restless but it did not seem to me that they had given away our position; however, they forged ahead and I took a shot at the first dog."

Roth was kept in prison from April 20 to July 8. According to CIA agent Eduardo González, he was released through the intercession of UK Ambassador in La Paz Ronald Bailey at the request of the Embassy of the United States.

Bolivian intelligence sources noted that George Andrew Roth was thought to be an alias, since no relatives had been identified as had been the case with the family members of Regis Debray and Ciro Roberto Bustos.

The United States sends Vietnam war experts to train Bolivian soldiers

Major Ralph W. "Pappy" Shelton, returned to Bolivia on April 23, 1967 to head the Green Beret training center at La Esperanza sugar mill, near Santa Cruz. He was to train soldiers in the use of the same techniques the US had implemented in Vietnam. Shelton had headed similar centers in the Dominican Republic and Laos.

He was accompanied by his aide, Captain Michel Leroy, just back from Saigon.

Other arrivals in Bolivia were Captains Edmond Fricke, William Trimble, Margarito Cruz and other advisors in different fields — weapons, communications, medical care, explosives, intelligence and political doctrine. This center trained 650 soldiers in counterinsurgency.

While the fighting went on, in Santa Cruz several US 4- and 12-seat helicopters were being equipped with gun emplacements to be sent into battle immediately.

On May 8, another combat resulted in the capture of 7 M-1 carbines and 4 Mauser rifles from the army. Ten soldiers were taken prisoners, 2 of them wounded. There was 1 death, that of Lieutenant Henry Laredo, on whom a diary was found where he described Bolivian workers as bone-idle and other insults. Regarding the troops, he commented on the lack of fighting spirit and on how the soldiers cried when they learned of the presence of guerrillas near by. Also he had on him a letter from his wife asking him for a guerrilla's scalp to hang in their living room.

The following day, the guerrillas released the soldiers after tending to the wounded and continued on their way while planes bombed the area.

This new defeat suffered by the army and its manifest incompetence riled the American advisors, who demanded the removal of Colonel Humberto Rocha Urquieta as commander of the 4th Division in Camiri.

Repression against mining, union and political leaders

While in the guerrilla zone the army suffered one defeat after another, in La Paz Barrientos ordered the immediate arrest of the main leaders of the Trade Union Federation of Mine Workers Víctor López, Simón Reyes, Arturo Crespo, Alberto Jara, and of political party leaders Mario Monje, Jorge Kolle Cueto, Guillermo Lora, Oscar Zamora Medinacellis, Carlos Serrate Reich, David Añez and Walter Vázquez Michel. The order also included Juan Lechín Oquendo, secretary general of the powerful Bolivian Workers'

Central (COB) and topmost leader of the National Leftwing Revolutionary Party (PRIN). Lechín, then in Chile, instructed the members of his party to integrate and to support the guerrillas. On May 1, 1967 he sent a message to all Bolivian workers:

"We are once again firm, manning our battle stations in the struggle for the working class and the liberation of our nation from the imperialist yoke.

"The only option is to defend democracy with guns in the hands of the workers and the unemployed. Guerrillas are struggling to free our homeland from the nefarious foreign yoke that has taken over the Presidential Palace and Miraflores Military Headquarters."

After delivering this message, Lechín went to Arica planning to cross the Bolivian border and to make a clandestine entry into his country. He traveled with two Chileans: Luis Valente Rossi, a Communist Party Member of Parliament, and Luis Hederman, a businessman. On reaching the Chilean control point, he was detained and questioned, despite the fact that he was carrying a valid passport in the name of Eduardo Manosera, No. 255717, issued in Buenos Aires in 1962 and renewed on October 31, 1966. The police reported that Lechín had undergone a physical transformation and was carrying a valid document, but that he had not succeeded in hiding his large teeth and two-colored eyes, which led to his detection. However, the Arica daily *La Defensa* revealed that the police was awaiting his arrival after receiving a phone tip that Lechín was on his way to the city accompanied by two individuals.

Lechín was taken to Santiago de Chile, where Senator Salvador Allende took steps to obtain political asylum for him. Barrientos protested irately and issued vulgar statements against Lechín and Chilean leaders. Allende did not deign to give an official response to the insults but, according to media sources, someone had tried to ridicule the Bolivian president by sending him five parrots in a cage, which, on arriving at the border, were confiscated for lacking the necessary health certificates. Three of the birds had been trained and incessantly squawked, "We are guerrillas! Long live Lechín! Long live Fidel! Down with Barrientos!"

Speaking about the guerrilla movement at Santiago, Lechín stated that it was the only path open to the workers for conquering their freedom.

The PRIN issued a document signed by leaders Lidia Gueiler Tejada and Carlos Daza, a blueprint for the establishment of a front in support of the guerrillas as the only way out for Bolivia.

Barrientos retaliated with further violence and repression and ordered that everything be done to capture Lechín Oquendo, Lidia Gueiler Tejada, Carlos Daza, Simón Reyes, René Chacón, Cirilo Valle and Rosendo García Maisman. García Maisman had been shot during the Night of St. John's massacre on June 24, 1967 and bled to death for lack of medical care denied to him by the authorities.

The prisoners in the concentration camps located in the jungles in eastern Bolivia, —named Pekín, Alto Madidi, Ixiamas and Puerto Rico— staged strong protests, denouncing the torture and abuse to which they were subjected. What they got in response was greater cruelty and repression, particularly against Alberto Jara, Reinaldo Veizaga, José Ordóñez, Luis Ninavia, Filemón Escóbar, Oscar Salas, Jorge Echazú, Sinforoso Cabrera, Nelson Capelino, Casiano Amurrio Rocha, Modesto Reinaga, Rudy Cuéllar, Mario Ortuño, Aníbal Vargas, Víctor Reinaga, René Olivares, Oscar Sanjinés, Walter Vázquez Michel and Luis Zaral. Barrientos was bent on wiping out the opposition at any price.

In the face of stepped-up repression and the mass transfer of union and political leaders to the concentration camps, university students immediately showed their fighting solidarity and, as a gesture of public support, agreed to have Ramiro Barrenechea, vicepresident de University Confederation of Bolivia, together with Raúl Ibarguen and Osvaldo Trigo, of the University Federation of La Paz, go to the concentration camps carrying letters, news and other requirements. When the young men came to Riberalta, the last village before reaching those isolated spots, they were questioned by the Army Intelligence Service.

For lack of roads, travel in the Bolivian Amazon jungle is done only by air or by river. The concentration camps were natural prisons. Nobody could get out. The jungle saw to that. Consequently, all the intelligence services had to do was control airports and landing strips. The student leaders learned that, in addition to

Ixiamas, Alto Madidi, Puerto Rico and Pekín, there were detention centers in the jungle named after cities or countries: Vienna, London, Argentina, Moscow and Paris, a curious paradox considering those dismal, isolated, godforsaken places. The horrors of the concentration camps were described at that time in several chronicles by journalists and many of them have been assembled in a book, *Alto Madidi*.

The young men also learned of the existence in the jungle of a secret US base, with landing strips, boasting 18-20 comfortable houses with air conditioning and intercoms. The base was off limits for Bolivians. According to Riberalta locals, the authorities claimed that the premises were the seat of a Language Summer School, but the residents were somewhat puzzled by the fact that during the night they heard planes flying overhead and that the people in the facilities even came to pick up bread in their light aircraft. Several sources noted that it was a radio communications base to spy on the guerrillas; others indicated that it was a geological exploration center whose task was to search the region for precious stones that were secretly transferred to the United States. Journalist Andrew Saint George —a confirmed CIA agent— revealed that the Americans followed the movements of the guerrillas with sophisticated equipment and instruments that measured body heat and the smoke from guerrilla cooking fires. Some time later it became known that this method had been used in Vietnam.

Other sources believe that the CIA got wind of potential guerrilla operations in the area of the department of Beni and that they started taking steps in preparation for that contingency. Obvious signs led them to fear the uprising of the indigenous groups. In the town of Ascensión de Guarayos, community leader Salvador Iraipí and his followers raided the office of the Criminal Investigation Division (DIC) and the police headquarters.

After the guerrilla-related events, there were statements claiming that the secret base or Language Summer Institute was located on the shores of Lake Tumichucua, which means "beautiful lake" in the Moxeña tongue.

The student and university movement, organized workers, peasants and intellectuals and community organizations incessantly criticized the local presence of the United States and publicly accused the CIA of using the institution to study native ethnic groups, their customs, languages and traditions. What generated utmost indignation was the revelation that in the indigenous communities the Americans were sterilizing women of reproductive age. This had such an enormous repercussions that the people went as far as to attack and kidnap several Americans. Bolivian filmmaker Jorge Sanjinés reflected these events in the film, *Yawar Mallcu,* which in Quechua means "blood of the condor".

In the wake of this scandal and pressured by the people, the facilities of the Language Summer Institute were placed under the Ministry of Education and Culture in 1982. Minister Alfonso Camacho Peña immediately legalized ownership by the Ministry and established the Rural Teachers' Training School.

The functions of the US secret base that operated all the time that the guerrilla movement existed in the Bolivian jungle have so far remained shrouded in mystery.

Barrientos orders the destruction of *Crítica*

Crítica, a magazine edited by Bolivian journalist Juan José Capriles, featured an article decrying the various crimes committed by the authorities and the internment of people in the concentration camps. The magazine later published that Che Guevara was in Bolivia. These reports incensed Barrientos, who told journalists that *Critica* was an infamous libel, an indecent and sensationalist rag, and its editor an immoral and unethical liar who, in order to boost sales, had resorted to fabrications by raising a dead body from the grave, for "Che Guevara has been dead for a long time".

From that moment on, Juan José Capriles was the butt of his enemies' jokes and derision. The magazine's premises were raided on more than one occasion, the editor received several death threats and his property was destroyed.

Some time later, when Capriles found out that Paraguayan Dr. Francisco Silva, had been arrested, charged with transporting weapons and organizing guerrillas in his country, Capriles considered that Silva might be connected with Che and decided to interview him. To that end, he negotiated with Colonel Fernando Pastrana, warden of the La Paz prison, a visit to that institution. Accompanied by photographer Antonio Equino, he toured the whole establishment and saw the inhuman conditions in which the Bolivian inmates lived. He managed to get into the concealed section, called Guanay, where there was practically no sunlight but where humidity was so great that, more often than not, if the prisoners did not die they left with pneumonia or tuberculosis. Capriles also visited other prisons in the country until he finally found Dr. Silva in an institution in Santa Cruz. Silva, however did not provide him with the information he was seeking. When Capriles learned about clashes with the guerrillas in Ñacahuasú, he set out for Camiri to report on the events.

In his article, Capriles described the terrible conditions the Bolivian soldiers had to put up with, their blistered feet, their bodies covered with rags, the lack of food and medical care. He also revealed that the two officers killed in combat on April 10 – Lieutenants Luis Saavedra Arambel and Jorge Ayala Chávez— had been sent to the theater of operations as punishment, because they were young officers who criticized the atmosphere of repression that pervaded the army. In his story, Capriles asserted that Che was with the guerrillas and published an anthem dedicated to him.

Barrientos, disgruntled once again, ordered that Capriles be detained and the all the issues of the magazine be seized. Capriles was taken to Santa Cruz for questioning. He was then brought before Barrientos, who said to him: "This time you told the truth — I wish it would have been a lie— but it will cost you more than all the lies you've ever told."

Capriles was sent to La Paz under arrest, charged with having links with Che and with serving as liaison with the guerrillas. CIA agent Julio Gabriel García questioned him. *Crítica* was dismantled and all its properties stolen. Capriles had two daughters in La Paz, aged five and seven, who were left helpless and destitute. In the end, after many efforts and complaints from all quarters, the girls were sent to their mother, then residing in Brazil.

All those in the opposition were branded as "guerrillas". For example, if someone wanted to ruin or destroy a rival businessman or small industrialist, it would suffice to report that person as a guerrilla collaborator and all the weight of the repression would fall on him, without any further investigation or inquiry into the charge. When a top official, politician, military or policeman coveted someone's wife or girlfriend, the man was immediately accused of being a guerrilla and was terrorized to such a point as to force him to leave town. If the interested party had enough leverage, he would pressure the individual into flying to exile. Houses were raided and normally ransacked, and all belongings and valuables were stolen.

The order came that Capriles was to be shot in the back while allegedly attempting to escape. The order was not executed because the military officer who was to do the shooting was acquainted with Capriles when they had been previously exiled together: He helped him escape and Capriles made it to the Uruguayan embassy, where he applied for political asylum.

The guerrillas arrive in Caraguatarenda

On May 28, 1967 the guerrillas captured the hamlet of Caraguatarenda. This event had great political and military significance because of the village's location, right on the road connecting Camiri and Santa Cruz. A short time later, two trucks and two jeeps carrying passengers and oil workers arrived; it was they who talked about what had happened. The army and the guerrillas clashed again on May 30, with a balance of two soldiers killed and several wounded. War correspondent José Luis Alcázar noted that all efforts and commands on the part of the military leaders failed to stop the panic-stricken soldiers, who fled in disarray. The following day they clashed once again. Several soldiers were wounded and a civilian guide was killed. A sense of defeat spread like wildfire among the military ranks.

Diego Martínez Estévez, a Bolivian military, wrote in his book *Ñancahuazú. Notes for the Military History of Bolivia* that a soldier cried out from a wrecked vehicle: "I'm a believer, for God's sake, don't kill me." An officer stopped firing and started kicking him to force him to take cover. Far from obeying, the soldier turned on his "protector" and attempted to hit him with the butt of his rifle while the other man was firing from a different angle. Observing the hysterical attitude of the soldier, the man jumped him and knocked him down. "For the next three days," he added, "this unit suffered from hunger and thirst; officers and troops, in an effort to survive, were obliged to hunt and to get water from the

35

carahuatas; some tried to assuage their hunger with coca leaves and most of them, unable to control themselves, wrested the caramañolas from the Trinidad Company, which was late in arriving at El Espino due to lack of transportation".

All throughout May, repression was rampant in the countryside: numerous groups of humble peasants put in prison, their livestock and crops stolen, their properties burned down. Owners of trucks and jeeps were forced to place them at the service of the army; farmhands and peasants had to march before the troops as guides. Terror reigned everywhere.

Several peasants from Masicuri and surrounding areas were arrested and taken to Vallegrande, where they were savagely tortured. CIA agent Julio Gabriel García took part in the questioning. Military control posts were established in all the accesses to cities and towns, as well as in the various highways and roads that led to the guerrilla zone. Bolivian journalist Jorge Rossa narrated that 18 military control barriers were set up on the Santa Cruz Cochabamba road, where passengers were subjected to a brutal search, particularly their documents.

"A young French ethnologist, a globetrotter," he wrote, "was detained as he sailed alone on his canoe on the Mamoré River, simply because he had a beard and was a foreigner [...]." "You were in mortal danger then if you grew a beard."

"A 14-year-old boy," he added, "was beaten in his own home by the thugs of the DIC simply because they had found a pair of Japanese rubber boots on the premises. What more evidence of the fact that he was planning to join the guerrilla and not simply that he was going fishing in the Yapacaní River?"

Despite the vicious repression, the peasants did not hide their sympathy for the guerrillas. In his summary of the month of May, Che wrote that the peasants were gradually growing less afraid and being won over. "It is a slow and patient endeavor."

Inti Peredo in his book *My Campaign with Che* stated that during the three months of fighting they caused the army more than 50 casualties, counting dead, wounded and prisoners, including three high-ranking officers. A large amount of weapons, ammunition, uniforms and food supplies had been seized. But the most noticeable achievement had been the demoralization and loss of fighting spirit on the part of the soldiers, which contrasted significantly with the aggressiveness and bravery of the guerrillas.

Meanwhile, the trial against Debray was commented throughout the world. Journalists, intellectuals, members of religious orders and government leaders manifested their concern for his life. A solidarity committee was established in Paris, according to a UPI news report dated May 9. The report indicated that a group of intellectuals made up by 38 scholars, three Nobel Prize winners, various academicians, writers, Catholic priests and Protestant pastors had sent a message to the Bolivian authorities in favor of Debray. Che wrote in his diary that the clamor around the Regis Debray case had contributed more to the prestige of the guerrilla movement than ten victorious battles.

The CIA devises a plan to interrogate Bolivian revolutionary Jorge Vázquez Viaña

On May 27, 1967 radio stations reported that guerrilla Jorge Vázquez Viaña had escaped from Camiri prison. He was wounded in a leg at the time he was captured on April 27. Subsequently he was taken to the barracks and tortured. Since the guerrilla refused to talk, the CIA devised a plan through a Cuban born agent to obtain information of the brave young man.

Bolivian war correspondent José Luis Alcázar wrote on the matter: "Radio Sararenda broadcast a 'protest' from a foreign journalist who said that Camiri military authorities had not authorized him to interview Vázquez Viaña."

Alcázar said that the alleged journalist was CIA agent Eduardo González and that the guards allowed Vázquez Viaña to overhear his protest. Thus, when the military authorized González to enter the prison, he "began the interview asking him about his health. Vázquez answered in monosyllables. Suddenly there was a change in the interview... In a whisper González tells the guerrilla: 'I am not a journalist. I am Fidel's envoy. I have come from Havana to find out what has happened to Che. We haven't heard from him'."

According to Alcázar, Vázquez Viaña was surprised, and although initially he did not believe González, the Cuban accent finally convinced him and he fell for the CIA's ruse.

On May 27, with the recording of the interview, Roberto *Toto* Quintanilla told Vázquez Viaña that the journalist was really a CIA agent and tried to blackmail him. Quintanilla suggested an escape plan and a later trip to the Federal Republic of Germany, where the guerrilla's wife and children were, in exchange for information on the urban support network and the location of safe houses. Outraged, Vázquez Viaña jumped on him, but Quintanilla and his assistants beat him and fractured both of his arms. Then he ordered his death.

His body was thrown in the jungle from a helicopter piloted by Jaime Niño de Guzmán and Carlos Rafael Estívariz.

The news about the escape was a cover for the murder.

The CIA and its Intromission in the Armed Forces and Other Bolivian sectors

Chaos, disorder, demoralization and murders in the army

On January, 1967, troops of the army's 4th Division with its seat at Camiri, included 10 commanding officers, 21 officers, 54 non-commissioned officers and 244 soldiers. The military command was the following:

Colonel Humberto Rocha Urquieta, Division Commander; Colonel Juan Fernández Cálzaga, Chief of Staff; Major Armando Reyes Villa, Operations; Lt. Col. Carlos Romero Arévalo, Intelligence; Lt. Col. Vicente Antezana Negrete, Personnel; Lt. Col. Carlos Klagges Strinford, Logistics.

All were appointed by General Alfredo Ovando Candia, Chief of the Bolivian Armed Forces. On discovering the guerrillas, troops of the 4th Division were increased significantly. In late March the division included 12 commanding officers, 42 officers, 93 non commissioned officers and 1,619 soldiers, for a total of 1,770 men. In May troops were increased to 2,500 men.

After the combat on March 23, the 4th Division's military command was seriously challenged because the guerrillas had been organized and set up in the area unnoticed, and in the first combat the division was definitely trounced.

Disorganization, chaos and demoralization were rampant in the army in an impressive manner; incompetence of the leaders was increasingly obvious. Yet, loyalty to Ovando was more important than military leadership, and for that reason they kept their posts with the exception of the chief of intelligence, who became the scapegoat and was blamed for all the errors. He was substituted by Capt. Hugo Padilla, also a trusted Ovando man.

When soldiers arrived at Camiri they found there were no barracks, dormitories nor the proper place to keep their belongings. When they returned for some reason, almost everything was missing, a fact that sparked serious conflicts.

The number of casualties due to sickness increased month after month. There were only three medics in the division. After the combat on April 10 there were more than 40 casualties due to diarrhea, intestinal disorders or dysentery. There were neither doctors nor supplies to treat the wounded and sick; according to military reports there was only iodine and ointments. The combat casualties were transported in makeshift stretchers through places where there were no roads.

General Gary Prado Salmón wrote: "These details undoubtedly affected the troops' morale, for a soldier that knows that he will be treated promptly and efficiently if he is wounded feels more at ease that the one that sees his comrades bleed to death without a dressing to staunch the blood."

Desertions, neglect of missions and mutinies reached dangerous levels, a fact that forced the military high command to open an investigation. According to intelligence reports the result was the following: alarming news about the number of guerrillas that were rumored to be 1,000 armed with modern weapons that included amphibious airplanes; their courage, daring and bravery that made them a disciplined, well organized troop; the number of dead and wounded in the army; the feelings of defeat and impotence communicated by officers and soldiers who had been prisoners of the guerrillas, saying that they were huge men immune to bullets because they were armored. Food was scarce because units usually were supplied by air due to lack of roads in the area.

When operations began, the army's 4th Division had only one helicopter for those missions, and usually it was being repaired, or the pilots refused to fly in bad weather, leaving the army units without food, which meant that soldiers had to fend for themselves, hunting and fishing or foraging for crops and animals from peasants, thus causing terror and indignation among the latter.

In his book Diego Martínez Estévez wrote that three soldiers told their comrades that once they were so hungry they killed and ate one of the scout dogs.

In military units there were soldiers from all over the country who were not previously registered. Thus there was no way to trace them. Also they had no transportation of their own, so they had to requisition trucks, thus creating new conflicts with civilians.

Soldiers had no identity tags and the dead and wounded were abandoned on the battlefield. There was the sad case of a father who came to identify the body of his son, killed on March 23. The army delivered the first corpse they found, but as it had only fifteen ribs the father did not accept it, for his son had twenty four. An officer ordered to give him nine extra ribs and the father left thinking that he was taking home his son's remains.

The case made a deep impression on the rest of troops, for they believed the same could happen to them. To this must be added that frequently officers beat their subordinates for any reason.

In his book *My Campaign with Che* Inti Peredo wrote about the March 23 combat: "We also cured the wounded and explained to the soldiers the objectives of our struggle. They answered that they did not know why they had been ordered to fight us, that they agreed with us, and asked us to execute Major Plata, a despotic officer."

Soldiers who were doing their mandatory military service in mid 1967 had their discharge postponed by decree, with no previous explanation or leave to visit home. Letters and packages accumulated and some officers burned them after stealing valuables from them.

Salaries and extra bonuses that had been promised were not paid and the soldiers' families were left without sustenance. Discomfort grew and mutiny broke out in isolated units, threatening to spread throughout the army at any moment.

Disorder and arbitrariness reached such levels that when the high command requested the names of those to be decorated for bravery in combat in order to boost morale, the first proposals were the paymaster and the dentist, who had not fired a single shot.

In late April an army company stationed at the calamine house mutinied and abandoned its officers. The soldiers were forced back to their post under threat of death.

Some units refused to fight and others mutinied. Diego Martínez Estévez wrote in his book that on April 22 the company led by Captain Fernando Pacheco sent a false report claiming they had clashed with guerrillas and killed 19 of them. Since the report was accepted, the following month he reported that they were chasing guerrillas in the Tirabuzón area, a place far away from where the unit actually was.

The 4th Division launched a big operation and it was discovered that Pacheco had lied. An investigation found that he frequently ordered his subordinates to turn off the radio so as not to receive orders, and also took great pains to avoid the guerrillas. Carlos Monge, one of the company's officers, wrote about Pacheco in his diary: "(…) in his face you could see nervousness and fear he couldn't control, and the worse part is that little by little he was infecting us with it." On another occasion, after an argument with him, he wrote: "It was a strong argument and I decided to leave the company, but when I did my entire platoon followed me, as well as Lince Hinojosa's, so I had to stay. From then on there was no peace in the company."

When Captain Mario Oxa Bustos found that the soldiers of the Bolívar Regiment had deserted he was beside himself and brandishing a pistol forced them back to their combat posts. The soldiers revolted and tried to lynch their officers. Due to the seriousness of the situation Captain Oxa sent a coded message to the high command: "Cif-87/67 Troops of Bolívar Regiment must be court martialed to find the guilty parties who wanted to instigate acts of military rebellion and kill their officers in a situation of international war against bandits."

Barrientos heard of the situation from a report by the US Military Mission at La Paz and in mid April he summoned Mario Agramont, who at the moment was a legal advisor with the traffic police at the city of Tarija.

Agramont received a memorandum with the order to travel immediately to La Paz for a very special meeting. When he reached the Bolivian capital he was received by his brother in law Col. Grover Ferrufino, a close friend of Barrientos and a member of his personal security, ordering him to meet with the President right away.

Barrientos was very clear and precise. He told him about his differences with Ovando, that he did not trust him or the information that Ovando gave him, so he had decided to meet Agramont in La Paz with the proposal that he carry out a very important secret mission. He would go to Camiri and transmit directly to the President from the field of operations all that happened and whatever transpired in the 4th Division. Agramont would transmit coded messages by radio from the Central Bank of Bolivia. Barrientos gave him a personal code for his exclusive use. He also commissioned him as a captain and warned him about the extreme secrecy of the mission, which nobody should know about.

Agramont went to Camiri as a command secretary, appointed to the Intelligence section. He began working with Captain Hugo Padilla, but shortly after Padilla suspected and later was certain that Agramont was working for Barrientos, and from that moment on contradictions and obstacles grew between the two.

During that period four people were arrested –a Brazilian, a Paraguayan and two persons with Uruguayan passports issued in the names of Carlos Alberto Aidar and Ventura Pomar Fernández. All were accused of liaising with the guerrillas, were tortured, murdered and their bodies left in the jungle. Agramont criticized Padilla for what he said were barbarous methods and called for less submission to the Americans and to CIA agents. This argument caused new contradictions.

A few days later there was a new arrival to Camiri in the person of Guido Benavides, a member of the Direction of Criminal Investigations. He was accompanied by several interrogators. Disagreements increased among them.

After several raids in Camiri and nearby towns Marxist literature was discovered at the home of Israel Avilez. Agramont kept some books. Weeks later Padilla made a secret search and on founding the books denounced him to the CIA agents as a Communist infiltrator and suggested a plan to eliminate him.

In June the command of the 4th Division was substituted almost completely. This was the result:

Colonel Luis Antonio Reque Terán, Division Commander.
Colonel Eladio Sánchez Suárez, Chief of Staff.
Colonel Juan Fernández Cálzaga, Logistics General Staff
Major Víctor Castillo Suárez, Operations.
Captain Hugo Padilla, Intelligence.
Captain Humberto Cayoja Riart, Personnel.
Lt. Col. Alberto Libera Cortez, Logistics.

Discord between Padilla and Agramont increased and reached its highest level after the arrest of an Argentinean girl from the province of Salta, who was captured with a handbag full of dollars. Padilla tortured and raped her. According to information in Camiri, the girl traveled every year to the areas where the guerrillas were operating to buy hair from Guaraní Indian women and sell it later to a wig factory. Agramont interceded and the girl was set free. But the Argentinean woman refused, because she said that all that were liberated were killed.

Intelligence sources said that Agramont promised her that he would take her to the border and she accepted. Before leaving they went to have dinner at Marieta, Camiri's best restaurant. They found Padilla there, who was drunk and pressed the girl to sleep with him. She accepted and both left for the Chapaco Hotel. The following day it was known that as soon as Padilla undressed the girl took his gun and killed him.

The La Paz newspaper *El Diario* reported that the commander of the army's 4th Division confirmed that the death of Captain Hugo Padilla was part of a guerrilla plot that also included him and other military officers, and that an investigation was under way, but that he could give no further details. He added that two suspects had been arrested and there were clues about a third, the main guerrilla liaison in Camiri. The other two were carpenters. It was also known that Captain Hugo Padilla had been killed with his own gun in a room at the Chapaco Hotel. A woman that had been found with the body inside the room was released later.

The military of the 4th Division launched a fierce repression. Zolio Claure, Miguel Bejerano, Jorge Paredes, and brothers Rogelio and José María Ovando were formally accused. The Argentinean girl, whose name remained unknown, was arrested again, tortured, murdered and her body left in the jungle.

Agramont was accused as an accessory to the chief of Intelligence's death, and only his friendship with the President saved him from prison.

Troops of the 8th Division at Santa Cruz were also increased. In April, 1967 the division's leaders were:

Colonel Joaquín Zenteno Anaya, Division Commander.

Colonel Ricardo González Lock, Chief of Staff.

Major Remberto Vilar, Operations.

Major Arnaldo Saucedo Parada, Intelligence.

Lt. Col. Hugo Ugalde, Personnel.

Lt. Col. Aldo Justiniano, Logistics.

Personnel of this division, a neighbor of the 4th, reached 1,200 including the 650 trained by US advisors.

To this number it must be added over 800 soldiers from other units: Trinity Company, with 5 officers, 6 noncom officers, and 160 soldiers; 76 from the Special Forces Instruction Center (CITE); 78 from Ustariz Company; 89 from Ingavic Squadron: 97 from the naval force; 154 from Florida Company; 91 from Roboré Company; and 119 cadets from different military schools.

The use of these units caused several problems. The men from CITE were deceived by Félix Villaroel, Barrientos' aide de camp. He made them believe that they would travel to the cities of Santa Cruz, Tarija and others in the southwest of the country to make parachute demonstrations, a kind of pleasure and recreation trip. The young paratroopers were eager to show off their training and skills.

War correspondent José Luis Alcázar reported that when the three C-47 airplanes, former bomber relics of the Second World War, were flying over the Bolivian jungle, Villaroel told them that they were going to Camiri to wipe out a guerrilla group. The journalist wrote that there was a deep embarrassing silence all over the cabin. The young faces were transformed: they were serious, pale, afraid; indecisive whether to believe or not what they had just heard. Incredulity. Alcázar wrote that "Everything had changed, except the rumbling of the old bomber's engines."

Diego Martínez Estévez wrote that the mothers of Trinity Co.'s soldiers demanded their sons' discharges, which were on the lists of the 1966 category.

"The case of this contingent was one of several who had been recruited after been discharged," he wrote.

"The upset mothers, when they found out that their sons would be flown to Choretty, the Camiri airport, went to the Trinidad runway and laid down to prevent the airplanes from taking off. It was to no avail, for the soldiers were taken to another runway."

Wives, fiancées, friends and other relatives joined the mothers in their protests, which finally forced the government to discharge them on the first week of August, 1967.

The presence of all these units caused new problems and ethnic discrimination made its presence. Soldiers from the Bolivian high plateau are used to cold heights and it was hard for them to adapt to the heat and humidity of the jungle. They refused to walk, which caused mocking from officers and soldiers from the East, already familiarized with high temperatures that in the area could rise to 38 degrees C (100 degrees F). Another element affecting soldiers from the plateau was scratches and insect bites, both of which were usually infected. When winter came, it was the turn of the Eastern soldiers to protest. The cold fronts, known in Bolivia as "surazos" (from the South) affected them considerably and they refused to walk in those conditions.

Captain Humberto Cayoja Riart, chief of Personnel at the 4th Division, sent the following report to his superiors:

"The intense cold of minus 5 degrees C, average humidity 90%, and the insects that abound at this time of the year, such as ticks in great numbers, may cause a decrease in the combat efficiency of the troops thus increasing the number of losses not due to combat. This is still more serious considering that troops have no warm clothes or sleeping bags, and even units like Braun's have blankets that look like mosquito nets, very old, probably supplied four years ago. To this must be added the inadequate equipment of some units that witness the disorganization of our army, as if it only existed for parades. It must also be considered that military medical service has not anticipated the effect of winter, which has a direct bearing on the combat efficiency of the troops."

Reque Terán himself, the 4th Division commander, wrote to Ovando communicating the serious situation, the deficiencies and improvisations inside the army.

On May, 1967, the military deployment of the 4th and 8th divisions reached 4,800 men for fighting a guerrilla of less than 50 men.

The CIA controls La Paz's central post office and telephones

By orders of the CIA, the mail interception service at the La Paz Post Office was reorganized and new employees were hired — paid for by the CIA—, after signing a loyalty agreement. Intervention reached the last details. Minister of the Interior Antonio Arguedas had Fidel Ríos in mind to appoint him as auditor of the post office, but the CIA was firmly opposed and sent him the following memorandum:

"This gentleman is a very active element of the MNR's cell at the post office and his political history is dangerous for that post in the information service, because personnel are managed by that post and they are main elements of the post office. He can even interfere with our work.

La Paz, May 31, 1967."

Fidel Ríos was never appointed as auditor.

The Technical Department was visited on several occasions by CIA Station Chief John Tilton, and officers James Holleran and Stanley Shepard, who concluded that many Communist pamphlets were circulating; so they ordered that measures be taken at Customs and airports. They ordered the appointment of Bolivian Jaime Terán as head of that control. Valuables articles that Bolivians received or sent abroad to relatives never reached their destination, a fact that caused a wave of protests and claims.

The Americans increased the number of units for telephone and personnel control units for tapping telephones, which also made the connections to automatically record conversations. Not only telephones of suspects and guerrilla sympathizers were bugged, but also those of politicians from the opposition, government officials, retired or active military officers, journalists, intellectuals and other targets of interest

Each day the head of the Ministry of the Interior's Technical Department delivered an envelope to the CIA with a photocopy of every intercepted letter, a transcription of telephone conversations, a copy of every book, magazine and pamphlet that entered the country. For receiving these and other equally important documents, the Agency used Víctor Quiroga, a Bolivian, who rented an office on the 7th floor of the Duery building, in downtown La Paz.

CIA agent Julio Gabriel García set up shop at the Ministry of the Interior, made Bolivian intelligence serve his interests, took up practically all the third floor, introduced his methods, systematically checked and controlled Bolivian personnel because he considered them inept, irresponsible, lazy and useless. He made no secret of these evaluations and soon Bolivians felt offended and began calling him El Gusano (The Worm).

Still unsatisfied, the CIA founded a front in Bolivia —Research Metal Company—, with alleged employees and experts on mineral sampling and quality analysis. All were CIA agents, trained in wire tapping installation, maintenance and repair, mail opening and sealing, and photography. They also mounted, installed and provided all kinds of equipment, furniture and writing material that included wire taps.

The CIA planted in the Bolivian General Staff a Cuban born agent by the name of George, who lived on 684 Rosendo Gutiérrez Street. George had the mission of evaluating telephone conversations, official and private mail of high ranking military officers and from the Ministry of the Interior. He also had President Barrientos, Juan José Torres, Ovando, Minister of the Interior Antonio Arguedas and other officers and officials under surveillance.

US intelligence agencies ordered the outlawing of the Communist Party, other left leaning parties and organizations, and increased their penetration. They also took several steps in order to create confusion and divisions among revolutionaries, labor unions and student organizations, and pressured for the need of neutralizing, repressing and exterminating the labor movement.

Particular emphasis was made on discrediting the guerrillas, accusing them of false crimes and outrages, presenting them as a handful of mercenaries, adventurers, rapists and foreign invaders, and hiding the fact that most of them were Bolivians. They even launched a propaganda campaign in the very area of operations presenting the guerrillas as Paraguayans, in order to fire up nationalistic feelings.

CIA officer John Maisto launched two terrorist attempts in the city of Cochabamba, one in a church and another one in the military club, with the intention of blaming guerrilla sympathizers and justifying an intense repression previously planned.

The CIA gets directly involved in control of the mail and of telephone tapping in La Paz

There were many irregularities and problems in mail control – protests from employees because of overwork, indiscriminate salary discounts and fines.

Complaints from citizens because of poor service increased — a fact that created restless and fear among intelligence operatives at the post office.

In view of such disorganization and lack of trust in Bolivian employees and in the Ministry of the Interior, the CIA station, without consulting or previous agreement with Bolivian authorities, took direct control of mail checks. Agents Julio Gabriel García, Luis Suárez, Miguel Nápoles and Hugo Murray were appointed to the mission. They set up a plan that began with surveillance of all employees for determining whom to fire or transfer. Alfredo Viricochea, head of recordings at the telephone plant, was also investigated.

From that moment on, CIA agents sent their orders directly to personnel infiltrated in those institutions, without previous knowledge of the Ministry of the Interior, as it had been agreed. Some of the orders were given through cards and handwritten notes.

The load work at the post office was heavy, for they had to sort out hundreds of letters and then report every month where they came from. Looking for efficiency, one of the CIA agents made a proposal:

"According to the work done up to the present, it is convenient to suggest the following plan for the sake of efficiency:

"It is impossible to check all the correspondence that arrives by airmail, particularly since the correspondence that has more interest for us is from Argentina, Paraguay, Uruguay, Peru, Brazil and Chile, discarding the rest of the sacks from other countries in order to be able to do our work without giving any hint to the public about our mission; I must say that this would be only for air mail, which is of the most interest to us. In reference to ground mail, I must say that with the employees under us and ourselves work is most effective, so in this section there is no need to take out correspondence.

"In order to carry out this work plan effectively and keep the public ignorant. I would suggest changing some employees at the

49

air mail section, because they have close relations with some members of the public and to avoid leaks."

One of the employees about to be changed was María Benquique de Sattori. The reason was the following report sent to higher authorities:

"Yesterday at 11 a.m., Mr. José Luis Cueto came to this office and personally asked for Mrs. María de Sattori, a clerk at the Certified Air Mail Section, inquiring why his mail does not arrive regularly.

"Also yesterday afternoon Mr. José María Alvarado came to see her to ask her about a letter from Cuba addressed to Mr. Gilberto Pedraza, which Mrs. De Sattori earnestly searched for and at the same time declared that it must be found, because no letter can be lost.

"In a conversation with another employee in our service, this same Mrs. Sattori told her, and I quote, that she is married to Jorge Sattori, who now calls himself José Sattori, a name change he adopted for receiving his mail and communist propaganda that he has not received for quite some time, so she is trying to find out the reason why he does not get his mail.

"According to the previous quote we find that he is a dangerous element for our work and the service's security.

"It should be known that Mr. Gilberto Pedraza is in our censorship list."

"The above is informed for the appropriate ends.

"La Paz, June 2, 1967."

The CIA ordered telephone taps on the premises and diplomats of the embassies of France, Mexico, Argentina, Peru, Uruguay and Brazil, as well as of top military officers of the Armed forces and the Ministry of the Interior.

A manuscript note by officer Hugo Murria ordered the surveillance of Colonels Fernando Sattori Rivera, León Kolle Cueto and Juan Lechín Suárez, including their bank accounts. The reason was that they were brothers of communist leaders Jorge Sattori Rivera and Jorge Kolle Cueto, and half brother of Juan Lechín Oquendo, respectively.

An intercepted letter addressed to Eduardo Olmedo López Muñoz had been sent from Lima, Peru, by former Bolivian President Víctor Paz Estenssoro. CIA experts forged the signature and changed the text with the purpose of discouraging López Muñoz, disheartening him, making him believe that Paz had repudiated him and embittering him towards Paz. Observing the letter it can be seen that besides forging the signature the second paragraph is modified and a new one added. This is clearly seen on collating the original with the forgery.

CIA agents rented post office boxes under assumed names or impersonating real people. One of these cases was that of Rodolfo Quevedo, who lived on 1476 Illimani St., identity card 305719. He was impersonated by Cuban born CIA agent Luis Suárez.

The disdain of CIA officers and agents for Bolivian officials under their command was so obvious that two of them, Ricardo Aneiva Torrico and Max Jaldin, agreed on putting up a common front to conceal information that was detrimental to the morality of many Bolivians, because CIA officers wanted to know the most intimate aspects of the people who were the subject of wire taps or whose mail was checked. Minister Antonio Arguedas himself claimed that Americans wanted to manage Bolivia's Ministry of the Interior as if it were a US consulate.

The CIA sends spies disguised as peasants and products buyers

CIA agents recruited soldiers and police officers born in the area where guerrillas were operating with the purpose of organizing groups of spies that disguised as peasants, peddlers or buyers of agricultural products would travel through towns, villages and fields. In those visits they collected information on guerrilla sympathizers or people who showed an inclination to help them. Later on the army would threaten, suppress, torture or kill them. Those who showed a disposition to collaborate with the military were appointed as mayors.

Mexican journalist Luis Suárez reported that in Camiri there were strangers that presented themselves as anything of an unexplained interest at the moment. Likewise there was talk of a Cuban American who was selling fabrics and socks.

On their part, the peasants informed the guerrillas about the presence of these spies. Pombo wrote in his diary on April 23: "At dawn we arrived to a place called Tapera. The peasants welcomed us and told us that a man that had been born there has recently arrived and seems to be an informer (...)"

Che wrote in his diary on June 20: "In the morning Paulino, one of the boys from the 'chaco' below informed us that the three individuals were not traders: there was a lieutenant and the other two did not belong to the guild."

A similar event happened on July 26, when peasants alerted them of the arrival of two new spies. On that matter Inti Peredo wrote in his book *My Campaign with Che:* "That same afternoon we took as prisoners two other spies, one of them a police officer (...)"

Spies were infiltrated even in the Bolivian capital. One day in mid 1967, Sonia Valdivia received the visit in her house of a man who claimed to be Che Guevara's brother. The man had a note of introduction from a good friend of Sonia's who was in jail. She received him affectionally and offered what help he needed. He confided in her and said that he came from Havana to organize a support network for the guerrillas and wanted to know whom he could trust in particular.

Sonia Valdivia was one of hundreds of people who were imprisoned in Bolivia, for Che's alleged brother was a CIA agent.

The US Embassy, an Instrument of Repression in the Mines

June was a critical month for the Barrientos regime, because the sense of unease was universal; demonstrations were common in spite of the permanent repression.

The miners of Huanuni were organizing a large demonstration against the government. Considering such an explosive situation, the government decreed the state of siege and suspended constitutional guarantees.

The regime's spokespersons declared that students were promoting a subversive plan to overthrow the government. Members of leftist organizations and parties were also implicated. Meanwhile, the workers at the Huanuni, Catavi, 20th Century and other mines raised their voices in protest over the violent repression against students. Likewise, tens of members of opposition parties were arrested and sent to concentration camps.

There were insistent rumors of a military coup, claiming that General Armando Escobar Uría and Colonels Joaquín Zenteno Anaya, Marcos Vásquez Sempértegui and Juan Lechín Suárez were plotting to replace Barrientos.

At La Paz and other cities of the country the repression continued, as well as surveillance of all kinds.

A very close source to the Bolivian president informed that in early June, 1967 the US Ambassador had met with Barrientos. Also present at the meeting were Colonel Juan Lechín Suárez, president of the Mining Corporation of Bolivia (COMIBOL), and CIA officer John H. Corr, who worked out of the US Embassy under the cover of attaché of labor affairs.

According to the source, the US attaché said that in Catavi, Huanuni and 20th Century mines there was an insurrection plot to overthrow the government, that the miners had agreed on donating a day's salary every month so that the guerrillas could buy weapons and medical products; that they were planning to declare the mines "free territories of Bolivia" and put up road blocks. He also claimed that a group of 20 miners were ready to join Che's guerrilla. Corr delivered a list with the names of the mines' leaders and workers that, according to his confidential sources, were part of the conspiracy. When Barrientos asked how the American had obtained the information the answer was an insult to the dignity of the Bolivian people:

"Bolivians are not characteristically reserved. A few drinks, the company of a friend or simply vanity to be believed important or knowledgeable are enough to make that information escape through the most unusual ways."

Subsequently the US Ambassador noted that it was necessary to take drastic measures to wipe out the source of subversion in the mines.

Some time later Barrientos met with the executive president of the Inter- American Development Bank (IDB), Alberto Ibáñez González, who informed him on all the projects for Bolivia. When he left, the US Ambassador once again was categorical:

"Those loans will be granted if there is peace and social ease in the country."

In view of such pressure, a massacre was unleashed at the mines: leaders and workers were murdered, arrested, jailed or exiled.

Labor unions were intervened and as usual there were mass dismissals. The victims were almost a hundred.

In his book *Galerías de muerte. Las minas bolivianas* (Galleries of Death: The Bolivian Mines) Father Gregorio Iriarte wrote:

"It is June, 1967. For three months the country has been rocked by the Ñancahuazú guerrilla. There is talk among the miners about the possible presence of Che Guevara in Bolivia. It is said that some miners have traveled southeast, ready to join the guerrillas [...]

"For the first time in Catavi, miners make the proposition of giving economic assistance to the guerrilla.

"This language seems to rock the very foundations of the Government and the Army. From that moment the High Command begins to plan a new punitive raid on the mines in order to teach a lesson.

"On June 3 the 20th Century and Catavi labor unions decree a 24 hour strike in order to make a peaceful march to the city of Oruro. The Government replies that it does not believe in the peaceful intentions of those marches and that they will not be tolerated under any circumstances.

"Some 800 miners wait impatiently outside the labor union building. They are ready to march on Oruro in any manner and at any risk. (The miners) decided to raid the hangars of the Company and seize a locomotive. They hooked up ten cars. The jubilant miners filled them completely and waving handkerchiefs and singing hymns, as if they were partying, left for Oruro amid the strident and continuous whistling of the locomotive [...]

"Halfway, near Huanuni, the Army had cut the tracks. The makeshift engineer was able to stop the train in time. The miners left the cars and marched in close formation to Huanuni's Square. There they improvised meetings, parades and speeches. The leaders were elated. Their words were full of enthusiasm and hope. The mining districts of Catavi, 20th Century and Huanuni were declared 'Free Territories' and the generous contribution of the miners was asked for the Ñancahuazú guerrilla.

"Simón Reyes, Secretary General of the Miner's Federation, had been for some days at the 20th Century mine. Together with Isaac Camacho and other Federation members they were giving the finishing details to a General Meeting that would be held at the 20th Century mine's labor union on June 25-26.

"The Government thought that the time had come to finish off the labor union once for all. The High Command made a thorough study of an attack plan on the mines. The efficiency of the operation would depend on the surprise factor. The Eve of St. John's Day, with its traditional bonfires, abundant punch and gay popular dances offered, according to the unsuspecting military planners, 'unbeatable tactical conditions' for their Machiavellian plan.

"In order to surprise the miners, nothing better than transporting the troops by train [...]

"Another 'surprise' factor was the timing. Four forty in the morning was Zero hour for the attack, an ideal moment to surprise the sleeping miners after a night of carefree joy.

"The previously reinforced Llallagua Police would serve as backup to the Army, particularly during the final assault to the labor union's building, and to identify and arrest union leaders. The orders were clear and categorical: not a single one could escape.

"General Amado Prudencio, Colonel Alfonso Villalpando and Major Pérez were directly responsible for the success of the operation. Lieutenant Segueiros commanding the National Guard and Alberto Zamorano the Llallagua detectives had the specific mission of arresting all leaders.

"General Barrientos also wanted to be present in a fashion at the saddest and most ignominious night of his presidency. He sent his most trusted man, the unavoidable Captain Plaza, as his personal representative to the horrible massacre.

"The High Command was satisfied. Never in Bolivia had a military operation been planned with such minute details [...]

"By the door of each house there was a bonfire. Intense cold, a quiet night, a star studded sky. It was St. John's Eve, a crystalline, cheerful and lively night, as usual [...]

"Some were surprised by the sudden arrival of a train and the silent deployment of the soldiers on the slopes of San Miguel Hill.

"It was still completely dark. All was shrouded in mystery. It was not worthy to alter the people's rest [...]

"Surprisingly the Camp is enveloped in a frightful shooting and each soldier's rifle vomits bursts of death in any direction.

"Both backup sections also open fire on the Camp, believing that the soldiers have been attacked. Bullets penetrate houses through windows and zinc roofs.

"Screams of horror from women and children silence for a moment the noise of machine gun fire. The hoarse report of mortars sends shivers of fear through the bravest ones. Major Pérez and his men see only enemies in each person hiding or at any door opening.

"The Government, unable to justify its actions, tries to confuse public opinion. Yet, those 26 corpses are there to prove their lies. The broken bodies of those children, of those peasants, of those women, of those night watchmen were evidence that at least at this time the miners had not clashed with the Army, nor were they the direct originators of the inhuman genocide [...]

"The funeral of the victims took place on the afternoon of that very day. Opposite the Racing Club gathered a huge crying and shouting crowd. It would be difficult to imagine a sadder and a more heartbreaking scene. Prayers and cries of pain were mixed with political slogans and subversive harangues. Insults to the Army were in the air, mixed with prayers from the faithful. At the cemetery, the leaders paid tribute to the victims from the top of its ancient walls announcing the coming day of implacable vengeance [...]

"Night fell to calm our nerves. The atmosphere was tense and the following day predicted new misfortunes [...]

"On the 26th the company wanted to resume work. Many miners come to the mine, but not to work. It is the only place where they could meet. They want to exchange impressions with their comrades, know exactly what happened, listen to the slogans from the leaders of the Miners' Federation. There was a long assembly at Level 411.

"Tempers were short, Many miners came to the meeting with dynamite sticks and bent on marching against the Army and even die if it were necessary, believing that in that manner they would take revenge for the St. John's victims.

"The government unleashed a systematic repression. At 20th Century 21 workers were arrested and deported immediately to concentration camps at the Beni jungle.

"Federation members and the main leaders at 20th Century and Catavi were able to leave the mines and escape from the Army. As an ultimate measure they declared the indefinite general strike.

"The company's answer was the dismissal of 200 miners.

"The strike lasted for 12 days. It was silent, sad and totally unfortunate.

"The Army's presence, now emboldened, enveloped everything, suffocating any attempt of struggle or organization."

Father Iriarte continues his narration:

"The ingrate visit of the military was also received by Huanuni, where hours of panic were lived. At four o'clock on June 25, after setting up its command post in Green Beach, the Army raids the town in order to occupy the labor union and strategic positions. At some moments shooting is intense.

"At Santa Helena Hospital Dr. Luis Valderrama tends to the first victims. Inside the operating room he is wounded by a soldier's bullet.

"At dusk workers have gathered near the National Radio station that is making urgent calls to several organizations of the country. Shortly after an army unit arrives and occupies the radio station. They blow up its equipment with dynamite.

"On the next morning, when an Army truck arrives to get supplies at a grocery store, women insult them and try to attack the soldiers. A small bridge is blown up at the moment that the army truck is about to cross it [...]

"COMIBOL, slyly managed by the 'Advisory Group' that serves interests alien to the country's, can feel satisfied: the labor unions have been destroyed, its leaders in jail or on the run, media have been confiscated or shut down, the Decree on Salary Decrease has been imposed to the letter, all democratic and revolutionary forces of the country have been overwhelmed."

In his book *Myth and Reality of Development in Bolivia*, Ramiro Villarroel wrote: "The policy of violence, used again in September 1965 and June 1967, is unparalleled in the country's history, not only because of the number of dead and wounded, but because its characteristics of premeditation, treachery and coldness with which they were executed. Training by Yankee advisors has transformed the military into an efficient repressive police force.

"Public reaction against the massacres at the mines was unanimous condemnation and repudiation. The Church raised its voice in protest. Student organizations, political parties, labor unions, and civic institutions were rocked by horror, and not willing to limit themselves to words sent generous assistance to the victims."

Father Gregorio Iriarte finishes this part of his narration with the following words:

"As a caricature of a sovereign and national entity, COMIBOL continued with its intransigent iron fist policy. 'Social peace' was imposed on the exiled, prisoners, wounded and dead. But it is the 'peace' of the cemetery."

The CIA and the US Ambassador in Bolivia attained "peace and social ease" demanded by them in exchange for the IDB's loans.

In other narrations Father Iriarte has expressed: "The case is that the CIA thinks that Che's main support is at 20th Century and Huanuni. And that at those places the urban guerrilla will be declared."

The attaché of Labor Affairs at the US Embassy in La Paz had close contact with Alberto Garza, a Mexican official with the domestic branch of the International Labor Organization (ILO), who was also an intimate friend of Larry Sternfield, known by all as a CIA agent, organizer of a network of American residents in Bolivia, headed by a man named Holt, a mine broker. These were the main informers, not the Bolivians, as the attaché of Labor Affairs at the US Embassy tried to make everyone believe.

The massacre at the mines was discussed in Parliament and several ministers were questioned. At one of the sessions, president of the Senate Hugo Bozo Alcocer granted the floor to Minister of Culture Roberto Prudencio, who wanted to answer Senator Raúl Lema Pélaez's remarks on the events. When he tried to justify the cruel massacres he said: "If the work of governing must be done, many times the sacrifice of killing will be necessary. Sometimes the Motherland demands it. And at the time (of the St. John's massacre) the Motherland demanded it."

Prudencio added that perhaps the measure adopted on the night of June 23 "was somewhat bloody." After justifying the gory intervention at the mines, the Minister of Culture explained his presence in the Cabinet. He said that he had "lived a long time in exile, and when he returned to the country he saw that General Barrientos' government had given back the country its freedom." About those who opposed the president in Parliament, he declared they wanted the government's loss of prestige, "revolution, revolt, putsch."

Bolivian intellectual René Zavaleta Mercado described Minister Prudencio as the philosopher of genocide, and that his attitude could explain the position of Barrientos and some of his officials against writers and artists.

Journalist Rubén Vásquez Díaz interviewed Sergio Almaraz Paz —one of Bolivia's topmost intellectuals—, who spoke about the government's hostile attitude against intellectuals and artists, and explained how the murals that famous artists Miguel Alandia Pantoja had painted in the Presidential Palace, Parliament and other important places of the Bolivian capital had been vandalized, that shortly alter the repression at the mines they had ordered the murals to be destroyed, for they could not stand them because they showed brutal generals walking on the heads of murdered miners.

Almaraz also said that from that moment on Alandia Pantoja was the victim of arbitrary actions; besides he also referred to the repression suffered by Bolivian members of the Institute of Cinematography who filmed *Ukamau*, an Aymara word that means "So it was". The film represents the sad story of Bolivian reality, which in itself was an accusation. For its high quality it was awarded prizes at several film festivals –Edinburgh, Karlovy-Vary and Cannes. But Barrientos was upset and banned the film in the country; he dismissed several artists and filmmakers, particularly Jorge Sanjinés and Oscar Soria, and others were forced to leave the country.

Trying to counter *Ukamau*'s image abroad, he hired North American Hamilton Corporation to produce a film on the country. The American company filmed *Unusual Bolivia*, at a very high cost. The film was considered mediocre and offensive to the Bolivian people.

Almaraz also told Rubén Vásquez that Barrientos personally banned the beautiful film *Dying in Madrid* as communist pro-paganda, and that rightist elements were openly threatening two of the country's most important intellectuals, Jesús Lara and Arturo Urquide, publicly calling for their killing as well as the killing of their children. The same threat fell on the prestigious and well known Bolivian writer Néstor Taboada Terán for his firm attitude in defense of Cuba and its revolution. Taboada had written, among others, *Chronicle of a Journey: Cuba, Dove of Popular Flight*.

The attitude of Bolivian intellectuals and artists against the Barrientos regime was one of public and constant criticism. The Congress of Bolivian Poets was held in July 23-29, 1967 at the city of Sucre, with the attendance of the country's most important ones: Yolanda Bedregal, Raúl Vázquez, Mary de Villena, Héctor Cossío, Antonio Terán, Rosa Fernández de Carrasco, Mario Lara, Amanda Arriarán, Jaime Choque, Jorge

Calvimontes, Luis Fuentes, Raúl Otero Reich, Raúl Jaime Freyre, Lidia Castellón, Gilberto Valenzuela, Mario Estenssoro, Álvaro Bedregal, Luis Villafani, Javier del Granado, Walter Arduz, Ambrosio García Rivera, Félix Pinto Saucedo, Héctor Borda Leaño, Heliodoro Ayllón and Alberto Guerra Gutiérrez, among others.

In the fully packed University's auditorium several of them read their poems of an antimilitaristic content. Jorge Calvimontes read "The St. John's Bonfire", a cry of condemnation of the miners' massacre, and it was a great hit. It created a tense atmosphere and those present agreed on condemning the government and the army for such a horrible act.

Immediately Barrientos declared that the congress was "dominated by a few communists" and "Fidel Castro-inspired."

The campaign that Che had been murdered in Cuba keeps on

Meanwhile the campaign that Che Guevara had been murdered in Cuba kept on and in late June, 1967 was still running. On June 29 Associated Press (AP) correspondent Robert Beprellez reported from Camiri that there were doubts whether Che was really in Bolivia or if Fidel's followers were taking advantage of his name in order to boost the guerrilla's image, provoke enthusiasm and promote similar movements in Argentina, Brazil and Paraguay. Beprellez wrote that Che Guevara had disappeared in Cuba on March, 1965 and that Fidel Castro claimed that he was on a revolutionary mission abroad. The AP correspondent also wrote that since that date it is said that he is in Congo, Argentina, Peru or somewhere else, but many believe that he was killed in Cuba by rivals opposed to his favorable attitude towards Chinese Communist ideology that disagrees with Moscow.
Barrientos repeated the same false and slanderous story.

Meanwhile, the Bolivian security services and the CIA were interested in keeping alive the idea that Che was dead, until they had finished their plan of destroying the opposition and arresting possible collaborators.

Bolivian journalist Jorge Rossa wrote that the media and the propaganda machine of General Barrientos furiously attacked the guerrillas with the object of poisoning public opinion with its hate, and claimed: "They said one word and... it was a lie. They issued a communiqué and... it was false."

The guerrillas present in Samaipata

On July 6, 1967 the guerrillas occupied Samaipata, the capital of the province of Florida, 120 kilometers from the city of Santa Cruz, by the Bolivia's main highway that links that city with Cochabamba, Oruro, Sucre and La Paz. It is a very traveled town where drivers stop for fuel and to eat.

The occupation was quite a feat, as well as a challenge, for the nearest garrison had been reinforced a few weeks before. In a swift raid six guerrillas took over the command post, disarmed the soldiers and bought medical products, food and clothing, talked with local residents and explained to them the objectives of their struggle.

US intelligence agencies considered the action as a defeat of the Bolivian army. With a different intention, military leaders of the 8th Division exaggerated the number of the guerrillas and reported that there were dozens of them, accompanied by Viet Cong commanders, all in order to justify the defeat and to be able to ask more assistance from the United States.

The information strengthened the testimony of the Ambassador at a hearing of a US Congressional committee on May 4: "They are part of a determined nucleus that will not be easily eradicated. It could take a long time. In that lapse of time funds for other purposes will necessary be diverted, and in my opinion that is the significance of the threat in the long term."

Discussion in US media agreed with that evaluation. On June 26 *US News and World Report* magazine reported that guerrillas were still operating, the country was facing the real danger of sliding into another military coup, uncontrollable inflation and even civil war. The Bolivian army felt frustrated after chasing the guerrillas for two months with nothing to show, and both Barrientos and Ovando had lost prestige due to their apparent confusion and indecision.

On its part, *The New York Times* reported in a Sunday edition that just by existing the guerrillas were winning from the military point of view. The newspaper then quoted a US military officer as saying that if they could move freely and get the support of more followers, a greater effort would have to be made to drive them from their positions.

Newsweek noted that there was a growing distrust from the US State Department regarding the ability of the Barrientos government to stand up to the guerrilla situation in the country.

These analyses and the taking of Samaipata alarmed the US, which evaluated the scenario of direct military intervention, since the Bolivian military proved incapable of stopping the guerrilla push, in spite of the advising and huge resources they had received.

The Bolivian regime was teetering because the successes of the guerrillas and its impact on public opinion, military failures and contradictions in the high command, the student movement in open rebellion, strikes by workers and teachers prepared to join them, mines and labor unions occupied by the military.

Several exiled opposition leaders declared that Barrientos should step down, because Bolivia was being "Vietnamized". They stressed that a government that is unable to keep order and establish its authority should step down, and if it refused to do so should be overthrown at any price.

General Alfredo Ovando Candia, together with 20 other high ranking officers, attended a general assembly of the Bolivian Socialist Phalanx and had a long and confidential conversation with the party's leader Mario Gutiérrez. Preparations for the coup were in motion.

Juan José Torres went to another highly secret meeting with the Phalanx leader. Several officers were plotting the coup with the approval of Ovando, even planning the possible contingency of Barrientos' death. While some were preparing the technical aspects, others established political contacts. According to Bolivian military sources, General Marcos Vásquez Sempértegui and Colonel Juan Lechín Suárez took part in the conspiracy. *Los Angeles Times* journalist W. Stephens was able to interview several top army officers and verified that the struggle among generals and other officers was fierce. Each one of them dreams of reaching the presidency, and doubts, suspicions, and intrigue form a closely woven net that also traps high civilian officials.

New problems were added on the international arena. On July 4 public opinion found out that train No. 503 with 28 boxcars that allegedly transported wheat flour was really loaded with arms. The information added that it was the fourth train arriving from Tucumán, Argentina to the border town of La Quiaca, and that Argentinean soldiers had protected the train up to the border town, where they were replaced by Bolivian soldiers.

Chile reacted strongly and demanded explanations from both countries. US and Argentinean military aid for Bolivia's rearmament was a danger that the Chilean military were not willing to tolerate. US authorities immediately assured them that the weapons would not be used against Chile.

A declaration by Paraguayan ruler Alfredo Stroessner that if necessary he was willing to send soldiers to Bolivia, because the guerrillas were a real threat to his regime and Barrientos seemed unable of controlling the situation, alarmed Bolivian public opinion that still remembered the consequences of the Chaco War, where Bolivia lost an important part of its territory and many of its brave sons.

The US was interested and pressured for a direct intervention by the armies of the neighboring countries, but contradictions, divisions and sensitivity among the military hierarchies of the respective countries prevented an agreement in that sense.

A meeting prepared by the US to be held in the city of Santa Cruz failed. The most they could attain was arms and provisions from Brazil and Argentina, and an understanding for the exchange of information related with the movement of guerrilla sympathizers and their identification.

Among Bolivian military there were sectors opposed to any commitment with Paraguay. For that reason the negotiations were held in secret, headed by General Samuel Alcáreza Meneses, chief of the military zone at the Paraguayan border, but with a clause that clearly established that it referred only to the increase of security at the common border, and that the Paraguayan army could not under any circumstance penetrate Bolivian territory.

Considering the difficulties and the worsening of the situation, US analysts believed that US direct military intervention was inevitable.

Students rebel against the Barrientos regime

The massacre at the mines and the ruthless repression had an immediate repercussion in universities, which held open assemblies to debate the event. Police closed the streets that accessed the universities and adopted combat positions.

At the Higher University of San Andrés at La Paz, on July 4 there was a combative meeting in which several points were agreed on: the immediate withdrawal of all troops from the mines; compensation on the part of the government to relatives of the dead on the Night of St. John; reinstatement of miners' salaries that the government had slashed; immediate release of arrested leaders and workers; return of occupied radio stations and labor facilities and compensation for those that were bombed or destroyed; guarantees for labor unions; lifting of the stage of siege; resignation of Barrientos; and intransigent defense of university autonomy.

Students took to the streets trying to reach the government's seat in the Quemado Palace. During the march they yelled: "Let's unite with the labor unions!" "All against the government!" "Miners' blood, guerrilla seed!"

The answer was brutal repression with high pressure hoses, tear gas and attack dogs.

The students at the Higher University of St. Francis Xavier of Sucre also took to the streets in a combative demonstration against the regime and supporting the miners. Several young people were arrested for putting up signs in the city's walls cheering the guerrillas.

On July 6 Bolivia's University Confederation inaugurated its 6th National Extraordinary Congress of University Student Leaders with the purpose of debating the national situation and the horrible events at the mines. At the meeting it was agreed to draft a political document assuring their commitment with the people and that the political, economic and social crisis of the country was only the result of the intensification of contradictions with the government. The document concluded stating that Barrientos was an enemy of the people and demanded his resignation.

An Assembly was held on July 7 at the San Simón University of Cochabamba. There was a similar resolution, but to the demand of Barrientos' resignation they added Ovando's.

At the University of Oruro they made public collections of food and medicines for the massacred mining centers. Also a delegation was sent to visit Catavi and 20th Century mines.

Middle and secondary level students in La Paz and Santa Cruz demonstrated against the regime: repression followed. On July 17 there were new demonstrations on the main Bolivian cities, where streets were blocked and traffic disrupted. Leftist parties who had gone underground made a call to the struggle stating that Bolivia was living a kind of civil war unleashed in the form of guerrillas in the southwest and in street actions in the main cities.

At Santa Cruz students raided and burned the seat of the Authentic Revolutionary Party, one of the government's backers.

Another event was the huge explosion that caused serious damage to a motel, home to US Special Troops' officers. All the windows were destroyed and the perpetrators left a sign that said: "Down with the Yankees, Long Live the Guerrillas."

In view of this attitude of the Bolivian people, the US Embassy in La Paz began the distribution at universities, schools, country towns, Indian communities, mines and cities of thousands of brochures with cartoon strips where Cuba was shown filled with jails, surrounded with barbed wire and weapons everywhere; bearded guerrillas with ferocious expressions, foaming at the mouth, devouring children, roughing up peasants, burning shacks, raping and murdering women, gagging students, old people and children.

Seeing such infamy, university leaders tried to counter the dirty anti Cuban propaganda. In a clandestine printing shop at Cochabamba they mimeographed several speeches by Commander in Chief Fidel Castro, Che Guevara and many other materials that could be of interests for students. One thousand copies were also mimeographed of Regis Debray's essay *Revolution in the Revolution*, but demand was so great that they had to make another 30 printings. Several student leaders participated, among them Jorge Ríos Dalence, head of the Cochabamba University Students' Federation, a great admirer of the Cuban revolution, Fidel Castro and Che Guevara.

Political activity among university students reached a high level on the occasion of the August 6 patriotic parade. As a protest, students looked away at the moment they marched past the stand. For this patriotic action they were immediately repressed by police forces.

CIA officer William Anderson must have felt very frustrated. He had traveled to Bolivia on several occasions and his mission was to recruit student leaders from that university with the purpose of dividing, penetrating and neutralizing the student movement.

Contradictions between US officials and Bolivians

Arrogance and contempt on the part of the US Ambassador and his officials towards Bolivian military created resentment among the latter.

In his book *Bolivia at the Time of Che,* journalist Rubén Vásquez Díaz writes about the situation: "There is a patronizing attitude and a badly hidden contempt from both sides, which severely limits efficiency in the collaboration. There is a general anti US feeling in Bolivia. Among army officers and government officials this is expressed in a very hypocritical manner. They slap Americans on the back, get what they can and thank them, and they talk about the great neighbor and of Western civilization and the free world. They know very well that what Americans give to Bolivia is nothing compared with what they have taken out, and even so they give it as very small loans.

"Bolivian officers also despised their US colleagues, because they know the Americans bad-mouth them and do not consider them real soldiers (...)"

He also pointed out that US diplomats said in public that "Bolivians are thieves, lazy and indolent people who can't be trusted, and also incurably nationalistic. Barrientos is a fool; Ovando and Defense Minister Guzmán are taking advantage of the US' goodwill and scheme against everybody –even the US."

Yet, since military assistance was necessary for US interests it kept flowing. On July 11, Reuter correspondent Christopher Rooper reported from Cochabamba that Colonel Joseph Rice had told him that US officers and non-commissioned officers in Bolivia numbered 50. Three days later two F-51 fighters and four T-28 trainers landed in Bolivia. But neither the active US participation nor the violent repression were able to eliminate demonstrations and the indignation of the people. Workers and students openly challenged the regime. The situation worried the Americans, who were concerned about Barrientos losing control and collapsing at any moment.

Fearing a situation of chaos, the United States began to create psychological conditions for an eventual direct military intervention. The CIA Station in La Paz was reinforced with new experts, who arrived in late July, 1967.

William Culleghan, the CIA coordinator for the area of military operations, took eight of his agents to meet Colonel Joaquín Zenteno Anaya. They would operate as advisors in the territory that was under the jurisdiction of the 8ᵗʰ Division.

Colonel Luis Antonio Reque Terán, the 4ᵗʰ Division's commander, planned a US advised military operation, codenamed Operation Cynthia. He publicly promised that he would wipe out the guerrillas in a few days, but it was a total failure. The US advisors valued the operation as a "complete chaos in the matter of organization, transportation and effective use of troops."

Meanwhile in the cities and the mines, repression went on. The previously mentioned Vásquez Díaz wrote:

"Arrests by DIC, Bolivia's political police, still continue at the mines. At least 200 miners and labor union leaders are estimated to have been deported to Puerto Rico and Pekín confinement camps, in the North and East regions of the country. An even greater number is persecuted and has been forced underground.

"In a general assembly on July 29, workers at the San José mine (an important mining center in Oruro) demanded from the government and COMIBOL the release of their comrades held in confinement camps."

By late July the guerrillas held two new victorious combats, a fact that made the idea of direct military intervention gain new adepts in Washington. But first they needed to prepare Latin American public opinion, because US intervention in Dominican Republic in 1965 was very recent and Washington feared a multiplied repetition of the wave of protests in all of Latin America.

Considering the deterioration of the situation in Bolivia and the active role of some journalists that sent censored information, Barrientos threatened foreign correspondents with expulsion.

At that time the United States decided it was convenient that the Bolivian President officially admit Che's presence in Bolivia, in spite of previously denying it on several occasions –also at the behest of the Americans–, for at those previous times they had feared the admission would have given hopes to the revolutionary movement and new strength to the opposition.

Nevertheless, accepting at the moment that Che was in Bolivia would be in favor of the government, for although the country was in a tense internal situation, the miners and the labor union movement had been massacred and were leaderless, students violently repressed, jails and concentration camps full and the main political leaders arrested or in exile. Terror was rampant in the country, the state of siege and suspension of constitutional guarantees had been declared.

The US Embassy in La Paz began a huge disinformation campaign as part of the psychological preparation to justify a possible US intervention. For that reason, it was convenient to accept that Che Guevara was in Bolivia and that Cuba was giving him full assistance.

The media began to saturate the public with the news that foreign forces formed by Cubans, Chinese, Europeans and Viet Cong commanders, all under Che Guevara, had invaded Bolivia. The calls to rabid nationalism were constant. To head the campaign of psychological and disinformation warfare, the Americans brought to La Paz from Saigon one of its topmost experts in the matter.

A disinformation expert arrives to La Paz

In late July Antanas Silvestro Dambrava Vitaustas arrived in Bolivia. Born in 1920 in Boranivich, Lithuania, Dambrava graduated in 1939 in Utena and went to law school at the University of Kaunas. In 1943 he got his law degree and an additional one in Drama at the University of Vilnius, the Lithuanian capital. A year later, when Nazi troops were defeated, Dambrava fled with them and eventually made it to a refugee camp in Salzburg, Austria, where he began working for the Americans. In Salzburg he edited a magazine for Lithuanian counterrevolutionaries. In the meantime he got a law degree from the University of Innsbruck. In 1947 he became a US resident.

By 1951 he got a job as radio announcer at the Voice of the United States of America (VOA). A year later he was appointed Secretary General of the International Federation of Journalists of

North America and took courses of International Law at the University of Columbia.

In 1955 he was writing programs targeting East European audiences from Munich, at the then German Federal Republic. He wrote slanderous stories and diversionist campaigns against the USSR, including programs in Lithuanian. Two years later he was appointed head of the section of special European events. When he returned to the US in 1960, he was appointed head of VOA's Latin American Section. The US government decorated him with the "Honor to Service" medal in 1962, for his disinformation work during the Cuban Missile Crisis.

From mid 1965 to early 1967, as information chief of the Voice of the United Status of America in Saigon, South Vietnam, he drafted the news that the world should know about that war. In July 1967 he was sent to Bolivia as an attaché at the US Embassy in La Paz.

In September Edward Fogler, a CIA officer and attaché of Public Affaire, introduced him to the editors of the main news media in Bolivia. Shortly after, on October 3 there was a reception to present Mr. and Mrs. Dambrava to the diplomatic set of La Paz.

With the arrival of Dambrava, a CIA structured plan was put into practice in order to increase agent penetration in the country's main media. Meanwhile a radio station and a newspaper, both wholly financed and managed by the CIA, were created. Some time later the project was blown due to leaks by Daniel Salamanca, Barrientos' private secretary and an official of the Presidency of the Republic.

Subsequently to the guerrilla events, Dambrava worked in the disinformation campaign against them. On leaving Bolivia, the US government once again decorated him for his exemplary performance. Barrientos also granted him one of the most important Bolivian decorations.

In 1968 he was appointed Consul and head of the United States Information Service (USIS) in Monterrey, Mexico. In 1970 President Richard Nixon appointed him as a permanent member of the Diplomatic Corps, which gave him the right to occupy posts in information agencies abroad, consulates or embassies. In September 1971 he was appointed first secretary and Vice Director of Public Relations at the US Embassy in Argentina, where he remained until being posted as first secretary in the US Embassy at Caracas, Venezuela. In 1977 he was transferred to El Salvador as counselor, where he remained until 1980, when he retired. Since then he has lived in Caracas, Venezuela, at Prolongación Los Manolos Street, Río Claro Building, La Florida, Caracas. The Venezuelan Lithuanian Union elected him as president in 1981.

The role of the CIA in Bolivia's repression

Control and repression against journalists from several news agencies

All journalists who arrived in La Paz or went to Camiri to report on Regis Debray's trial and the guerrillas were submitted to systematic surveillance by the CIA and the Bolivian intelligence agencies. In May Ovando declared that special security measures would be taken to prevent the entry of individuals who acted as accomplices of the guerrillas. The first ones affected were Soviet journalists Karen Jachaturov, director of Novosti press agency, and Vitali Borowski, *Izvestia*'s correspondent.

Regis Debray's trial and declarations by Barrientos that a law would be enacted that included the death penalty spread alarm in many sector all over the world. French President Charles de Gaulle wrote a personal letter to Barrientos, who answered it with insults and new threats on Debray's life.

Intellectuals from France and other countries were mobilized as token of solidarity with Debray, concerned by the expectations raised in relation to the lack of guarantees for the trial. Several traveled to Bolivia. Constant criticism to the regime in Europe forced the Bolivian government to issue visas to some journalists.

A group on European intellectuals arrived in La Paz as a gesture of solidarity with Debray. They were French publisher François

Maspero, together with his countryman lawyer George Pinet and Belgian attorney Roger M. Lallemand, who represented the Human Rights League, and Jacques Vigneron, from the Science Department of the University of Paris.

Bolivian intelligence agencies arrested Maspero and submitted him to a harsh four hour long interrogation trying to force him to declare that Debray was a liaison of Fidel Castro's policy in Latin America. Because of the French publisher's firm denial, they threatened to involve him in a conspiracy against Bolivia and include him as an accessory in Debray's trial in Camiri. Seeing that Maspero would not give in to their threats, the authorities expelled him from the country on July 8, 1967. He left for Lima, Peru at 11:39 a.m. in a Braniff International flight.

Among other things, Maspero told that on the old adobe walls of La Paz he saw graffiti that said, "Long live Debray," "Long live the guerrillas," Long live the people's armed struggle." He also said that filmmaker Chris Marker wanted to film at the mines and went to COMIBOL for authorization. He was received by an American who said to him: "Film our miners? No way! That would be bad publicity."

In early August a group of journalists arrived from London: Perry Anderson (*New Left Review*); Robin Blackburn (*Tribune* and *Sunday Times*; Taring Ali Khan (*Town Magazine*); and Ralph Schoenman, (Bertrand Russell Foundation). At a stopover in Lima they met Mariano Baptista Gumucio, ex secretary of the Bolivian embassy in the UK and former private secretary to past Bolivian President Víctor Paz Estensoro, who arranged an interview for that very evening with Dr. Paz and with his Minister of Interior Ciro Humboldt Barrero, both exiled in Peru. The former Bolivian president received them in a very kindly manner and advised them to try to get to Camiri..

Baptista Gumucio traveled to La Paz and put them in touch with Jorge Canelas, the AP's chief correspondent in Bolivia, and introduced them to several intellectuals that were sympathetic to the guerrillas —René Zavaleta Mercado, Félix Rospigliosi Nieto, Sergio Almaraz Paz and his wife Elena Osio Sanjinés, Jaime Otero Calderón, and Argentinean exile Adolfo Perelman, among others.

With the help of Baptista Gumucio and several Bolivians the journalists managed to get a permit from military authorities to travel to Camiri. Before leaving they met with Janine Alexandra,

72

Regis Debray's mother, and with the French consul in La Paz, Therese de Leoncourt, who were both under surveillance by the CIA. From that moment on, the four journalists were considered as suspects by the US intelligence agency and a search was conducted in their rooms at the Copacabana Hotel, located on the Prado Promenade in the Bolivian capital.

Schoenman, Taring and Blackburn went to Camiri, where they were arrested. They were interrogated by Colonel Reque Terán, the commander of the 4th Division, who told them that Debray should have been shot as one does with a snake in the grass, and that he would have already done it if the decision were up to him. He pointed out that he did not like the Constitution, because it permitted journalists to write any sort of bad things, that he preferred a dictatorship, because in Bolivia there were many slackers and people who did not want to work should be flogged.

This was not a first for Reque Terán. Previously he had said to a group of university students that the blame for Bolivia backwardness fell on its people. The only solution would be to change the race, force it to crossbreed with Europeans, particularly Germans and South Africans. The statement earned him both the condemnation and the mockery of the students for placing South Africa in Europe.

About Ciro Roberto Bustos, he claimed that he was a guerrilla and should also die; nevertheless, he told them that he had allowed him to be visited by his wife in order to listen in to their conversation. He burst out laughing. Subsequently, he gave them the assurance that they were free to do their work.

After leaving the division the journalists went to the Marieta Restaurant, where they were subjected to an obvious provocation. A man told them that "Debray's head would be chopped off as a chicken's", and he also insulted the British and even pulled one of them's long hair. Nearby a police officer was watching, waiting for their reaction to arrest them if they answered the provocation. A short while later the police officer approached them and warned them to get a haircut and a shave, because if they didn't they could be mistaken for guerrillas and shot to death.

Schoenman, Taring and Blackburn were arrested again and taken to the 4th Division's headquarters, where an officer interrogated them, until Reque Terán arrived and ordered their release.

Contradictions among different Bolivian intelligence agencies surfaced even in the presence of foreign journalists. Military Intelligence, the Ministry of Interior's secret service and the Criminal Police each went its way. Relations among them were terrible. Through prisoners they tried to find out what the other services were doing and obtaining, thus creating constant contradictions and rivalry.

As the journalists were leaving the division's headquarters they were intercepted and taken at gun point before Minister of Interior's official Hugo Peñaranda to be questioned again.

Through these events they found out about the arbitrariness, violations and crimes committed by Bolivian military authorities, among others the placing of a bomb in the jeep that would transport Walter Flores Torrico, Debray's attorney, in order to blow him to pieces. Another time a man approached them and called them "Castro-communists" who soon would be "castrated communists". Several Bolivians present apologized to the journalists and beat up the intruder, but soldiers who were in the vicinity interceded on behalf of the provocateur and arrested those who were partial to the journalists.

Subsequently Lothar Mennen, Perry Anderson and José Luis Monje arrived in Camiri and were also put under surveillance. These systematic controls were done on all whom they suspected. In a long list there were journalists from several countries, such as Mexican Luis Suárez (*Siempre* magazine); Chilean Augusto Carmona (*Punto Final* magazine); Britishers Richard Gott and Christopher Romper; Jean Stage (Denmark), Jorn Kumm (Sweden), Frenchmen Phillipe Noury and Frederic Pohecher; Sergio de Santis (Italian TV); Franco Pierini (*L' Europeo* magazine); photographer Paul Slade and journalist Jacques Chupus (Radio Luxembourg). All were under some form of surveillance. Their belongings were searched and their telephones bugged. The CIA ordered their rolls of film fogged.

Taring Ali Khan was arrested again and threatened to be sent to La Paz for a thorough investigation. Dutch archeologist John Buywisveld was kidnapped in Camiri by DIC agents, taken to Cochabamba and accused of being a guerrilla liaison. Buywisveld had arrived to Camiri from Paraguay.

All telephone calls in Camiri were under CIA control. On one occasion, when Ralph Schoenman telephoned Belgian lawyer

Roger M. Lallemand in La Paz, his call was intercepted and Lallemand was subjected to a long interrogation. Foreign journalists that reported from Camiri received help from their Bolivian colleagues, such as Gustavo Sánchez, Enrique Araoz, José Luis Alcázar, Oscar Peña, Carlos Salazar, Humberto Vacaflor and Jorge Canelas, among others, but the last two were expelled from Camiri. A similar measure was taken with Brazilian AFP correspondent Irineu Guimaraez after he reported that the military court was not prepared for a trial of such importance, but that it continued for political reasons.

Alfred Hopkins, the New York's *National Guardian* correspondent, reported that when Ralph Schoenman tried to read a document that questioned the trial against Debray he was expelled from the court room. After the incident, several journalists had their passports confiscated. DIC agents arrested Hopkins and kept him detained for two hours.

Feltrinelli arrives in La Paz

As a gesture of support and solidarity towards Regis Debray, Italian publisher Giangiacomo Feltrinelli went to La Paz. A millionaire and owner of the Feltrinelli Publishing House, one of Europe's finest, he had a library specialized in the international labor movement, considered by experts as the best of its kind in the world, containing documents of unique historical value. Very well known in Italian high society, Feltrinelli was a favorite subject of magazines, where he was regularly featured for his hobby – neckties. When Feltrinelli found out about Debray's trial in Camiri, he decided to travel to Bolivia together with his female companion Sibilla Melega.

When both applied for visas at the Bolivian consulate in Milan, consul Bruno Vailati processed them because of Feltrinelli's prestige. His publishing house was dedicated to Third World issues, frequently published speeches by Fidel Castro, Ernesto Che Guevara and different materials on the Cuban revolution. The company had branches in several European cities and New York and was planning to expand to South America. A group of brilliant experts in social, political and technical subjects were his contributors.

In spite of his prestige, the CIA Station in La Paz warned Bolivia's Ministry of the Interior that Feltrinelli was a dangerous character, an international communist, a leftist publisher, a Communist Party sympathizer partial to Fidel Castro and Che Guevara, and who had in his passport several courtesy visas from Socialist countries. The Agency informed that he was a guerrilla liaison, so since arriving in La Paz from Lima, on August 8, 1967, he was put under surveillance.

While he waited for Miss Melega, who had previously traveled to Ecuador and had planned to arrive in La Paz a week later, he stayed at Room 311 of the La Paz Hotel. During that time Feltrinelli toured the city, visited some people, met with others, among them Humberto Vázquez Viaña, who promised to give him some photographs of his brother Jorge Vázquez Viaña, a member of the guerrillas, and information on how he was murdered.

Subsequently he met with Bolivian Colonel Carlos Vargas Velarde, who offered to give him evidence on the CIA's intervention in Bolivia, where the agency was planning to introduce from Miami several Cuban mercenaries and present them as guerrillas who had fallen prisoners, with the purpose of launching a provocation against the Cuban revolution.

Colonel Vargas explained to Feltrinelli that among CIA plans was the organization of several groups –formed by the military, police, agents and DIC members, under the advise of Cuban born counterrevolutionaries—, with the mission of committing criminal acts against the civilian population in the area where the guerrillas were operating, in order to blame those crimes on Che and his followers.

Feltrinelli also met a French Argentinean by the name of René Mayer, who on behalf of Colonel Luis Antonio Reque Terán, offered him valuable documents related to the guerrillas in exchange for an important sum of money. Mayer gave him two addresses in case he accepted the offer —Monsieur Rives 3 Rue Camartin, Paris 9, telephone OPE 3343, or through Meyer himself at Encon Street, in Buenos Aires.

The CIA ordered George Andrew Roth —British Chilean journalist who had been detained with Debray and Bustos— to meet with Feltrinelli and offer him several writings about his jailing in Camiri, with the purpose of compromising him and mount a provocation against the Italian publisher

On August 18, at 5:30 p.m. two men who identified themselves as DIC members knocked on Feltrinelli's hotel room and asked him to come with them. He asked permission to get his cigarettes, a ruse to warn Sibilla Melega and warn her to go to the Italian embassy and tell what was happening. Sibilla also went to several journalists who were staying at the Copacabana Hotel and informed them of the arrest.

Feltrinelli was taken to the Ministry of the Interior, where he was interrogated for approximately two hours. Subsequently he was transferred to DIC headquarters and finally to jail.

In prison he found several inmates, among them mining labor leader Filemón Escóbar, and knew of how the CIA, in cahoots with the Bolivian Interior Ministry, had tried to buy labor leader Federico Escóbar for $6,000 dollars. Escobar was later murdered for threatening to denounce the Agency. Feltrinelli was interested in this case.

A prisoner promised to send him a manuscript where he would reveal what he knew about Escóbar's murder, and also of how US intelligence services were working against Bolivian labor unions, trying to corrupt its leaders, and promised to give him names so that the practice were denounced. He also explained that an American named Tony Freeman was at the US Embassy under the cover of attaché of Labor Affairs, but actually was in charge of bribing mining leaders. About Freeman, Father Gregorio Iriarte wrote the following in his book *Galleries of Death. The Bolivian Mines*: "He made many trips to the mines. The management opened its doors to him and he was well received, even with some fear.

"He met with miners, particularly those who had attended IRWO (Inter American Regional Workers Organization) courses and who were considered potential labor leaders. Freeman was the strategist that would take them to power.

"But his principles were elementary and pragmatic and based, above on all, on the power of the dollar. He belonged to the kind of people that believe that every man has a price, especially if the man is poor and oppressed, as miners were. Freeman offered and gave money freely. He did not understand that in the midst of hunger, resentment and humiliation, dignity could exist. That was the reason for his failure."

Mainstream media published the news of Feltrinelli's arrest and soon it was known all over the world. It had great impact. Italian newspapers such as *Il Giornale d'Italia, Il Tempo, Il Messaggero, Corriere della Sera, L'Unitá* and *La Stampa* made it front page news. *Avanti* and *Il Popolo* placed it in its inner pages. *Avanti* headlined its piece with the title "New Arbitrary Act of the Military in La Paz."

According to Italian TV, the President of Italy was concerned about the publisher's fate. It also broadcast several photos of Feltrinelli. *Paese Sera* headlined, "Mystery about Italian Publisher Missing in La Paz after Questioning", and added: "Feltrinelli's friends informed that he was questioned by two plainclothes police officers on Friday at 18:00 hours."

Another headline: "Darker Still Mystery about Disappearance of Feltrinelli. Bolivian Authorities, Pressed by Italian Embassy in La Paz, Said They Don't Know Where Italian Publisher Is."

All news media published the fact and some did not hesitate to call the Bolivian ruler a fierce dictator.

Italian President Giuseppe Saragat called Barrientos and asked him to spare Feltrinelli's life. It was the second European chief of state to call the Bolivian president, because previously Charles de Gaulle had voiced the same concern about Regis Debray. In Paris and in Rome it was known that both were in danger of death so they decided to intervene on their behalf to avoid their murders.

While Feltrinelli was interrogated and kept in prison, two plainclothes policemen arrested Sibilla Melega when she arrived to the hotel and ordered her up to her room. Once there she found eight other policemen. Everything was in complete disarray, the result of a thorough search. Subsequently she was taken to DIC headquarters, but she was not questioned because none of the policemen spoke Italian. Next day she was taken back to the hotel and kept under strict surveillance.

On the morning of the 19th, Italian Ambassador Pietro Quirino Tortoricci went to DIC headquarters to tell Feltrinelli that President Saragat and Foreign Minister Amintore Fanfani had taken much interest in his case and had agreed with Barrientos that he and his companion would leave the country immediately. After the Ambassador left, a policeman posing as a journalist tried to question Feltrinelli

At 2:00 a.m. on August 20 he was put in a red DIC jeep, together with several plainclothesmen, and taken to his hotel, where Sibilla was waiting for him, their bags packed, and left for La Paz International Airport.

The intelligence officer who accompanied them aroused their suspicion, because he did not look like a Bolivian and spoke English very well. Before boarding the plane, the man approached Feltrinelli and said: "You should thank your country's authorities for being very energetic in asking that you were taken out of Bolivia. If it had depended on us, you would have stayed here forever. If you come back, you won't leave this country alive."

At 3:30, Feltrinelli and Sibilla left for Lima, and from there returned to Italy.

The story of Federico Escóbar Capata's death, which so impressed Feltrinelli, was picked up by Father Gregorio Iriarte, who had personally talked with Barrientos to plead for Escóbar's freedom. Escóbar died in unknown circumstances, in spite of calls by several labor leaders for a thorough investigation. In his book Iriarte quotes from José Ignacio López Vigil's work *Radio Pius XII, a Mine of Courage:*

"I believe not 15 days had passed since his return. One night, when he was coming back from a party in Uncía (an important Bolivian mining center), the pickup in which he was traveling ran off the road. Nobody died, but almost all the leaders were wounded. Federico broke an arm. He was taken right away to the hospital in Camiri, where he was treated. They put his arm in a cast. Nothing serious, they said

"They say that he received orders from the party to go to La Paz. They suspected that perhaps he had not been well treated at the company hospital. That he should see another doctor in La Paz [...] And thought that the cast was wrong. That he needed surgery for the arm.

"His wife tells me that she was with him that day, strolling in the street. Next morning, at the clinic, they gave him general anesthesia. And he died on the operating table.

"The strange thing is that there was no autopsy. I asked his mother, an old lady, and she told me that it was not allowed. A commission was formed to investigate, but it never worked.

"It is very hard to accept a crime [...] There always have been doubts about his death.

"It was almost a national day of mourning. They brought him from La Paz. And a lot a people went to wait for him. Many, many people. And so many dressed in red! There was a guard of miners and of girls in red overalls, waving red flags. It was impressive.

"He is buried in Llallagua, where Sanjinés later filmed *The People's Courage*."

Father Iriarte narrates on:

"The movie theatre was named after him, they put up that bronze statue at the Miner's Square, and there was nothing but praise for him. But what nobody has done, nor the Miners' Federation, nor the Bolivian Workers Confederation (COB), nor his own party is ransom his life's history, write about what he did, what he spoke of, what Federico Escobar was. And it is necessary", concluded Father Iriarte.

It would have to be said that the strange circumstances of his death should be investigated, because similar events have happened systematically in Bolivia's political life.

Colonel Carlos Vargas Velarde, who promised Feltrinelli documental evidence on the CIA's intervention in Bolivia, was found dead in his office at the Ministry of Defense. The high military command informed that Vargas had shot himself. His death caused a wave of rumors that he had links with the guerrillas and for that he had been murdered. On October 28, 1967, the military high command issued the following press release, published by *El Diario* newspaper in La Paz.:

"In relation to a mistaken version published in a local morning paper, the Military High Command considers its duty to clarify the following:

"The tragic disappearance of an Army officer on the 25th of the present month, was not related in any manner to possible links or concomitances with the guerrilla actions that the country had to endure;

"The deceased Army officer has always deserved, for his military and civilian conduct, the full confidence and respect of his superior officers and his peers that considered him an honorable and selfless server of the Armed Institution."

For the Bolivian military high command it was very difficult to admit that Colonel Carlos Vargas Velarde could be related to the urban network that supported the guerrillas, and that he was determined to deliver documents that so compromised the Bolivian army and its links with the CIA. According to intelligence sources,

Vargas was found out and murdered by orders of the Agency, but both facts had to be concealed.

The alleged suicide was the least compromising justification to cover up the crime.

The strange death of Italian publisher Feltrinelli

After the guerrilla events, Feltrinelli published *Che's Diary in Bolivia* and was very interested that Inti Peredo write his memoirs. Feltrinelli even met him to try to convince him. He also wanted the world to know the methods used by the CIA in Bolivia and the manner in which Federico Escobar had been murdered. He had received some letters and manuscripts on the subject.

Feltrinelli asked Chilean journalist Elmo José Catalán Avilés to write about the Agency's participation against the guerrilla and in Che's murder. He never could make his wish come true. On March 15, 1972 he was found dead in the outskirts of Milan by a high tension pylon that had been dynamited. It was informed that his death had been caused by an explosion when he placed the charge in order to commit a terrorist act. His death was never sufficiently explained and there were many unanswered questions about a possible murder. One of them was the implausibility that someone like Feltrinelli would attempt a terrorist act alone, and additionally, unarmed, for there were no weapons at the site. Another suspicious detail was the fact that the Milan police called an undertaker to remove the body one hour before it was discovered. Indeed, the body was sent to the morgue without a magistrate being present at the scene, as required by Italian law.

Feltrinelli's eyeglasses were not found at the site. He was so nearsighted that he could not even walk without them, much less plant an explosive. The night of the bombing was totally dark and there was no moon. No light source was found at the site. The blown up pylon was substituted without a fingerprint check and without observing legal procedures. The van in which he allegedly had gone to the scene had no ignition or door keys.

It was known that documents found on Feltrinelli were gross forgeries, which was absurd in the case of such a very well known man.

Another element that reveals the possibility of a crime is that if he died as a consequence of the explosion, as it was claimed, his hands and face should have been burned. But they were intact. Instead there were several contusions on his head and internal lesions that suggested that he had been beaten or tortured.

It was also said that he carried compromising documents in his pockets, but one of the undertakers that removed the body said that the documents were planted by Milan police superintendent Luigi Calabresi, who on May 17 of that year was shot to death by unknown assassins when he was leaving his home.

Another two prisoners are questioned by the CIA

US military assistance to Bolivian rulers continued. On August 1 a US military airplane Star C-141 landed in El Alto International Airport at La Paz with 15 tons of war materiel. Eight days later journalist Álvaro Murguía reported that Bolivian troops were being newly equipped with Argentinean PAM and Ballester Molina machine guns and automatic pistols, FAL automatic rifles and the small and light Swiss UZI submachine gun.

In late July two of the guerrillas that had stayed with Joaquín, considered part of the dregs, Eusebio Tapia Aruni and Hugo Silva Choque (aka "Chingolo"), deserted and were made prisoners by the army. They were sent to Lagunillas, where CIA agents questioned them. After being tortured by Reque Terán, Hugo Silva agreed to guide Captain Rolando Saravia, together with an army company, to where the caves and deposits of the guerillas were.

On August 14 radio stations broadcast the news that weapons, medicines, valuable documents and photographs had been seized by the army. In his diary Che jotted down an entry: "(...) someone talked. The question is who."

All the documents that were found were sent to the US for its evaluation and analysis. The bearers were Colonel Manuel Cárdenas Mallo, chief of Department III (Operations), and Mayor Quink, of the US military mission in Bolivia. Both were accompanied by a CIA officer in their La Paz-Miami-Washington flight. The documents were delivered to a Pentagon office. The following day, Colonel Cárdenas went to a meeting with a group of

Agency experts, some of them Cuban born, whom he briefed on the guerrilla events in Bolivia. Up to that moment some Agency analysts had claimed that Guevara was not in Bolivia. Such was their arrogance for the manner in which Che had evaded them that they refused to admit it.

On August 26 General Charles Porter, Chief of the US South Command headquartered in Panama, arrived in Bolivia accompanied by two US generals and two colonels, with the objective of evaluating the guerrilla situation.

Visits by US personnel were frequent. Every two weeks the Bolivian military and the US mission in La Paz met to evaluate events.

August was the most difficult month of the whole guerrilla campaign, as Che wrote in his diary:

"Undoubtedly it was the worse month we've had in the war up to now. The loss of all the caves with its documents and medications was a hard blow, particularly from the psychological point of view (...) The lack of contact with the outside and with Joaquín, and the fact that some of his men have been made prisoners and have talked, also demoralized the troop somewhat. My illness has sown uncertainty on several others and all this was reflected in our only encounter, in which we should have made the enemy several casualties and we only wounded one of them."

On the last day of the month, traitor Honorato Rojas took Joaquín's group to Puerto Mauricio's Ford on the Grande River, where troops of the 8th Division under Captain Mario Vargas Salinas were ambushed. When the guerrillas were fording the river the soldiers opened fire from both banks. Several were killed and others murdered after being taken prisoners. Freddy Maymura, a Bolivian guerrilla, was unharmed, but he refused to answer questions, identify his comrades and cheer the army. He was murdered.

The only survivor of the group was José Castillo Chávez, aka *Paco*, who was taken to Vallegrande to be interrogated by CIA agent Julio Gabriel García. The Bolivian military also delivered to the Americans documents found in the backpacks and clothes of the guerrillas for its evaluation in the United States.

Meanwhile in Camiri, journalist and poet Arnulfo Peña —owner of the only weekly paper in the area that he himself wrote, edited, mimeographed and sold— published a beautiful legend in which a flower emerged from the Grande River.

Through the writing readers knew of the life of Tania, the Guerrilla, her heroics and her death, which differed from the official versions. The legend of the Flower of the Grande River moved the townspeople. A short time after, Arnulfo Peña was arrested and tortured. His mimeograph, files and documents were violently destroyed.

Tania, the Guerrilla

Tania, the Guerrilla, aka Laura Gutiérrez Bauer, was the cover for Haydée Tamara Bunke Bider, born in Buenos Aires, the daughter of a German father and a Soviet mother living in Argentina. At the triumph of the Cuban revolution, Tania decided to live in Cuba and help in the defense of the socialist revolution. In 1963 she began a rigorous training as an intelligence operative that would prepare her for complicated and risky missions, lead a solitary life, silence her true feelings and not be able to share her revolutionary joys.

She learned to change her language and attitudes for those of bourgeois society where she would carry out her mission. On February 20, 1964 she finished the first stage of her training and moved to the city of Cienfuegos to develop her practical and operative plan. In late March Commander Ernesto Che Guevara explained to her the undercover work that she would carry out and the need to move to Bolivia. Che warned her that no matter how difficult her situation she should not contact any leftist organizations or parties or any people related to them, nor ask for help or reveal her true identity. Compartmentalization had to be total.

On April 9, 1964, she left for Western Europe using a passport in the name of Haydée Bider González. She also had two different sets of papers, one as Vittoria Pancini and another as Marta Iriarte. Among her various missions she was supposed to take several photographs of a village in a certain region, which she later would claim to be her hometown, and also of an elderly married couple, previously studied, that she would claim to be her parents.

On August 5 she arrived in Frankfurt, Federal Republic of Germany, where she adopted the identity of Laura Gutiérrez Bauer, her permanent and definite cover. In early October, 1964 she left for Bolivia as an ethnologist specialized in archeology and anthropology. On November 5 of that same year she arrived in Peru. From the Peruvian capital she traveled by plane to Cuzco, by train to Puno and in a van to Yunguyo, the last Peruvian town on the Bolivian border. From there she easily entered Bolivian territory, stayed at a hotel in the town of Copacabana and the next day went on to La Paz.

At the Bolivian capital she connected with painters Juan Ortega Leytón and Moisés Chire Barrientos, the latter a relative of the Bolivian president. Both of them introduced her to other artists and intellectuals. She established a close relationship with Gonzalo López Muñoz, head of the Presidency's National Direction of Information and Barrientos' trusted friend. López was part of the President's inner circle with free access to any premise in the presidential palace, including the Bolivian ruler's private quarters. Secret and extremely sensitive documents passed through his hands, many of them even before the President himself saw them.

López Muñoz gave her a credential as a subscription agent of the weekly *IPI*, a confidential publication that he published, to which only officials, politicians and important figures of Bolivian society were suscribed. This job gave her valuable relations and access to the office of the head of information.

Tania befriended Dr. Julia Elena Fortín and through her became part of a numerous group of experts in the research committee attached to the Ministry of Education's Department of Folklore. To legalize her admission to the committee she needed a letter of recommendation from the Argentinean Embassy. The letter was given to her by Ricardo Arce, secretary of the diplomatic mission, with whom she had established a close relationship. Arce introduced her to the embassy's personnel, including Marcelo Barbosa, Consul of Argentina in Santa Cruz.

She also became related with the government's Department of Planning; with Ana Henrich, former secretary of the Senate and a close collaborator of Minister of the Interior Antonio Arguedas; with top government officials, rightist political parties, top military officers and many other important figures, such as the well known and Falangist oriented journalist Mario Quiroga, who got her a work permit and offered her a job as proof reader in the newspaper *Presencia*, the most important in the country.

Tania began teaching German to the children of the local bourgeoisie, a fact that allowed her to visit their homes, connecting with their parents and other relatives.

Another very valuable relation was with lawyer Bascopé Méndez, who introduced her to a large number of his friends.

On the occasion of attending a party at the exclusive La Paz Club, her escort Ricardo Arce introduced her as a member of the Argentinean embassy's personnel. This fact opened many doors and connected her with new and interesting fiends.

With Ricardo Arce and Mexican Juan Manuel Ramírez she went to another party on the shores of Lake Titicaca. Present at the party was General Barrientos, top army officers and government ministers. Tania met the President, who was very impressed by her, and both stroke up a lively conversation. Those who met Tania have said that she was beautiful and very attractive, a cultivated woman who played the guitar and the accordion and also could sing. Her black hair and her deep green-blue eyes captivated all. The party provided her with an ample circle of friends and she linked with members of the Foreign Ministry's protocol office, where she became very well known.

On January 20, 1965 she was already in place and had established relations with important government figures –top military officers such as General Ovando, diplomats, artists, researchers, journalists and rightist and reactionary political leaders. Laura Gutiérrez Bauer had become a star in the Bolivian political jet set.

She studied Bolivian folk art with scientific rigor, set up the first ever exhibit of Bolivian typical costumes, toured tne Bolivian altiplane collecting popular songs, and represented the Department of Folklore in a festival held in Salta, Argentina.

She married Mario Martínez, a student of electrical engineering and the son of an important mining engineer. The wedding was celebrated at the home of artist Yolanda Rivas de Plaskonska. Through the marriage she obtained the Bolivian citizenship and passport.

On January 1, 1966 the representative of an important and famous firm of beauty care products arrived in La Paz. His cryptonym was Mercy and his real identity was never discovered by the CIA or by Bolivian intelligence agencies. Mercy's mission was to contact Tania, know how she was, bring her news from family and friends, review her operative know how and deliver new techniques for secret communications.

Mercy also gave her additional training in surveillance and countersurveillance, invisible ink, information collecting and analysis, counterintelligence and its working methods, observation, cartography, microdot, security measures, radio reception, karate, locksmithing, communication links, dead drops, and coding with interspersion. Mercy gave Tania's assimilation and training a high evaluation. Once Mercy finished his work with Tania, he performed other missions and returned to his country of residence.

Some months later Tania traveled abroad and held several secret meetings with a new liaison who informed her that a comrade who like her was residing in La Paz would contact her. From that moment on she would be under his command.

Back in Bolivia, in May, 1966 after receiving the agreed on signal, she went to the appointed meeting place and established contact with her new handler.

On July 10, 1966 Tania received a message. Immediately she began to make preparations for the arrival of the guerrillas. For that purpose she rented safe houses and facilities that could serve as warehouses, made "sausages" for coded messages and performed other missions. When Che arrived he met with her and gave her new orders.

On December 20, 1966 Che wrote in his *Campaign Diary* that it had been decided to press the contacts with Coco Peredo's man who was working in the Presidency's information office and talk with Megía (a Peruvian revolutionary whose identity has not been revealed) so that he would serve as contact between Ivan and the man in the presidency. He pointed out that Ivan would be in contact with Tania, Megía and "Sánchez" (Julio Dagnino Pacheco), another Peruvian revolutionary that was part of the underground in Bolivia, and also with a comrade from the Bolivian Communist Party. The urban support network was being structured at a fast pace and included Dr. Hugo Lozano as radio operator, Rodolfo Saldaña, doctors Walter Parejas Fernández and Humberto Rhea Clavijo, and Loyola Guzmán, as well as other comrades.

In late December, 1966, Tania traveled to Ñacahuasú and on the 31 she met Che. She spent New Year's Eve with her comrades in the Bolivian jungle. On January 1, Che entrusted her with several secret missions in Argentina. She left for La Paz the next morning and from there continued to Buenos Aires.

Tania carried out her missions and returned to the guerrilla camp in March, 1967, in order to take out Regis Debray and Ciro Roberto Bustos. While they were waiting for Che, who was reconnoitering, Vicente Rocabado Terrazas and Pastor Barrera Quintana deserted the guerrilla. Subsequently they informed the Bolivian army, their intelligence service and the CIA about the presence of Tania in the guerrilla camp, and that she had traveled by jeep to Camiri. The vehicle was located and Laura Gutiérrez Bauer identified as linked to the guerrillas. Che wrote on his diary: There is sure indication that Tania's cover is blown, which means that two years of good and patient work have been lost."

Bolivian intelligence agencies and the CIA Station at La Paz did not know about Laura Gutiérrez Bauer's secret and undercover activities until the revelations by the two deserters gave them an important lead. She worked in the high spheres of Bolivian society unsuspected. When her apartment was raided, all they found were photographs with important figures of the cultural, political and social circles of Bolivia, including Generals Barrientos and Ovando, which baffled CIA officers and the Bolivian intelligence service. Names, addresses and telephone numbers found were of people that were above suspicion of being linked to the guerrilla operations or the urban support network, and although repression was applied to some of them, they were released immediately, for they were influential and had government connections.

The life and personality of this extraordinary internationalist revolutionary was depicted in the book *Tania, the Guerrilla,* by Cuban Marta Rojas and Mirta Rodríguez Calderón, published in 1970 by the Cuban Book Institute, with a foreword by Inti Peredo.

The Bolivian people faced intense repression

Taking advantage of documents and photos found at the caves and those obtained when the army ambushed the rear guard group on August 31, intelligence services and the CIA implicated and compromised a large number of people that they wanted to repress. In collaboration with Bolivian secret services they prepared an intense and calculated operation that began in early September.

Dr. Hugo Lozano's residence and office were raided on September 5, but the radio operator of the urban support network managed to go underground. On September 14 they arrested Loyola Guzmán Lara, a student of Philosophy at the University of La Paz and in charge of the guerrilla's finances. From the first moment she was subjected to a permanent surveillance in order to detect her contacts. When CIA agents showed the military and intelligence officers some photos found at the caves, one of them recognized her. Two other women were arrested with Loyola, distinguished University of La Paz Professor Paquita Bernal de Leytón, and mining labor leader Norberta de Aguilar. Immediately university students demonstrated in the streets demanding their release.

The media reported that Loyola Guzmán tried to commit suicide when she jumped from the second floor of the Ministry of the Interior, but she fell on a ledge and then on a tree, a fact that saved her life. Once again she was apprehended. Other strange "suicide" attempts at the ministry were reported. It was also informed that Roberto Moreira Montesinos, a young law student, tried to "kill himself". At his trial, Judge Clara Torres de Oporto asked him his opinion on Fidel Castro. The young man answered bravely: "He is a very just head of state that I admire very much", and then he added that he believed in the guerrillas, because they were the salvation of the country, that he knew Coco and Inti Peredo and admired them. After his deposition he allegedly fell from the second floor of the Ministry of the Interior. In the fall he suffered several fractures.

Professors César Chávez Taborga and Gonzalo Ramírez Alcázar, as well as several other professors and teachers, were arrested under the accusation of liaison with the guerrillas. This caused a general and indefinite general strike among his comrades. The same solidarity attitude was adopted by rural teachers. Professor René Higueras del Barco, a leader of rural teachers and head of Hugo Dávila High School in the Miraflores quarter, was arrested together with some of his colleagues. Immediately Hugo Dávila students began a hunger strike in support of their teachers.

In Oruro, 270 kilometers from La Paz, there was a violent demonstration. The incident began when Army Sub-lieutenant Esedín Alarcón gave a public beating to university student Néstor Nogales. His schoolmates took to the streets and the police attacked them with bombs, gunfire and tear gas. Several students were wounded. One of them, Justino Duran Illanes, died at 4:00 a.m. at Oruro General Hospital.

The death increased the tension and demonstrations, and other city sectors joined the protests. Students decreed 48 hours of mourning, and Durán's wake was held at the university's auditorium with a permanent guard of honor. All the country's universities supported the mourning.

The government held the communists responsible for the violence. In an meeting granted to several chiefs and officers of the security guard, Barrientos told them that the armed forces and the police were the institutions charged with keeping the stability of the nation.

"We might take extremely drastic but definite measures," he added, "because although there are armed guerrillas in the southwest jungle, here in the cities the guerrillas use strikes, violence, and commotion."

He also said that at the moment both the army and the police were on the defensive. In relation to the guerrillas, he said: "They are doing what they please. They raise one flag and then another."

From that moment on repression particularly targeted relatives of the guerrillas. Humberto, Jorge Vázquez Viaña's brother, was accused of liaising with the guerrillas and of operating a clandestine radio equipment. His house was raided and he was tenaciously harassed until he was forced to go into exile.

Rosa Maymura Hurtado, the sister of a guerrilla known as Fredy, was dismissed from her job at *El Diario* newspaper. Two other brothers, Antonio and Ángel, as well as their aunt Rogelia Hurtado, were thrown in jail. Still another sister of Fredy, Mary Maymura, was put under surveillance, and her husband Héctor Solares was fired from his job at Illimani National Radio.

Doña Isabel Marchetti, secretary general of the Widows of the Chaco War Association in Santa Cruz and mother of guerrilla Lorgio Vaca Marchetti was arrested and held in solitary confinement. The ladies member of that prestigious institution protested for the arrest of a seventy year old frail woman. The authorities turned a deaf ear. In view of the situation the widows prevented that she was taken to La Paz, as the police had attempted to do. They vented their frustration on her children. Hugo was arrested; Olga was fired from her teaching post, and later was arrested and charged with agitating the widows of the Chaco War in defense of her mother. Isabel and her children were questioned by CIA agents.

The family of Marlene Uriona, Lorgio Vaca's wife, was also persecuted. Her brother Guillermo was fired, her sister Mary was placed under close surveillance, but influential relations in political and military circles prevented her arrest.

Likewise Modesto Reinaga and his wife Raquel Barriga, brother and sister in law of guerrilla Aniceto Reinaga, were persecuted.

Repression against the family of Moisés Guevara began from the very instant in which the intelligence agencies knew that he was in Nacahuasú. His parent's home at the mines of Cataricagua was raided systematically and everything in it destroyed. On one occasion the house was machine gunned. Because of the constant psychological pressure against the family one of Moisés' brother was driven to insanity. They terrorized everyone in such a manner that friends, comrades and even relatives could not visit the house, because they were accused of complicity with the guerrillas or of being sympathizers. Prior to the September repression, close friends found out that the army had a plan for exterminating the whole Guevara family. Because of the tip they were able to hide elsewhere.

Elvira Valdez, linked to Peruvian revolutionaries, was tortured and lost her mind. Vicenta Guzmán Lara, Loyola's sister, was also persecuted. There were dozens of people arrested for allegedly being linked to the guerrillas, being a sympathizer or simply out of suspicion.

Many revolutionaries were tortured and subjected to fierce questioning. Others managed to go into hiding, apply for political asylum or leave the country in secret. Most of the members of the urban network went underground.

Mireya Echazú, Coco Peredo's wife, was tenaciously persecuted, and when she was not found the repression was applied to her family. Her father, Dr. Alberto Echazú, was detained and his house raided. He was released thanks to Dr. Javier Torres Goitía, President of the Bolivian Medical Association, for Dr. Echazu was one of the institution's most prestigious members. Subsequently the authorities arrested Torres Goitía and other doctors and accused them of being linked to the guerrillas.

Jorge Echazú, Mireya's brother, was also arrested and sent together with several of his comrades to a concentration camp in East Bolivia.

From the very first moment that the army knew there were guerrillas in Ñacahuasú, Inti Peredo's wife Matilde Lara was persecuted, but she managed to go underground. Her father Jesús Lara, one of Bolivia's top writers, was put under systematic surveillance. He was not arrested because the intelligence services thought that through him they would find his daughter's hiding place.

Antonio Peredo, Coco's and Inti's brother, was dismissed from Radio New America and Illimani National Radio, where he worked as an announcer and journalist. He was charged of transmitting coded messages. Peredo was forced into exile. His sister Emma was fired from her job at the Ministry of Agriculture; another sister was expelled from Simón Bolívar Teachers' College, where she was Head of the Language Department. Doña Selvira Leigue, the Peredo brothers' mother, was placed under systematic control and police surveillance.

Repression was brutal. Anyone suspected or family related to a guerrilla was accused as such. Safe houses set up by the CIA at Isabel la Católica Square and in the Sorata tourist sector were permanently occupied, and Agency's agents personally did the questioning.

The list of arrested people was long. Bolivian authorities admitted the arrest of Loyola Guzmán, Germán Salinas, Gonzalo Ramírez, Roberto Moreira Montesinos, Félix Mendoza, Efraín Cabrera, Fredy Valdivia, Norberta de Aguilar, José Luis Valencia, Willy Calvo Ricaldi, Víctor Hugo Fernández, Marcelino Flores, René Higueras del Barco, César Chávez Taborga and Paquita Bernal de Leytón. They publicly accused King Palenque, Guido Quesada Gambarte, Jesús Taborga and Justiniano Ninavía, among others, of being guerrilla liaisons. On September 18 the government announced the discovery of a guerrilla liaison network and the arrest of its members —Enrique León, Florencio Lezcano, Víctor Pacheco, Emilio Padilla, Víctor Salazar, Manuel Romero and Juan Ríos Encinas. Three days later several women were detained in Cochabamba, including Carmen Eguez de Rico, who was pregnant, a fact oblivious to DIC chief Alberto Díaz Siles and his agents when they questioned her.

In spite of his age and former high position,—father of Esperanza Butrón (married to guerrilla Mario Gutiérrez Ardaya) and former Labor Minister under Víctor Paz Estenssoro—, Germán Butrón was submitted to constant police control.

Repression went rampant in the rest of the country. At Trinidad, capital of Beni department, relatives of guerrillas Julio Luis Méndez Korne and Mario Gutiérrez Ardaya were under the control of the intelligence services, particularly Mary and Pura, Mario's sisters, two very prestigious teachers, as well as their father Elías Gutiérrez, a decorated hero of the Chaco War and benemérito de la patria.

Permanent control was established at Tarija against Fabiola Campero and Marta Arana, respectively mother and sister of guerrilla Jaime Arana Campero, aka *Chapaco.*

In Camiri all the documents for the defense of Regis Debray were stolen. Shots were fired against Debray's father to intimidate him and force him out of the country. Since the month of May Bolivian intelligence agencies and the CIA had placed Janine Alexandra, Debray's mother, under rigorous control. Special instructions were given to intercept all telephone calls both in Bolivia and in Paris.

French Ambassador Dominique Ponchadier and Cultural Attaché Gerard Barthelemy were also under surveillance and their telephones tapped by the CIA. Agency officers believed that Barthelemy was not trustworthy, because he expressed sympathy towards Debray in private. They called him pejorative names and made contemptuous remarks of the fact that he had married a Haitian.

The CIA kept Ana María Castro, Ciro Roberto Bustos' wife, under special surveillance and bugged her house. They did the same in the case of Elizabeth Burgos, Regis Debray's companion.

Repression did not end in September, but grew in intensity. More than 200 people were charged with being liaisons to the guerrillas.

Americans inspect arms remittances to Bolivia

In August, 1967 there were insistent rumors that US military advisors were implicated in shady arms dealings with traffickers and smugglers. The scandal grew after a cargo that sailed from the Chilean port of Arica never reached Bolivia. According to Bolivian intelligence sources, the CIA Station informed Washington about this profitable affair. There was much rivalry and turf warring between the Agency and the Pentagon, so when the scandal broke contradictions heightened.

On September 2 the US government sent Patrick Morris, director of the State Department's Office of Bolivian and Chilean Affairs, to investigate the agency's reports and discuss existing problems among US officials.

On that same day Bolivian media reported the discovery of an important cache of weapons at the Huanuni mines. According to the same sources the information was a false leak in order to mislead Morris and make him believe that the weapons had been stolen by miners that supported the guerrillas. In that manner the smuggling would be justified.

On September 19 French teacher Susanne Robert was apprehended and charged of links with the guerrilla and arms trafficking. The following day, a diplomatic pouch from the US Embassy with documents and checks disappeared en route from the US mission to the Branniff International Airlines office in downtown La Paz.

According to Bolivian sources, a fourteen year old boy stole the pouch for a few pesos and delivered it to two plainclothesmen that were waiting for him in a military jeep at a street near Camacho Avenue. It was said the report written by Patrick Morris on the arms smuggling and trafficking plus his conclusions on the issue were in that pouch. The reason for the robbery was that US military advisors needed time for explaining to their superiors in Washington and influence them.

On September 21 a mission of the US Armed Forces arrived in La Paz with the purpose of investigating complaints, and to oversee the transportation and delivery of a new 15 ton shipment. The Bolivian media reported that the arms would come by way of the Peruvian port of Arequipa. Nevertheless, a US ship, the "Marfac", docked at the Peruvian port of Matarani, 950 kilometers from La Paz, where the shipment was loaded and supervised by the controlling commission. It was later known that the report in relation to Arequipa was a deliberate misleading leak.

On its part, Bolivian intelligence sent Captain Humberto Aliendre Mercado to receive the shipment as guarantee that it would be fully delivered. The arms were flown to Bolivia in a US Air Force Hercules cargo plane.

The investigation of the missing shipment caused rumors about different versions among the Bolivian military, US advisors and CIA officers. The former claimed that the arms were never sent or that the Americans sold them elsewhere. They also accused the Chilean armed forces as the perpetrators of the robbery because they were concerned about Bolivian rearmament.

Another matter of friction was the robbery of the diplomatic pouch, for the US Embassy pressed the police to find the guilty parties. For that reason an internal and criminal repression began against shoeshine boys, newspaper vendors or child beggars on Camacho Avenue and its surroundings. A group of these poor kids were arrested, beaten and tortured in order to find information about the incident. Repression reached such degree that groups of parents, neighbors and relatives of those poor boys went to penal district attorney Juan Rivera Antezana to make a formal complaint. They charged members of the army and the police of the outrages and physical damage inflicted on the boys. But the public prosecutor accused the Bolivian Communist Party of masterminding a systematic smear campaign against the Armed Forces of the nation, that all accusations were false and part of a communist plan to present the military as abusing citizens.

Relatives and neighbors protested to the judge, and presented the beaten youngsters so that he could see for himself. Rivera Antezana claimed that the damage was self inflicted in order to accuse army officers of those crimes, and declared: "We will not allow that the Nation's Armed Forces be vilely slandered and discredited by reds." Then he concluded: "Those responsible for this campaign will be suppressed according to the law."

On October 11, 1967, the police informed that citizen Leandro Goyzueta had been arrested on Camacho Avenue when he tried to exchange 26 US checks for Bolivian currency. According to the police, Goyzueta declared that he had found them in a garbage dump on Los Andes Street. Since he had given no other information the investigation continued, because it could mean a sure lead for arresting the guilty parties.

On that same day La Paz press reported a bizarre suicide –a fourteen year old youngster had lost his life playing Russian roulette at the Alonso de Mendoza Square. On the next day the newspaper

Presencia reported the following news. "Yesterday, at 20:00 hours, detectives of the Crime against Persons section found the body of Oscar Cordero Zapata, 14, who according to police authorities accidentally killed himself while he was playing with a firearm. The bullet was lodged in the right temporal region [...] Police are investigating where the boy could have gotten the revolver with which he accidentally took his own life."

Neighbors declared that on that day several DIC and Ministry of the Interior members, commanded by Colonel Rafael Loayza, had gone to the boy's house and beat him savagely, warning relatives and neighbors not to intervene or denounce the event under threats of death. Another neighbor who remained hidden in her house saw through a window when Colonel Rafael Loayza shot the boy. Hours later the body was found at Alonso de Mendoza Square.

Bolivian sources claimed that the boy knew who had stolen the diplomatic pouch. His murder erased the possibility of finding who had masterminded the robbery.

Teachers protest in La Paz

In mid September Bolivian teachers and professors decided to go on strike demanding higher salaries and in protest for the outrage and repression against several of their arrested colleagues, charged with links with the guerrillas. Since the authorities turned a deaf era to their demands, they decided on a large demonstration in the Bolivian capital. The La Paz newspaper *El Diario* reported that "Groups of teachers yesterday threw downtown areas into confusion when they held isolated demonstrations against the government. They were vigorously repelled by the police, who used a large quantity of tear gas, attack dogs and water hoses. An urban and two rural teachers were wounded [...]"

The newspaper report underlined that teachers opted for a new tactic to express their protest. They grouped hundreds of protesters that went to different parts of the city. "A well organized group was dissolved in its attempt to reach Murillo Square [...] In a few seconds the police routed the group with tear gas. A grenade wounded teacher Emel Calderón, who was taken to the Medical and Surgical Service [...]"

There were also bloody clashes at Santa Cruz Avenue, and at Potosí and Yanacocha Streets. Stores and offices were forced to close down because the abundant amounts of tear gas prevented pedestrian traffic. The same press reported that due to that police attack, the teachers tore out paving stones to defend themselves.

In Cochabamba students, teachers and professors also protested. Ramiro Barrenechea, vice president of the Bolivian University Confederation, explained:

"At the civil parade of September 14, the Cochabamba commemoration of the struggle against Spanish colonialism, we had noisily shouted 'Long live the independence guerrillas.' For the chaste ears of the pious this could be taken for a student metaphor that alluded to the well remembered 1810 guerrillas. But the police did not believe in literary figures and attacked with systematic effort and meticulousness those of us who marched by with our raised fists and looking away from the authorities, who shockingly exhibited in the 'patriotic altar' their rotund fury for that intolerable act of rudeness. Three military bands simultaneously roared: the 8th Division's, formal and in dress uniforms; the CITE's in camouflaged battle dress; and the police band. It wasn't that they were accompanying the passage of the university, but had received the order to drown with their bass drums and trumpets the battle cries and a few bold mentions to those at Ñacahuasú, Che and the thunderous 'Down with the military boot.' Those more formal and disciplined sang The Marseillaise, particularly the stanza:

'Against us tyranny's
Bloody standard is raised [...]
To arms, citizens,
Form in battalions,
March, march!
Let impure blood
Water our furrows!'"

In order to justify repression, the police informed of "A wave of student provocation generated by professional agitators that caused meetings, demonstrations, rock throwing and street war."

Inside important government and Armed Forces circles alarm grew concerning the grave consequences of the use of napalm.

From the eastern jungles of Bolivia came the report of a great fire that lasted weeks, devastating virgin forests and local wildlife. The information raised great concerns that forced the military command to admit the seriousness of the situation and point that only the onset of the rainy season could end the catastrophe.

While more Americans arrived in Bolivia, journalist Jorge Rossa wrote about the coming of a strange Colonel Owens from South Vietnam, where he had been in charge of the invaders' supply trains, accompanied by two other Americans named Lee and Donovan. According to the Americans, they were in Bolivia to study the modernization of the Santa Cruz-Yacuiba railroad. The journalist's report said that when they passed by the railway workers' thatched huts they muttered, "This bloody bastard people."

US presence in Bolivia and reaction by the population

On September 18, 1967, the La Paz newspaper *El Diario* reported that Vice president Luis Adolfo Siles Salinas and US instructors had been present at the closing ceremony of the Ranger Regiment's training course and had awarded diplomas to chiefs, officers and soldiers

Regiment commander Colonel José Gallardo said in a speech that US advisors were the architects of the Bolivian soldiers' new personality. Major Ralph Shelton spoke on behalf of the 15 American experts who trained the Bolivian army. In his speech he said that in a struggle such as this one, soldiers needed to be very tough. On addressing them he said: "I am very proud of you. Now you are combat ready."

Zenteno Anaya called Shelton "a dear friend of Bolivia" and congratulated him on his work. Then Vice president Siles Salinas made a speech. The act ended with a parade by the 640 rangers with their uniforms and green berets in the style of US Special Forces.

At the capital, Sergio Almaraz Paz, together with intellectuals René Zavaleta Mercado, Jaime Otero Calderón, Raúl Ibarnegaray Téllez, María Elba Gutiérrez, Félix Rospigliosi Nieto, Horacio Torres Guzmán, Guillermo Riveros Tejada, Jorge Calvimontes Montes, Sergio Virreira, Eusebio Gironda and Enrique Fernholds Ruiz, created the National Coordination of the Resistance, and wrote the "Manifesto to the Nation" that began to circulate clandestinely. Among other issues, it pointed out:

"The time has come to call on the peoples to defend the Bolivian homeland. Indeed, the country is more occupied than ever, and this fact is ignored only by those who refuse to see things as they really are or by those who want to mask them. Never have the fate of Bolivians, the supreme interests of the Nation as a Nation, and even the lesser operative details of the administration been so directly placed in the hands of foreigners. Today it can be said that nothing belongs to Bolivians in Bolivia, except poverty, persecution and death."

The signers of the document pointed out that they were men born of the flesh of this land, from several sectors of opinion, from different political organizations, considering that "we undoubtedly are forced now to make a dramatic call to our people, judging exclusively in our names and as absolutely responsible, but before the entire Nation, this conspiracy of imperialism and the anti-country that even if it passes and reigns triumphantly in Bolivia today, will only be preserved if the country renounces forever to be its own master."

In another part they wrote: "It is the American plan, and not Barrientos nor Ovando that rules this country. It is a plan that is designed for directly occupying the strategic sector of our economy, for the destruction or immobilization of the social composition of the country's strategic sectors and, in short, for the later, gradual and systematic denationalization of Bolivia as a whole (…)"

In relation to repression on the workers, and particularly on miners, the Manifesto said:

"For the counterrevolution it was necessary to destroy that essentially dangerous class, and in so doing they proved they were willing to go to the most terrible extremes, unparalleled in the terrible history of our country.

"The history goes back to the previous regime. For more than a year and a half, the US Embassy pressed the Paz Estenssoro administration through Mr. Henderson with an almost weekly regularity, demanding the entry of the army in the mining districts, otherwise the third stage of the Triangular Plan would be suspended. It was known that military presence in the mines would not be possible without bloodshed, but they argued that the result of the previous stages could not be checked, for their officers were taken hostages by the miners, as it had previously happened on some occasions. Perhaps in order to pay the price of the power that he had received, Barrientos finally gave in to this demand, not very enthusiastic about the actions, .as reported by the press on those tragic days [...]"

The Manifesto also denounced the cruel massacres carried out during the Barrientos regime at Villa Victoria, Munuypata, El Tejar and other La Paz neighborhoods, at the Milluni, Kami, Atocha, Telamayu and Catavi mining centers. It revealed the use of artillery and air attacks against open towns, and added: "But this was not enough: on June 24, 1967, the mines are again the scene of new genocides, christened by the people as the St. John's Massacre. This time because the regime's inconsistency and decomposition were shaken by a perturbing element that forced it to attain unity based on the compromise with a crime. It is common knowledge in Bolivia that after the massacre itself the workers were massively dismissed, salaries of the remaining ones reduced by half, and their organizations submitted to rules compared only to the existing ones in Franco's Spain and Oliveira Salazar's Portugal. This is a curious developing policy for men that have a life expectancy of thirty years. Barrientos had said it: 'We will repress with the most brutal violence.'

"What is the explanation for this furious aggressiveness towards a class that is also the most tragic one in a tragic country?"

In relation to the army the Manifesto claimed: "Thus the occupation plan by the Americans is continued within the army itself, which is today an occupied army, just as Bolivia is an invaded country.

"In the name of the army, in the midst of bribery, binges and nepotism of a despicable lineage, there has been a conspiracy against the very essence of the army –which is none other than the defense of territorial and economic sovereignty of the nation, the protection of its inner and outer double border.

"Today on behalf of the army, which after all is none other than the guerrilla of our forbearers turned into an institution, speak the ones who have handed over the army, the ones who trade their country for Mercedes Benz automobiles. Suffice to say that for decades the senior year of the Military Academy is done at US facilities in Panama.

100

"The occupation is such that our present army, in relation to equipment and even in relation to its very military doctrine, is not designed to defend Bolivia as Bolivia, which is a determined territory and human field, but for the safeguard of this part of the continent as a section of the US Empire."

The Manifesto ends with the following paragraph:

"It is time to organize ourselves with the only goal of reducing to its proper limits a foreign invader that despises us and spits on our most intimate symbols. It is time for Bolivians to join their efforts to expel the intruders. And no matter our subsequent fate, we call on our people to spurn factions and unite exclusively with the Nation. Let us resist those that occupy our homeland!"

While the *Manifesto to the Nation* was distributed in a clandestine manner, US military advisors and Marines were still arriving. On October 5, 1967, *El Diario* reported from Cochabamba that a US Air Force Hercules airplane had landed at that city with army doctors and spare parts for the helicopters that operated in the southwest of the country against the guerrillas. According to the report the news was confirmed by Major Víctor Lora, chief of the city's Air Base No. 2. It also said that witnesses of the landing of the airplane at the base informed that it also carried Navy officers and troops.

While the rangers were arriving to the zone of operations, on September 22 the guerrillas took the Alto Seco hamlet and subsequently moved on towards El Picacho and the surroundings of La Higuera, where they arrived on the 26th. On that same day they continued on to the hamlet of Jagüey where the army was ambushed. Coco Peredo, Manuel Hernández Osorio and Mario Gutiérrez Ardaya were killed in combat. The military loaded the bodies on donkeys and took them to Pucará. The population was shocked seeing the bodies treated as if they were sacks, and not human beings. Subsequently they took them to Vallegrande. The documents were delivered to CIA agents Julio Gabriel García y Félix Ramos, who sent them to the United States.

After the ambush, guerrillas Antonio Domínguez Flores (*León*), and Orlando Jiménez Bazán (*Camba*) did not regroup with their comrades. The former surrendered to the army and the latter was made prisoner on the 28th. When they were taken to Vallegrande, Barrientos met with them and guaranteed their lives in exchange for their collaboration. CIA agents Félix Ramos and Julio Gabriel

García began torturing and questioning them, and told them not believe Barrientos, because they were the ones that made the decisions and did not care about another dead guerrilla. *León* gave valuable information about the composition of the guerrilla, the exact number of those left, the state of health of each one of them, particularly Che Guevara, of whom he said that his cryptonym was Fernando, and answered all questions. He accepted to testify against Debray and Bustos and to everything that the authorities understood was necessary and useful. He was taken to Camiri and placed in the same cell with Ciro Roberto Bustos, with the order that he should inform about everything that Bustos said and did.

The September 26 ambush, the death of three valuable comrades, Camba's detention and León's desertion were severe blows to the guerrillas that was forced to change plans and follow an unforeseen route. Additionally, León was carrying most of the medicines and part of the food that the sick or those in bad shape could not carry. All of that meant new difficulties for the guerrilla.

The urban support network

The Bolivian secret agencies and the CIA arrested some members of the guerrilla's urban support network, but most of them went underground, thus escaping from the intense repression. With the purpose of reorganizing the network Rodolfo Saldaña, Estanislao Villca, Juan Martín Tejada Peredo, Horacio Rueda Peña and Osvaldo Ucasqui Acosta remained in La Paz, but in very difficult conditions. They in turn received the support, help and solidarity of relatives, friends, comrades and sympathizers in the Bolivian capital, who collaborated with them even at the risk of becoming victims of the intense repression. A prominent role was played by Geraldine Córdova de Coronado, mother of guerrilla Benjamín Coronado.Some of the premises and safe houses were raided, but others went undiscovered. Such was the case of a mechanical workshop in the Alto Obrajes neighborhood where weapons sent to the guerrilla were prepared and adapted. At the shop M-1 carbines were converted to M-2s, clips were manufactured for several weapons, as well as rifle grenade launchers. On one occasion the workshop's guards observed unusual police surveillance, so immediately they warned Rodolfo Saldaña, who ordered the weapons moved in a station wagon to a safe place. Saldaña later recalled that when they arrived to the important Hernando Siles Avenue they found extreme security measures because of a caravan of vehicles that escorted President Barrientos. Right away they joined the end of the caravan as if they were part of it and took advantage of the expedient flow of vehicles to avoid possible controls and leave the area that was occupied by security forces, soldiers and police, all armed to the teeth. After moving the weapons they returned and also moved lathes, machinery and soldering equipment to avoid discovery of the place and the equipment by the repressive forces.

Members of the urban network who worked as truck drivers from the cities of Sucre, Santa Cruz and Camiri to important points of the guerrilla area were never detected, in spite of the intense and systematic controls at all roads, towns and cities

In the midst of the intense repression and severe controls in airports and border points, a guerrilla liaison came to La Paz, Her cryptonym was Natacha and she secretly met with Rodolfo Saldaña at a tailor shop in one of the capital's poor neighborhoods.

The authorities never knew of the existence of this shop or the identity of two comrades that worked there as members of the urban support network. Escaping detection, a group of 50 trained Bolivian revolutionaries were ready to join the guerrillas.

The Bolivian intelligence agencies and the CIA never detected the clandestine radio station in La Paz that was able to communicate even with Argentinean radio hams, nor were they able to arrest the radio operator .

The arms caches in the areas where Che's guerrillas were planning to operate or those in La Paz were not discovered.

Several contacts with people that worked in military barracks, government offices and of the Ministry of the Interior, who supplied information, arms and provisions, are still unknown. A backup group of the urban support network in the city of Puno, near the Argentinean border, was never identified. Likewise the ones in Argentina and Chile or in other Bolivian cities such as Santa Cruz, Oruro, Cochabamba, Tarija, and Sucre.

Support networks were created in towns in the vicinity of the guerrilla area. Such was the case in Lagunillas, capital of the Cordilleras province, where guerrilla camps were established. On December 20, 1966 Che wrote: "Finally it was decided that Ricardo, Iván and Coco fly from Camiri and that the jeep stays here. When they return they will telephone Lagunillas and warn that they are there. Jorge will go that night in search of news and will look for them if there is anything positive."

This entry assumes that someone who had a telephone in Lagunillas was a liaison with the guerrillas or was trusted by them: otherwise Che would not order them to call when they reached Camiri nor to guerrilla Jorge Vázquez Viaña to go at night in search of news.

Among those who received telephone messages were David Herrera, the town's chief of police, and his wife Rebeca Bello. They were not the only ones that helped the guerrillas, but also Dr. Hugo Bleischner Taboada, a military doctor, and Mario Chávez, who appears in Che's diary as "the explorer" or "the man from Lagunillas."

On that day Che also wrote: "At one we were unable to receive anything from La Paz." Obviously someone from La Paz was sending radio messages to the guerrilla zone.

Before the combat at Quebrada del Yuro

The guerrillas stayed in the vicinity of La Higuera on the first days of October. On the 6th they reached a stream and cooked all day under a ledge. They continued their advance in the early morning. On this occasion Che wrote:

"We set out on the 17th with a very small moon and the march was very tiring (…) At 2 o'clock we stopped to rest, for it was useless to continue moving forward."

The march was not only tiring but extremely difficult, because Chino, the Peruvian, lost his eyeglasses and was practically blind, and in that condition he was unable to walk. Several of the guerrillas were ill. The vegetation was tough and thorny. Even by day the conditions were very complicated, because on top of all this there was the lack of trees and the vegetation was almost leafless.

On the last paragraph written by the Heroic Guerrilla in his campaign diary on October 7, he said: "The army gave a strange

104

information about the presence of 250 men in Serrano to prevent the passage of the 37 surrounded guerrillas, and gave the location of our refuge between the Acero and the Oro Rivers. The news seems a disinformation."

According to Bolivian sources, the information was Ovando's idea for reinforcing the order given by the commander of the 7th Division in late September that the units stationed in the vicinity of La Higuera should be deployed towards the area of the Acero and Oro rivers. There was news that the guerrillas were headed in that direction.

Likewise it was known through other sources that Ovando believed that the guerrilla should be engaged from the periphery and at a distance, avoiding frontal clashes, that advantage should be taken of the circumstances and the possibilities that the Americans were granting to train and properly supply the army. He thought that if the guerrillas were wiped out at that moment, US assistance would cease. He claimed that finishing off Barrientos was a matter of a short time. Ovando felt that eventually the guerrillas would be for his own benefit, and that after eliminating Barrientos the absolute control of the army would be in his hands. At that moment, the different fractions of the Revolutionary Nationalist Movement would join him. Military and political control would allow him to become president, and for both objectives the presence of the guerrilla at the moment was important. Ovando's strategy was shared by other officers.

Ovando's order that troops should retreat from the vicinity of La Higuera before October 5 was not carried out. Their leader, Major Miguel Ayoroa Montaño, was against it and thought it was illogical and irrational. As there was a deadline for the order, Major Ayoroa requested permission to express his contradictory point of view, and argued that if on September 26 there had been a combat in the vicinity of La Higuera, no information, no matter how reliable, could convince anyone that in such a short time the guerrillas could have gone as far as the Acero and Oro Rivers.

Considering Ayoroa's intransigent attitude, Ovando sent Reque Terán to meet with him and impose discipline. Ayoroa was ordered to Vallegrande, to where Reque Terán arrived accompanied by Alberto Libera Cortez, chief of logistics, and Víctor Castillo Suárez, chief of operations. Ayoroa stated that his troops had been immobilized for a week because of the order of redeployment. He considered the decision as a lack of respect to his military integrity and claimed that the Commander in Chief did not know what was really happening. He explained why he disobeyed the order and how instead stipulated that no one could move from the area of operations. Reque Terán ordered him to obey, but again Ayoroa refused to comply and said that he would leave the area only if the information was confirmed.

After returning to Pucará to await the final decision he received a message from Captain Gary Prado informing that one of his men had seen the guerrillas. Captain Prado asked for instructions and Ayoroa ordered him to take command of A and B Companies.

On October 8, at 12:30 a.m., he left for La Higuera together with Captain Celso Torrelio. When they arrived the combat was in full swing.

The role of the CIA in Che's Murder

October 8, 1967

In relation to that day's events, Inti Peredo wrote: "The early morning on October 8 was cold. Those of us who had jackets put them on. Our advance was sluggish, for Chino walked very slowly at night and Moro's illness was getting worse. At 2:00 a.m. we stopped to rest and at 4 we resumed our hike ..."

When the guerrillas stopped for water at a stream they were seen by Pedro Peña, one of the army's spies that roamed the area dressed as a peasant. Peña put out the lamp he was carrying and hid in order to pinpoint the exact place. He went to La Higuera, looked for Sublieutenant Carlos Pérez Panoso, platoon leader in Company A, and informed him of the situation. Pérez radioed his superiors who were stationed in the vicinity of the area with two Ranger companies of 145 men each and a 37 men squadron, all trained by US advisors. Other companies were also deployed to Quebrada del Yuro (Yuro Ravine).

At five thirty in the morning, the guerrillas reached the confluence of two streams. According to Inti Peredo, "The morning was lit with the beautiful sun that permitted us to closely study the terrain. We were looking for a crest to proceed later to the San Lorenzo River. Security measures were maximized, particularly because the ravine

107

and the hills were almost bare, with low shrubbery that made hiding almost impossible."

According to Inti and other guerrilla survivors, Che decided to send three pairs of scouts: to the left *Urbano* and *Ñato*; forward *Aniceto* and *Darío*, to the right *Benigno* and *Pacho*. All returned with the news that the soldiers were closing the passage. Che recalled the scouting parties and ordered the retreat to another ravine, but after more reconnoitering *Pacho* and *Benigno* found that the ravine ended in a cliff and there was no way out. In his book *My Campaign with Che*, Inti wrote:

"What possibility did we have? We couldn't go back. The way we had taken, much unprotected, made us easy prey of the soldiers. Nor could we go forward, because it meant marching into the soldiers' positions. Che made the only possible decision at the moment. He ordered everybody to hide in a small side canyon and organized the defense. It was approximately 8:30 a.m.. The seventeen of us sat there in the middle and on both sides of the canyon, waiting.

"Che made a quick analysis. If the soldiers attacked us between 10 a.m. and 1 a.m. we were at a disadvantage and our chances were few, for it was very difficult to resist for a long time. If the attack came between 1 and 3 p.m., we had better chances of neutralizing it. If the combat was held from 3 a.m. on, we had the best possibilities, for night falls quickly and is the natural ally of the guerrilla."

Pombo mentioned that Che organized the scouting, ordered in which direction each had to go and where they should regroup in case of dispersion. He also organized the defense with *Antonio, Chapaco, Arturo* and *Willy* in the rear, placing *Benigno* at the entrance and subsequently Inti and *Darío* on the left flank, with the mission of protecting the entrance and if necessary the retreat. *Pacho* was posted on the right flank with a mission of observation. Urbano and Che himself would remain on the upper end of the ravine.

The orders were: if the army entered the ravine, to retreat by the left flank; if they attacked on the right flank, to retreat down the ravine, and in the same direction if the attack was through the upper end. Regrouping would be on the left slope. They were at Quebrada del Yuro, some 1,500 meters long, 60 meters wide, with a stream bed 2 to 3 meters wide.

The combat begins

Inti Peredo explained in his book:

"About 11 a.m. I went to replace (*Benigno*) in his post, but (…) he stayed there lying down, because the wound in his shoulder had suppurated and it hurt him very much. Finally *Benigno, Darío* and I stayed there. On the other end of the ravine were *Pombo* and *Urbano*, and Che in the center with the rest of the combatants.

"Approximately at 13:30 Che sent *Ñato* and *Aniceto* to replace *Pombo* and *Urbano*. In order to reach that position we had to cross a clearing that was covered by the enemy. The first to try it was *Aniceto*, but a bullet killed him. The battle had begun."

Pombo, Urbano and *Benigno* have added that the army controlled a part of the stream bed, so the guerrillas' positions were isolated one from the other.

The firm resistance of the guerrillas checked the advance of the army. The possibilities of exit in the daytime were remote because, as it has been said, the slopes were steep and ended in naked areas where the guerrillas could become easy targets.

The then Captain Gary Prado, Company B's leader, rushed to the combat area and radioed Vallegrande that he had engaged the enemy and needed helicopters, airplanes and reinforcements. AT-6 planes were sent to the area, but were unable to drop their napalm bombs because of the proximity of the soldiers to the guerrillas. They turned back.

The survivors recounted that two hours of intense combat passed, and about 4 p.m. *Ñato* relayed signals that made them believe that Che had made his exit. *Pombo* went out first and a hail of bullets fell on him. The soldiers saw *Urbano*'s shoulder and focused their fire on him, but he was not hit. One of them threw a grenade that raised a cloud of dirt and smoke, a circumstance that *Urbano* took advantage of to get out.

Intense shooting was heard down the ravine. *Pombo* and *Urbano* made it to the command post, but on arriving they saw the rest had already retreated.

Che's combat at the Yuro

The sad events at Quebrada del Yuro have been reconstructed by the survivors of the guerrilla in several interviews.

"We had to reconstruct what happened at the moment that Che was wounded based on deductions and on the posts where we were, because from the individual positions that the three of us occupied we could not directly see what happened. You have to imagine what those places are —a very rough terrain, full of zig zags, of hills grouped in such a manner that even if we were 300, 400 or 500 meters away we couldn't really see each other ... when the army made its entry in the ravine and controlled it, Che decided to retreat. He must have realized that the army was surrounding us and must have concluded that he had with him a group of comrades that were in no condition to fight.

"We believe that he decided to split the group in two, so that those who were sick could leave, while he remained with the rest to cover them. This would allow the sick ones to exit before being completely surrounded, and Che probably thought that afterwards his group could shoot its way out, or whatever was possible.

"He made the decision to take that risk in order to save the lives of *Moro, Eustaquio* and *Chapaco*. He ordered *Pablito*, who was fit to fight, to go with them. This group was advancing, trying to leave the cordon while Che was holding off the army. He stays back with *Chino, Willy, Antonio, Arturo* and *Pacho*.

"When Che tries to get out, he realizes the soldiers have totally surrounded him. He meets head on with Sergeant Bernardino Huanca's platoon, which has machine gun emplacements, and he is wounded

"*Antonio, Arturo* and *Pacho* resist, while Che, helped by *Willy*, manages to climb the slope where he had planned to retreat. They hide, but shortly after are discovered. It seems that it was a chance encounter, not that they were tracking him, but that a group of soldiers were going to position a mortar when they clashed with Che's group."

Thus ended their recount.

Che, who had a leg wound, kept on fighting until his carbine was rendered useless and was out of bullets for his pistol. *Antonio, Arturo* and *Pacho* were caught in a crossfire, but concentrated their fire on the soldiers causing several casualties, until a grenade exploded on them.

The soldiers who were at the place where Che and *Willy* had climbed were three —Balboa, Choque and Encinas. Some time later they told how they saw two guerrillas climbing, one of them Che Guevara. They explained that Balboa was the first to see them, took aim with his rifle and told them to stop. He saw how *Willy* took care of Che, who was wounded. Balboa was joined by the other two soldiers and saw that Che's M-1 carbine had been rendered useless by a bullet that hit the chamber; his pistol had no magazine and he only had a dagger. They recalled that Sublieutenant Bernardino Huanta arrived, approached Che and hit him in the chest with his rifle butt; then he pointed his weapon at him, as if he intended to shoot him, but *Willy* Cuba stepped in front of Che and shouted: "Damn it! This is Commander Guevara and you have to respect him!"

Huanta was not sure if it was really Che, so he communicated with Captain Gary Prado who ordered him to take the two guerrillas under a tree some 200 meters away. Prado radioed the army's command post at Vallegrande to report on the combat and on Che's detention. The information was retransmitted at 15:30 hours, and the text was the following:

"Time: 14:50
"Today, 7 km NW of Higueras, at the confluence of Jagüey-Racetillo Ravines, at 12:00 hrs, there was action, 3 guerrillas dead and two seriously wounded. Information confirmed by troops assure fall of Ramón. We still have no confirmation. On our side 2 dead and 4 wounded."

"Time: 15:30
"Prado from Higueras. 'Fall of Ramón confirmed awaiting orders what must be done. He is wounded.'"

At 16:30 a helicopter overflew the combat zone, but was unable to land, because the guerrillas that still were in the ravine shot at it. Then the pilot flew to La Higuera and returned to Vallegrande with the wounded soldiers.

At 17:00 hours a message is sent to La Paz that read: "Fall of Ramón confirmed. Condition will be known in another 10 minutes."

On the road to immortality

The soldiers carried the bodies of Antonio and Arturo, as well as Pacho, who was seriously wounded. Che was moved when he saw him and asked to be permitted to cure him. The soldiers refused.

At 17:30 the army left the area of operations and returned to the town. During the difficult march Che was guarded by several soldiers. Behind him went Willy Cuba, with his hands tied the same as Che's, then Pacho, helped by some soldiers, for he was seriously wounded, and finally the dead.

Before reaching the hamlet they met Ranger Battalion commander Miguel Ayoroa, and the Vallegrande Engineers Regiment commander Andrés Sélich, who had arrived by helicopter. Also with them were mayor of La Higuera Aníbal Quiroga and some peasants leading mules to carry the dead.

Andrés Sélich insulted and threatened Che. Two soldiers took their watches and other belongings.

According to Mayor Quiroga, "When we were en route to Quebrada del Yuro, on hearing gun fire Andrés Sélich and the military with him ran for cover, but the shots were from the soldiers, and they remained hidden until we civilians came out and checked.

"Che walked out of Florencio Aguilar's vegetable garden; he came first and behind him Willy, and further back the mules with another wounded guerrilla. Then other dead guerrillas.

"I saw Che. He was a big man, with a penetrating look in his eyes, and his height was imposing."

At 19:30, when the caravan ended its march to the hamlet, night had fallen. In the dark, the feeble lights from rustic kerosene lamps or candles illuminated the humble huts. The silent and frightened townspeople watched from their homes; others approached slowly like shadows to see the guerrillas.

The soldiers took Che to the ramshackle school of La Higuera, made of adobe, straw for a roof and a dirt floor. Two classrooms separated by a wooden panel. Day after day Élida Hidalgo, Juana Carrizales, Julia Cortés and Cacho Talama taught there. Che was left in one of the classrooms with the dead bodies of Arturo and Antonio on the floor. In the other room they put Willy and Pacho, the latter in very serious condition.

In relation to the wounded guerrilla, La Paz magazine *Enfoque* published an interview with Sub-Lieutenant Mario Eduardo Huerta Lorenzetti, who said that "the guerrilla's pain was growing and he whispered some words. I leaned towards him and heard that he was saying 'I feel terrible, please, do something to relieve my pain'. I did not know what to do, but he indicated himself: 'There, in the chest, please,' he said."

The night of October 8 at La Higuera

Witnesses to what happened on the night of October 8 at the hamlet of La Higuera were the military, Che, Willy Cuba, Mayor Aníbal Quiroga, the teachers, the telegraphist, his wife Ninfa Arteaga, and the townspeople.

After the military left the guerrillas in the school, Andrés Sélich, Ayoroa and Gary Prado went to have dinner at the mayor's house. Afterwards they went to the home of telegraphist Humberto Hidalgo and began to make an inventory of the guerrillas' belongings.

Approximately at 9 p.m., Andrés Sélich and Gary Prado went back to the school with the intention of questioning Che. Miguel Ayoroa joined them later. They wanted information, details that would allow them to annihilate the rest of the guerrillas and to know the exact spot where they should have regrouped. Che remained silent.

Sélich insulted him again and pulled his beard so hard that he uprooted part of it. Che had his hands tied, but he was outraged and reacted, almost hitting Sélich in the face with his bound hands. Sélich rushed Che with the intention of beating him. Che reacted in the only way he could: he spat him in the face. Sélich jumped on him again. Then they tied Che's hands behind his back.

They returned to the telegraphist's home, where Sélich took the guerrillas' belongings. The most valuable were distributed among the officers according to their rank: 4 Rolex watches, a .45 caliber German pistol, 1 Solingen steel dagger, 2 pipes, 1 altimeter and other objects. Sélich gave the officers the US and Canadian dollars and Bolivian pesos, after they promised not to report it to their superiors, for if the money fell on Zenteno Anaya's and Arnaldo Saucedo Parada's hands they would keep it.

At that moment Private Franklin Gutiérrez Loza arrived and demanded his share. Sélich gave him 2,000 pesos and 100 dollars to keep him quiet. But some time later, feeling he had received too little, Gutiérrez reported them to Saucedo Parada, who informed his superior officers. Private Gutiérrez was accused of desertion, giving information to the guerrillas and selling their possessions to journalists. He was tried and sentenced to prison.

Sélich also kept Che's backpack, several rolls of film and a notebook with green covers in which Che had copied several poems: Pablo Neruda's "General Chant"; and Nicolás Guillén's "Aconcagua" and "Furnace Rock." Subsequently the notebook was given to Major Jaime Niño de Guzmán, who apparently still has it.

The officers made the inventory that they would give to the command. Among other objects:

—An address book with instructions.
—Two notebooks with copies of sent and received messages.
—Two small codebooks.
—Twenty maps of different areas, updated by Che.
—Several books with notations on the margin.
—One M-1 carbine
—One 9 mm pistol.
—Twelve undeveloped 35 mm rolls of film.
—One radio.

The rest of the less valuable possessions were distributed among some of the soldiers. Ninfa Arteaga, the telegraphist's wife, kept some of them. The military gave Mayor Aníbal Quiroga a mule, the saddle and a flashlight.

After 10 a.m. of that October 8, a message was received at La Higuera from Vallegrande with orders to keep Che alive. The message was as follows:

"Keep Fernando alive until my arrival by helicopter tomorrow morning. Colonel Zenteno Anaya."

Once more Gary Prado visited Che, who told him that two soldiers had taken his watch and Tuma's. According to Prado's own testimonial, he went looking for the two soldiers and made them return the watches, claiming that Che wanted Prado to keep them for him, because probably they would be taken away again. In this manner Prado kept both watches. Subsequently he kept Che's for himself and gave Tuma's watch to Miguel Ayoroa.

October 8 in La Paz

Approximately at 6:00 in the evening there was a meeting in La Paz among Barrientos, Ovando and Juan José Torres with the purpose of discussing the messages received from La Higuera and Vallegrande.

A source who had access to what was discussed at the meeting said:

"They did not know what to do and no decision was made. They just evaluated the events and the information obtained up to the moment and asked for further clarification and new details of what was happening. After the meeting Barrientos went to the residence of the US Ambassador and from there they called Washington.

"At nine o'clock the President was interrupted with a message from Vallegrande, in which they asked for instructions on what to do with the prisoners.

"He had not yet decided what to do and the answer was that they should be kept alive until further instructions.

"The high command transmitted the instructions to Vallegrande and from there they were relayed to La Higuera."

The source added:

"It would be idiotic to deny that the United Status was not consulted, and since I am not willing to be considered an idiot, I declare that the consultation was made."

Decision in Washington

The decision to assassinate Che had been taken in Washington since 1960. After the fiasco of the Bay of Pigs mercenary invasion, Richard Helms was appointed Deputy Director of the CIA. He kept Project Cuba, which included the assassination of Fidel, Raúl and Che, and the imposition by force of arms of a government in Havana according to US interests. They claimed day in and day out that the Cuban revolution would be defeated in a matter of months. The elimination of the main Cuban leaders was part of their plans.

In 1962 Washington established a special augmented group to implement Project Cuba, headed by the Attorney General Robert Kennedy and composed of McGeorge Bundy, Special Advisor on

National Security; CIA Director John McCone; General Lyman Lemnitzer, Joint Chiefs of Staff, Chairman; General Maxwell Taylor; Alexis Johnson, State Department; and Edward Lansdale, CIA Special Group's Operative Office.

On January 19, 1962 the Special Augmented Group met at the office of the Attorney General, where they were informed that Project Cuba was a top priority of the Administration and should be implemented with no regard for time, money, effort and resources. Several actions designed to destroy the Cuban revolution were also agreed at the meeting, particularly the elimination of Fidel, Raúl and Che.

Thus, when on October 1967 the information that Guevara was wounded and held at the La Higuera school reached Washington, it was not necessary to discuss the issue. The CIA, the State Department, the Pentagon and the President of the United States had made the decision long time before.

A Message from Washington

Approximately at 11 o'clock on the night of October 8, the Bolivian President received via the US Ambassador a message from Washington that Che should be eliminated. Among the arguments given by the Ambassador to the President were that in the struggle against communism and international subversion it was more important to present Che as totally defeated and dying in combat, because it was not advisable to keep such a dangerous prisoner alive. Allowing it would mean keeping him in prison, with the constant risk that groups of fanatics or extremists would try to liberate him. Then there would have to be a trial, public opinion would put pressure and the Bolivian government would not be able to cope with it because of the country's convulsed situation.

The Ambassador mentioned Regis Debray's trial in Camiri and the negative consequences for their common interests. He insulted French President Charles de Gaulle for interceding in favor of Debray, and pointed out that if he had been eliminated when taken prisoner, all the scandal caused by his trial could have been avoided. Leaving Che alive, he said, would be to freely offer him a platform to express his ideas, against the interests of Bolivia and the United States. He pointed out that Che's death would be a very harsh blow against the Cuban revolution, and particularly against Fidel Castro.

An exceptional witness later informed that Barrientos, Henderson and their closest collaborators agreed on those opinions. The meeting ended a few minutes after midnight.

Midnight at La Higuera

At the hamlet of La Higuera, Ayoroa went out for a stroll around midnight. He was checking his troops when suddenly he heard a racket coming from a place where several Rangers were drinking with the town's mayor Aníbal Quiroga. All were drunk and inflamed. When he approached them he heard them say that they were going to kill Guevara. Present among the officers were Mario Terán and Bernardino Huanca, who previously had insulted Guevara and threatened to kill him.

Considering his orders to keep Che alive, he rushed to the place. According to La Higuera's townspeople, about that time the wounded guerrilla, Alberto Fernández Montes de Oca (*Pacho*), died without receiving medical attention.

Ayoroa and Prado made officers Tomás "Toty" Aguilera, Carlos Pérez Panoso, Mario Eduardo Huerta Lorenzetti and Raúl Espinosa responsible for Che's life. They would take turns guarding and protecting him.

When it was the turn of Mario Eduardo Huerta Lorenzetti, a 22 year old young man and a member of an honorable family from Sucre, Guevara had a long conversation with him. Huerta later told several friends that Che's figure and look had made a deep impression on him. On occasions he almost felt hypnotized. Che spoke to him about the extreme poverty of the Bolivian people, about the respectful treatment the guerrillas had given to officers and soldiers made prisoners by them, and asked him to compare it with the manner in which the guerrillas had been treated. Huerta said that he felt that the way that Che spoke made him feel that he was talking with an older brother. Seeing that Che was cold, he got a blanket and wrapped him in it, lit him a cigarette and put it to his mouth, for Che's hands were tied behind his back. Che thanked him and explained the objectives of their struggle, and the importance of the revolution against imperialist exploitation exerted on our peoples.

Huerta asked him about his family and Che told him about his five children, his wife, and also about Camilo Cienfuegos and Fidel. He told Huerta how fond he was of them and how much he respected them, of how they had liberated Cuba and of the Cuban revolution's achievements.

Che asked Huerta to untie his hands and help him escape, and Huerta later said that he had been tempted to do it. He went out of the school to observe the situation and talked to Aranibar, a friend nicknamed "The Bear", and asked for his help. But Aranibar told him it was too dangerous, that he could be killed. Huerta hesitated, fear gripped him and made him desist. He later confessed that Che looked him into his eyes and said nothing, but that he could not hold his gaze.

October 9 at La Higuera

At dawn on October 9, Julia Cortés, one of La Higuera's teachers, went to the school. Che had passed the night in her classroom. Julia, influenced by the military, went with the intention of insulting him and asking him to leave. As soon as she entered she shouted a string of abuses. Che spoke softly to her; then there was an exchange of questions and answers. He clarified a spelling error she had made on the blackboard, spoke about her work as an educator and of the formative influence that she would have on Bolivia's future men and women, of the importance of her work, of that event in the history of Latin America that was happening in her school and that she was witnessing. The teacher was astounded and convinced that she was in the presence of a man totally different from what the military had made her believe —a fine person, upright and noble. This she said later to the soldiers and to La Higuera's townspeople. For those words she was accused of sympathizing and collaborating with the guerrillas. For years she was slandered, in retaliation for telling what she thought about Che. Branded as a communist, on several occasions she was threatened that her kind of talk would lead her to be banned from teaching.

The teacher left the classroom when the officer that had allowed her in asked her to leave the premises, for a helicopter was going to land. It was 6:30 a.m. Zenteno Anaya and another man climbed down from the helicopter. The civilian was a Cuban born CIA agent using the name of Félix Ramos. Before taking off from Vallegrande he had been the apple of discord, when Zenteno left behind Saucedo Parada, the 8th Division's Chief of Intelligence. There was no room for the three of them in the helicopter and Zenteno had believed that Ramos would be more useful. His Bolivian intelligence chief was left behind in Vallegrande.

Zenteno received the reports and went to the home of telegraphist Humberto Hidalgo, where they showed him a list with the guerrillas' belongings. Together with the CIA man and his officers he went to see Che and spoke briefly with him. Once Zenteno had gone out, the CIA agent went in and began insulting Che and attempted to mistreat him. The military that witnessed the encounter said that Commander Guevara seemed to know him and his counterrevolutionary background, because he answered his insults with contempt, calling him a traitor and a mercenary.

Zenteno went to see the bodies of Antonio, Arturo and Pacho, mistaking the latter with Bolivian guerrilla Aniceto Reinaga. Approximately at eight thirty, Zenteno Anaya went with Ayoroa and Prado to the scene of the previous day's combat.

Soon the CIA agent had installed a long range radio transmitter to send a coded message to the CIA. Subsequently he set up a camera on a table out in the sun. The purpose was to photograph a German agenda with red covers, some 30 by 20 centimeters, that was Che's diary. A soldier helped him holding down the pages and his finger was photographed on many of them. Ramos took more than 300 photos, two pages at a time.

The morning of October 9 at La Paz

On the early hours of October 9, Barrientos received a telephone call from Bolivian Foreign Minister Walter Guevara Arce, who was in Washington at a meeting of the Organization of American States. On their conversation, Guevara later said:

"When news broke that Che was a prisoner, I called Barrientos and told him: 'I believe it is critical that Che Guevara is kept alive. It is necessary that no mistakes are made in this sense, because if we did we are going to get a bad image that nothing will be able to destroy, not anywhere in the world. Instead, if you keep him imprisoned in La Paz for a time, as long as necessary, it would be more convenient, because people get lost in jail. Time passes and they are forgotten.' The answer came back immediately. He told me: 'I am very sorry, Doctor, but your call is late. Che Guevara died in combat'. That was his answer.

"I was really sorry, not only for the man, his characteristics, the resemblance in our names, but because it seemed to me a very serious political error, and I still believe it was a very serious political error, with many external influences to force that mistake.

"I stayed a little over a week in Washington and began to perceive a great deal of events as a consequence of Che's death. Che was wounded, was taken prisoner. He spent all the night of October 8. The news reached La Paz and beyond. The sub-lieutenant fired his gun, a tragic and absurd thing.

"In all this absurdity," concluded Minister Guevara Arce, "extraordinary foreign forces played a role; there is no question about it."

Early in the morning on October 9 at La Paz, Ovando arrived to the Miraflores Barracks and went up to Department III (Operations) on the second floor. David La Fuente, Marcos Vásquez Sempértegui, Federico Arana Cerrudo and Manuel Cárdenas Mallo had arrived earlier. Ovando told them that Che was a prisoner at La Higuera.

León Kolle Cueto, Commander of the Bolivian Air Force, Horacio Ugarteche, of the Naval Force; and Juan José Torres arrived some time later, and finally Barrientos, who immediately went to a small meeting room of Department III with Ovando and Juan José Torres. After a brief conversation they called in Marcos Vásquez Sempértegui, David La Fuente, León Kolle Cueto and Horacio Ugarteche. Barrientos, with the deliberate purpose of compromising the members of the military high command, presented the issue of Che's assassination. He talked about it as a firm decision, not as something to be discussed. After the meeting, a coded message was sent to Vallegrande. Ovando went to the airport and took off for La Higuera in a TM-14 airplane. Rear Admiral Horacio Ugarteche, Colonels Fernando Sattori and David La Fuente, Lieutenant Colonel Herberto Olmos Rimbaut, and Captains Oscar Pammo, Ángel Vargas and René Ocampo were also in the plane.

The CIA agent receives a coded message

Approximately at 10 a.m. at La Higuera, CIA agent Félix Ramos received a coded message with the order to assassinate Che Guevara.

While a soldier went looking for Colonel Zenteno, the CIA agent headed for the school together with Andrés Sélich. On guard was young Mario Eduardo Huerta Lorenzetti, the same officer that gave Che a blanket and talked with him. The CIA agent ordered him out of the room. The young officer obeyed, but saw that when Ramos tried to question Che he shook him by the shoulders trying to make him talk, pulled his beard and screamed at him that he was going to kill him. Huerta later told his friends that since he had orders to protect Che's life he tried to prevent the CIA's agent abuse. In the scuffle Ramos fell, and from the floor shouted at him: "I'll get you for this really soon, you Bolivian piece of shit, stupid savage Indian!" Huerta tried to hit him, but Sélich interceded.

Some minutes later the body of the Bolivian guerrilla Aniceto Reinaga was brought from the combat zone, as well as the almost blind Peruvian Juan Pablo Chang Navarro, *Chino.* The CIA man used violence to make the guerrilla talk, but he did not succeed. The Spanish magazine *Interviú* —which gained access to a CIA report— said that Ramos used a bayonet against the Peruvian guerrilla.

About eleven o'clock Zenteno Anaya returned with Ayoroa and was informed by the CIA agent of the final decision to kill Che. Ramos also said that he would gladly shoot him himself.

Some time later Ninfa Arteaga, together with her daughter, teacher Élida Hidalgo, went to the school in order to give Che and the other two guerrillas some peanut soup.

Zenteno Anaya told Félix Ramos to execute the order, that if he wanted to do it, fine with him. But the CIA agent finally decided with Sélich and Ayoroa to ask among the soldiers for volunteers. Mario Terán, Carlos Pérez Panoso and Bernardino Huanca, all them trained by US advisors, accepted.

In a later interview Mario Terán declared that when he entered the classroom Che was sitting on one of the rustic benches of the school, and even though he knew he was about to die, kept his calm. Terán helped him up and was impressed. He could not shoot him and his hands were trembling. He saw that Che's eyes had an intense shine, and imagined him very, very tall, walking towards him. He felt fear and his eyes clouded, while he heard the others shouting at him: "Shoot, you idiot, shoot!" Terán was given a drink, but even so he could not shoot.

Officers Carlos Pérez Panoso and Bernardino Huanca shot Peruvian guerrilla Juan Pablo Chang Navarro and Bolivian Willy Cuba.

Once again the Bolivian officers and the CIA agent pressed Mario Terán to shoot. He later told journalists that he closed his eyes and shot Guevara, and afterwards the rest of those present did the same.

It was 1:10 p.m. on October 9, 1967. The CIA agent Félix Ramos also shot Che's body. After the murder, Zenteno Anaya returned to Vallegrande.

The townspeople, terrorized by the army's actions, slowly approached, disconcerted by the incredible event that they had witnessed. For the people that lived in La Higuera, a peaceful, religious and superstitious hamlet, it was unchristian to murder human beings, and they began to whisper that God would punish La Higuera on account of the military..

Che's body is taken to Vallegrande

Around 2:00 a helicopter landed at Vallegrande with Zenteno aboard. He was received by Roberto "Toto" Quintanilla, Arnaldo Saucedo and CIA agents Eduardo González and Julio Gabriel García. Zenteno went to where Ovando was with the rest of the entourage that had come from La Paz.

The CIA agents gathered the documents and belongings of the guerrillas. The helicopter went back to La Higuera to bring the dead guerrillas, with express order to bring Che's body last.

At La Higuera the events had shocked the townspeople. Ninfa Arteaga helped Father Roger Schiller close Che Guevara's eyes. This was in contrast with the attitude of the soldiers, who dragged the body before putting it in a stretcher and carrying it to where the helicopter would pick it up

People at La Higuera and even some military were outraged when a soldier tried to hit Che's body with a stick. They then covered the corpse with a blanket. The priest said a prayer and went to the school, where he cleaned the blood and picked up the cases of the bullets with which Che had been murdered.

At four in the afternoon, the helicopter took off, piloted by Major Jaime Niño de Guzmán. The Heroic Guerrilla's body lay in a canvas stretcher. Half an hour later they landed at Vallegrande.

Repercussion on the arrival of Che's body to Vallegrande

Through several reports by press correspondents the repercussion caused in Vallegrande due to the arrival of Che's body was known. Daniel Rodríguez, reporter of the La Paz daily *El Diario*, wrote that the news of the arrival shocked the population that flocked to the helicopter pad and then to the hospital. The crowd attempted to take Guevara's body and Army troops had to make an effort to avoid the assault. The whole town was in the pad and determined not to allow the military to take the body anywhere. After the helicopter landed, the military untied the body that was fixed to one of the landing skids and immediately put it in an ambulance that took it to the Lord of Malta Hospital.

Christopher Rooper, a Reuter correspondent, transmitted the following from Vallegrande:

"The body was taken from the helicopter and placed in a Chevrolet van that, followed by anxious journalists that had taken the first available jeep, went to a small facility that is sometimes used as a morgue. Efforts were made to prevent spectators and journalists from entering the premises. An individual was particularly active. He was plump and bald, about thirty years

123

old, and although he had no military insignia on his olive green fatigues, he seemed to be in charge from the moment that the helicopter landed. This man also went with the body in the Chevrolet van.

"None of the military revealed the man's name, but local versions claim that he is a Cuban exile that works for the Central Intelligence Agency (CIA)."

The Camiri journalists go to Vallegrande

When news circulated about the La Higuera combat, some of the journalists that were in Camiri left for Vallegrande. *The Guardian* British correspondent Richard Gott reported the presence of the CIA, when he wrote that from the moment that the helicopter landed the operation was placed in the hands of a man dressed in fatigues, who everybody thought was one of the representatives of US intelligence agencies, and probably a Cuban. Gott wrote that "The helicopter landed on purpose far from where a group of people had gathered, and the body of the dead guerrilla was put in a truck. We commandeered a jeep to follow them and the driver managed to pass through the gates of the hospital, where the body was taken to a colorless shed that served as morgue.

"The doors of the truck opened and suddenly the American agent jumped shouting a war cry: 'We are going to take him the hell out of here!'

"One of the correspondents asked him where did he come from. 'From nowhere!' was the insolent answer.

"The body dressed in olive green and a zippered jacket was taken to the shed. Undoubtedly it was Che Guevara.

"I am perhaps one of the few people here that has seen him alive. I saw him in Cuba in a reception at the Embassy in 1963, and I am positive that it was the body of Che Guevara.

"As soon as the body arrived at the morgue, doctors began to inject him with prophylactics. The American agent was making desperate efforts to keep the masses at bay. He was a very nervous man and gave angry looks every time a camera was pointed at him. He sensed that I knew what he was, and he also knew that I thought that he should not be there, for this is a war in which the United States should not be involved.

"Yet, there was this man, who has been with the troops at Vallegrande, talking with high ranking officers on a first name basis."

Richard Gott assured that Commander Ernesto Che Guevara would go down in history as the greatest man since Bolívar, and then added: "He was perhaps the only person that tried to channel radical forces of the world in a campaign focused against the United States. He is dead now, but it is difficult to imagine that his ideas will die with him."

CIA agents and Bolivian officers celebrate Che's Death

CIA agent Eduardo González, together with Toto Quintanilla, took the body to the Lord of Malta Hospital's laundry. When they put it on the floor, the agent, showing his lowly condition, kicked it. After the body was raised and put on the washing board, he hit it in the face. Toto Quintanilla took the body's fingerprints and ordered that a nurse be called.

Susana Osinaga was on duty that night. With the help of Graciela Rodríguez, a laundress at the hospital, she washed Guevara's body. Doctors José Martínez Caso and Moisés Abraham Baptista made out the death certificate. By order of the military they did not include the time of death. Likewise the doctors were forced to perform an autopsy and inject the body with formaldehyde, pending the arrival of a team of Argentinean experts.

In order to make an identification of the other dead guerrillas, deserter Antonio Domínguez Flores, aka *León*, was brought from Camiri.

At the Santa Teresita de Vallegrande Hotel, CIA agents and Bolivian military celebrated Che's death. Félix Ramos opened a bottle of whisky and served all those present. Meanwhile, at La Higuera, Father Roger Schiller invited the townspeople to a mass for Che Guevara and his murdered comrades. All went carrying candles. There was an impressive silence. No one understood why they had been murdered. The priest said the following words: "This crime will never be pardoned. The guilty ones will be punished by God."

On October 10 the body was exhibited to the townspeople at Vallegrande.

At 11 a.m. Zenteno Anaya and Arnaldo Saucedo held a press conference, where they showed Che's diary and made declarations concerning the day, time and circumstances of Che's death, claiming he had died on October 8 from wounds received in combat. Ovando also had made declarations, but when journalists compared them with those made by the military at Vallegrande the contradiction was obvious, which caused skepticism. Doubts and confusion increased, as well as suspicions that Che had been murdered.

CIA agents controlled telephone and post office services in Vallegrande. They censored news that correspondents sent out to the world. Control was so strict that journalists had to ask permission from the agents to make a phone call.

Che's body was exhibited at the hospital's laundry that served as morgue. People respectfully filed past in silence.

María Muñoz, a nun, said that "Che was as if he were alive. There was an impressive silence. I did not hear anyone talking, and he, looking at us with his eyes open, seemed alive."

Eugenio Rosell, a teacher that in 1967 was twenty years old, said that "The population was very respectful because of his background, his intelligence, his ideals, his struggle, because it is not easy to analyze and deduce that a man that was not born in Bolivia had truly come searching for the best solutions for the oppressed, who are most of the population, and that he came to stay with us eternally, and that is appreciated by the people of Vallegrande (...)

"Many people here compared him to Christ, but really, when I looked at him I saw that he had the looks of the Guerrilla Commander, and I began to cry. Many people cried also."

From Argentina, news services reported that the authorities feared that the guerrilla's grave could become a place of pilgrimage, for that would become a new political problem that would be added to the existing ones faced by General Onganía's government. One of the reports said that "Probably Che's grave will never be known", and a top military officer recalled that was precisely the reason that the exact place where Eva Perón's remains are has never been revealed.

Che's hands are cut off and the body disappears

After the Heroic Guerrilla's murder it was impossible for the Bolivian President to erase his crime. Barrientos knew that Che's relatives would claim the body, could challenge the autopsy and request clarifications on the circumstances and manner of death. He also feared that Latin American medical doctors would protest in a similar manner. He had already received information that the Medical Association of La Paz was on that track. There was the additional concern of the presence in Bolivia of Che's brother, Roberto Guevara de la Serna, a Buenos Aires lawyer who had traveled together with journalists from Argentinean Channel 13 to Santa Cruz.

Press coverage increased information on the murder. The contradictory declarations of top military officers, investigations by journalists and press reports based on testimonials from soldiers and townspeople at La Higuera and Pucará, were further evidence that military authorities were lying about the manner and date of death.

Barrientos wanted to prevent Che's burial place from becoming a shrine for the neighbors of Vallegrande and revolutionaries the world over. Considering the delay of the Argentinean experts that would definitely identify the body, he ordered that the hands and the head be cut off and the remains cremated.

There are several versions in relation to this ghastly order. CIA agent Félix Ramos said the decision was taken by Ovando. Saucedo Parada wrote that Toto Quintanilla had orders from Minister of the Interior Antonio Arguedas to cut off Che's head and hands and take them to La Paz, possibly following orders from General Barrientos, and that Zenteno Anaya agreed that only the hands would be cut off for identification purposes, which was done by Doctor Moisés Abraham.

Arguedas declared that it was not fully discussed by the military high command, for it was a decision of those present at La Higuera, probably meaning Vallegrande. He said that since the body showed a bullet wound in the neck and another impact near the heart, and considering that for political reasons they had invented the phrase, "I am Che. I'm more valuable alive than dead", it would be unbelievable that a man shot in the neck and the heart could speak. This was the reason why the body could not be exhibited in front of too many people. Since the problem of identification was still unsolved, the decision was to cut off his hands.

Arguedas claimed that Quintanilla had said that at the request of the Cuban American CIA agents, Che's hands had been cut off and hidden.

There is confusion about the origin of the order and contradictions have not been clarified. Some sources claimed that there was an agreement between Toto Quintanilla and the CIA agents at Vallegrande to make it look like an order from above. According to these sources, the following is what happened:

Toto Quintanilla, Saucedo Parada, CIA agents Eduardo González and Julio Gabriel García met to discuss how to comply with the orders. Nevertheless, they consulted Zenteno Anaya, who decided that only the hands would be cut off for identification purposes. CIA agents insisted that the head be cut off too and sent to the United States for laboratory analyses. For this end they ordered the presence of Doctors José Martínez Caso and Moisés Abraham Baptista, who refused for different reasons. Doctor Martínez was drunk at the agreed time to perform the ghoulish task and it was imposed on Doctor Moisés Abraham Baptista, who was assisted by the CIA agents and Toto Quintanilla. The body was taken in a jeep to the Pando Regiment barracks in Vallegrande. It was 2 a.m., October 11.

The military had four gasoline tanks for the cremation, but they were unable to do it because it was close to daybreak. They also were concerned about the reaction of the townspeople of Vallegrande and about the presence of foreign correspondents. These two factors were decisive and the body was buried in the same ditch made with a tractor for the rest of the guerrillas. Che's body was carried by Andrés Sélich and Major Walter Flores.

Information collected gave two probable burial sites for the guerrillas, one in a plot behind the dormitory at the Pando Regiment barracks, and the other besides the runway at Vallegrande's airport, a few meters away from the head of the landing strip. Both sites are 200 meters apart. Nevertheless, the Bolivian Army maintained the official version that Che had been cremated and his ashes scattered in the jungle.

On October 11 the Argentinean team of experts flew in to La Paz from Buenos Aires. The team was formed by Inspector Esteban Relzhauzer, Deputy Inspector Nicolás Pellicari and fingerprint expert Juan Carlos Delgado, of the Argentinean Federal Police's Departament of Investigations. Shortly after, the hands were delivered to them for the purpose of identification.

The following is the declaration made by those experts:

"In the city of La Paz, Republic of Bolivia, today, Saturday, October fourteen of the year one thousand nine hundred sixty seven and at sixteen hundred hours, the officials signing the present document, Officers Inspector Esteban Relzhauzer, in his capacity as scopometric (sic) expert, Deputy Inspectors Nicolás Pellicari and Juan Carlos Delgado, dactylographic experts, all from the Argentinean Federal Police's Department of Investigations, for the appropriate purposes, declare that: by order of the Chief of the Argentinean Federal Police, Division General Mario A. Fonseca, following a request of cooperation by the Ministry of Foreign Relations and Worship, they traveled to Bolivia and place (sic) themselves at the disposal of the Embassy of Argentina in this city, which give (sic) the orders to be kept. For that purpose they were informed that they should proceed to a dactylographic examination and examination of documents that would be delivered to them. (In the company of Captain Carlos Mayer, Naval Attaché at the Embassy of Argentina), Embassy Secretary Jorge Cremona and the Vice Consul in charge of the General Consulate at La Paz Miguel A. Storppello, they went to a building of the Miraflores Bolivian General Headquarters, where they were received by Lieutenant Oscar Pamo Rodríguez, Adjutant to General Alfredo Ovando Candia, Commander in Chief of the Armed Forces, and Major Roberto Quintanilla, from the Ministry of Government. They give to the experts and the above mentioned a closed cylindrical metal container, which was opened, and contains two hands submerged in a colorless liquid, with an odor similar to formaldehyde, a strong disinfectant used to preserve the conditions of the offered elements. For that purpose the above mentioned dactylographic experts, Officers Deputy Inspectors Nicolás Pellicari and Juan Carlos Delgado, proceed to carry out the appropriate technical operations for the purpose of arriving to the identification through the 'Juan

Vucetich' dactylographic system, used by the Federal Police, of the papillary designs on the fingers of the amputated hands that are exhibited to them. They follow the technique transcribed below for the correct information of the process and the results obtained:

"The papillary tissue, due to long action of the formaldehyde in which the hands were submerged, showed deep wrinkles in the fleshy region, a circumstance that restricted the inking and lifting of fingerprints. Since the advisable technical procedures in such cases showed no results, the fingerprints were obtained with polyethylene sheets and in some cases with latex, which were classified and will be taken to the Laboratory of the Argentinean Federal Police's Identification Section, with the purpose of submitting them to the practice work. Once the replicas were obtained in the indicated manner from the above mentioned hands, they were collated with the dactylographic individuals on the photocopy of the card (ten fingers) that corresponds to the original present on the Identity Card File granted by the Argentinean Federal Police, number 3.524.272, in the name of Ernesto Guevara, thus establishing its perfect identity in indubitable manner and according to the postulates of the Argentinean Dactylographic System, that is, that they belong to the same and only person. It is placed on record that in this act we deliver to Major Roberto Quintanilla, Adjutant General to the Minister of Government, Justice and Immigration, a photographic copy of the decadactilary dactylographic card that corresponds with the original in the above mentioned Ernesto Guevara's file. Likewise we receive from the above mentioned official a decadactilary dactylographic card obtained on day 9 of the present month at Vallegrande, Santa Cruz Department, from a male cadaver that in this act is identified as the above mentioned Ernesto Guevara. Additionally, scopometric expert Officer Inspector Esteban Relzhauzer, of the Argentinean Federal Police's Scopomatic Section, receives for the purpose of examination two notebooks: one of them containing standard sized manuscript notes, 20 cm by 14.5 cm, with plastic covers, wine dregs colored, with a bas-relief inscription on the cover that says '1967', and on the lower edge, to the right of the spine of the above mentioned element of analysis there is a notch probably due to heat. Said notebook is in a good state of conservation, no visible stains nor tears of the sheets. On the interior (inner side of the cover) there is a small adhered seal in red that reads: 'Carl Klippel   Kaiserstrasca (sic) 75   Frankfurt a. M'. The printer's signature is: 'Hartellung A.N/', all of which confirms the German origin of said element. Sheets are of smooth white paper with the daily dates of 1967 printed on them, and individually with a description of the hours. (It is doubly indicated.)

"On each of the observed pages the presence of manuscript text can be seen that corresponds with annotations made describing operations and movements of the mentioned persons. Said cycle begins on January 1 of the present year and ends on October 7, from which date on the following sheets are blank. With the use of the identifying technique known as 'scopometric study of documents', and in the presence of collating elements that undoubtedly belong to the Identity Card file number 3.524.272 of the Argentinean Federal Police, in the name of Ernesto Guevara, in the form of manuscript signatures and writing made at the time of application of documents on the part of the above mentioned Guevara to Argentinean authorities, all elements that were brought to this place as photostatic copies of the original have been collated. In said study we have taken into account: date of production of the above mentioned authentic writings, the circumstance that we have on one part signatures and writings (only the words 'Guatemala – Panama – Chile and Colombia'), compared to writings only on the other, and that the authentic signatures present the strokes and typical structure of pure literal forms with some tendency to simplification that do not affect the general examination, and therefore are suitable for the formal basic extrinsic and intrinsic collation of the scopometric identification; simultaneously an adequate optical element is used. Under the above mentioned conditions the authentic elements constitute a negligible part of the material presented to the expert for its investigation, and thus it has been necessary to make a statistical examination of the characteristics of the writing in the presented notebook and the folder with the brown plastic cover with the inscription 'Elba 66509' that contains 44 sheets of manuscript writing. With the afore mentioned technique and through its principles we established a significant writing regularity, structure, graphic culture and the existence of characteristic formations that made possible a relation of the presented notebooks (that) reproduce the same graphic characteristics of the writings found in Ernesto Guevara's file. We document that copies of the sheets of writing discussed in this act were not obtained, but that same will be sent later to the Federal Police for a better documentation of the investigation. –And with this we finish this event. It is read to those present, who sign it for the appropriate end, and in the order in which they were mentioned. Agreed. Certified.

(Signed) Esteban Relzhauser. — (Signed) Juan Carlos Delgado."

Minister of the Interior Antonio Arguedas ordered that the hands and the death mask be delivered to him. He hid them for some time, until he was able to send them to Cuba, where they are at present.

Four guerrillas are murdered

The surviving group conformed by Jaime Arana Campero (*Chapaco*), Octavio de la Concepción de la Pedraja, (*Moro*), Lucio Edilberto Galván Hidalgo (*Eustaquio*), and Francisco Huanca Flores (*Pablito*), went to the contact point ordered by Che in case the guerrillas were dispersed.

Army Company C. commanded by Captain Ángel Mariscal, followed the group's tracks and on the evening of October 11 saw a small fire at a point near the Grande and Mizque Rivers, which permitted to pinpoint the site. They thought that the guerrillas were cooking, or perhaps warming themselves by the fire, for it was very cold.

At dawn on the 12th they saw a guerrilla coming out of the bush and go to the river for water. The Company deployed and began to surround them, even by the opposite bank of the river.

When the guerrillas noticed the presence of the army, they prepared for their final resistance. It was an unequal combat — 145 soldiers against 4 guerrillas, three of them very ill. They fought until they ran out of ammunition. The combat started at 11:00 a.m. and ended one hour later at the area known as Cajones. When the soldiers arrived at the scene, they found one dead guerrilla, *Moro*; two others were slightly injured —*Pablito* and *Eustaquio*—, and *Chapaco* seriously wounded. The soldiers also found three M-2 carbines and a Winchester rifle, as well as backpacks and personal belongings.

The surviving guerrillas were tied up and taken to a beach at the Grande River, where they were told that they would be taken to Vallegrande for questioning. When the helicopter arrived, they were machine gunned down without a single word. The bodies were flown by helicopter to Vallegrande. At 6:00 a dump truck picked up the bodies and left en route to Guadalupe, to Vicente Zavala's hacienda, where they were secretly buried.

At Tarija, Fabiola Campero, accompanied by her daughter Marta Arana, hired an air taxi for Vallegrande with the purpose of claiming the body of her son, but military authorities forced them to return. The press later reported that the crying mother begged to know the place where his son was buried to plant a cross on his grave, but Zenteno Anaya told her that crosses were already in place at all burial sites, which was untrue. The events shocked the population of Tarija, for the Arana Campero family was highly respected.

In the meantime, Inti, Pombo, Benigno, Urbano, Ñato and Darío ran several military cordons, made several casualties to the army and approached the vicinity of Mataral, on the Cochabamba Santa Cruz Highway, where they held another combat in which Ñato died. A few days later they arrived to the house of Víctor Céspedes, a farmer. He and his family protected them until January, 1968, when they left for Cochabamba.

Repression against journalists

Control and repression against journalists continued. At Camiri, British reporter Ralph Schoenman was the subject of a new provocation when he was accused of endangering national security, disturbing the peace and compromising Bolivia's relations with the UK. For that reason, he was arrested and sent to Army's Headquarters in La Paz. There he was submitted to questioning under the pretext of suspicions and evidence gathered by Army Intelligence. The explanation given was that Schoenman served as secretary in a political trial at Stockholm against US President Lyndon B. Johnson for the Vietnam War. Bolivian authorities also informed that he was US born, but a British citizen, and that he had intentions of compromising relations with that European country. Finally he was expelled from Bolivia.

Meanwhile, at Vallegrande, not even Bolivian journalists where free to do their work, because they were under CIA surveillance. The Agency obstructed the work of *El Diario* reporter Daniel Rodríguez, and of Erwin Chacón and José Luis Alcázar, from *Presencia,* for its agents acted as the owners of Vallegrande shouting rudely at them that they did not want to see them around. On several occasions Bolivian military authorities had to intercede with the aim of easing tensions.

The three Bolivian reporters decided to get even. On October 11, at the Teresita Hotel, where CIA agents had lunch every day, they put up a sign with the following words: "Motherland or Death, We Shall Overcome. Long Live Cuba."

When Félix Ramos saw it he became furious. Getting up from the table, he ripped down the sign and stormed out of the hotel.

Many other journalists were controlled by the CIA. French Michelle Ray's room was searched several times. She also received death threats and the French Embassy had several anonymous calls saying that it was very dangerous for her to remain in Bolivia. When she left La Paz, all her belongings were stolen, including her clothes and handbag. But what the Agency ignored was that Jorge Torrico, a Bolivian army officer, was three meters away observing everything, with his papers at hand, ready to board the same plane. His plan was to fly to France, seek political asylum and reveal secret information about what had happened at La Higuera and Vallegrande.

International repercussions of Che's assassination

Cuba corroborates Che's assassination

On October 15, Commander in Chief Fidel Castro addressed the people of Cuba through national TV and radio stations and the international broadcasting station Radio Habana Cuba. Fidel analyzed in great detail the news, wires from various news agencies and other considerations regarding the assassination of the Heroic Guerrilla. To assert that the news was painfully true, in his address Fidel said that

"[...] the duty to tell the truth overrides what may or may not be convenient —and such was our attitude [...]

"[...] We know that revolutionaries have confidence in the Cuban Revolution; revolutionaries all over the world have true confidence in the word of the Cuban Revolution [...] And no matter how bitter it may be, how painful even [...], we shall not hesitate to fulfill this duty. But, also, what would be the logic for revolutionaries to keep up false hopes? What would we stand to win? Is it not true that revolutionaries should be those best prepared to face all circumstances, all vicissitudes, all setbacks if need be? Could it be said that the annals of the revolutions or of the revolutionary peoples have been characterized by the absence of heavy blows? Is it not true that genuine revolutionaries are those who have overcome those blows, those setbacks, and have kept their spirits high? Is it not precisely we the revolutionaries who extol the value of moral principles, the value of setting an example? Is it not true that revolutionaries are those who believe in the durability of the works of mankind, of the principles of mankind? Is it not true that revolutionaries are the first to begin to acknowledge the ephemeral nature of men's physical life and the durability and lasting nature of men's ideas, behavior and examples, examples that have inspired and guided peoples throughout history?"

Fidel Castro announced that the Council of Ministers of Cuba had agreed on the following:

"First: That for 30 days, as of the date of this agreement, the national flag will fly at half mast, and that for three days, as of 12 a.m. tonight, all public entertainment will be suspended.

"Second: The day of his heroic fall in combat is declared a day of national commemoration, and to that effect, October the 8th is established as the 'Day of the Heroic Guerrilla'.

"Third: Any and all activities tending to perpetuate his life and his example in the memory of future generations will be carried out."

Likewise, the Central Committee of the Communist Party of Cuba agreed on the following:

"First: To set up a committee made up by Commanders Juan Almeida, Ramiro Valdés, Rogelio Acevedo and Alfonso Zayas, headed by the first of the aforementioned comrades to coordinate and direct all the activities tending to perpetuate the memory of Commander Ernesto Guevara,

"Second: To summon the people for next Wednesday, October 18, at 8 p.m., for a solemn evening in Revolution Square as a tribute to the unforgettable and heroic fighter fallen in combat."

The world condemns Che's assassination

When news of the assassination of Commander Ernesto Che Guevara was broadcast to all corners of the earth, it generated a wave of repudiation and condemnation never to be effaced from history. Workers, students, peasants, professionals, intellectuals and progressive governments all over the world expressed their indignation. Demonstrations of disapproval and condemnation reached diplomatic missions of Bolivia in major cities of the world, as well in the United States itself.

The press at the time is an invaluable source of information regarding the repercussions of that crime.

From Paris, AFP reported: "The European media has provided extensive coverage and, regardless of their leanings, recognize in general the enormous prestige of a man whose deeds matched his words.

"In France, a country that is particularly sensitive to the events in Bolivia, due to the procedure against intellectual Regis Debray, detained last April in the guerrilla area, all newspapers gave pride of place to the news regarding the death of Ernesto Guevara."

L'Humanité said that all newspapers shared the view that Guevara was an exceptional man, regardless of his political views.

Journalist Marcel Niedergang wrote in *Le Monde,* the Parisian daily: "First citizen of the Third World and ardent defender of the oppressed peoples."

World-famous Josephine Baker and her children sent a message of condolence to Commander in Chief Fidel Castro.

Larousse Publishing House carried out a popular survey on the 150th anniversary of its founder, Pierre Larousse, which showed that Che Guevara should be the foremost international personality to be incorporated in the famous dictionary.

In Colombia, the communist weekly *Voz Proletaria* published in its front page an article under the headline "Che Died Fighting for the Freedom of the Americas".

In Santiago de Chile, students took to the main streets and avenues to pay homage to Che; in the School of Medicine they held a solemn ceremony to his memory. The Chilean Parliament also paid tribute to Che; among those who took the floor were Salvador Allende, Volodia Teitelboim, Tomás Chadwick, Baltazar Castro and Fernando Luengo. The Christian Democratic Party also paid homage to his memory.

Students of Tegucigalpa held demonstrations condemning the crime and agreed to declare Che a National Hero of Honduras.

In an important soccer game in Peru, the players marched in wearing black arm bands as a sign of mourning. College students in Lima and in other Peruvian universities condemned the murder of the Heroic Guerrilla and paid tribute to his memory. At the Greater University of San Marcos' campus of La Cantuta, the 12th Congress of Peruvian Students was being held. Participants decided to give the Congress the name of 'Commander Ernesto Che Guevara' ".

Brazilian workers unveiled a plaque in the Cascadura district. The police raided the universities of Espírito Santo and the Social Studies Institute of Rio de Janeiro to prevent public demonstrations and tributes. Bishop Antonio Batista Agoso, senior hierarchical personality of the Church, condemned the murder of Che. Hélder Cámara, Archbishop of Recife, Brazil considered Che a martyr of the Americas. In the towns of Sataozinho Santos, there were mass demonstrations. The municipal houses of Niteroi and Campos, in Rio de Janeiro, extolled Che. Thousands of students demonstrated along Rio Branco Avenue, in Rio de Janeiro.

In San Juan, Puerto Rico, pro-independence leader Juan Mari Brass spoke to hundreds of people who met to pay homage to Che.

The Embassy of Bolivia in Uruguay was surrounded by groups of demonstrators. A solemn ceremony was held at the University of Montevideo in which Rector Oscar J. Maggiolo said: "History will reserve a privileged place for Commander Guevara among the greats of our Americas." Over 1,000 students chanting slogans against the United States took to the streets despite the state of siege in the capital city. Communist leader José Luis Massera addressed the demonstrators.

A bomb exploded at the Bolivian diplomatic mission in Quito, causing serious damages; also several Bolivian offices were burnt down. Big demonstrations took place in Ecuador's major cities. In Quito, Guayaquil, Loja and Cuenca, hundreds of students and Che sympathizers filled the streets. His name and the date of October 8 appeared profusely in streets and highways.

Also in Quito, the Law School's main lecture hall at the Central University of Ecuador was named Che Guevara, and a picture of him was unveiled. At the Ecuadorian House of Culture a commemoration was held and Benjamín Carrión addressed those present. Students in Guayaquil, the second most important city in the country, also took to the streets with a huge picture of Che painted by artist Antonio del Campo. The picture was carried aloft and deposited at the university. Among the demonstrators were Dr. Fortunato Safadi and his wife Ana Moreno, who had met Che when he visited Guayaquil with his friend Carlos Ferrer.

In Loja, the university campus was named Ernesto Che Guevara. There was also a national tribute to his memory in which the keynote speaker, Nela Martínez, a prestigious Ecuadorian, said among other things:

"I saw his picture published under headlines of joy in the international media and I cried. Who was not moved by the news? Even the very accessories to the crime tried to find a way to wash their hands. The mask of Pilate once again hides the miens of the executioners throughout time.

"Lying on a washing stone, his corpse was not a corpse. The open eyes stared at us. His grimace did not reflect the mark of death. His attitude, a challenge to the very end. A victorious smile, for his other triumph, lit up the day. His combatant's face remained for ever imprinted in the Andes.

"Old legends, of those who will return to continue the war that was started, will circulate by word of mouth and heard in the long silence of the fields, in the mud and thatched hut hamlets, in the other history of the illiterate. ¿How long did Tupac Amaru wage a war against the Spanish Crown, the enemy of the Indian? Long was the wait, until not once, not twice, but a hundred times, he returned. All the commotion of the greatest uprising against colonial power was not lost when his body was severed and cast to the four corners of the Tahuantinsuyo. New silenced epics, silent in and of themselves, had shaken the entrails of the peoples of the Andes.

"Fires remain within, like in volcanoes. When the continent is shaken, you can sense lava going to the conscience of men [[...]]."

In Quito, street demonstrations continued, including the firebombing of the Ecuador-US Center. Famous painter Oswaldo Guayasamín stated: "Ernesto Guevara is not dead; no one can kill him, the soil of the Americas is flooded with his presence; guerrillas will multiply; courage and heroism will once again be the bread of the humble. Tyrannies and coup perpetrators will fall."

In Georgetown, the capital of Guyana, Janet Jagan exalted Che's personality.

In México, the facade of the Academy of Art was covered by a cloth that read: "Che Lives On". *Siempre* magazine devoted him four pages. All the media –radio, TV and the press– covered the news extensively. Dailies like *La Prensa, Ovaciones, El Nacional, Excelsior* and *El Día* featured the item.

139

Journalist Leopoldo Zea wrote in the morning paper *Novedades:* "All the peoples of the Americas, all the peoples of the world that struggle for their liberation and their freedom, feel in their hearts profound grief over the death of Commander Guevara, fallen while facing the common enemy of the peoples and of men."

In the capital city of Mexico, a large number of friends of Cuba —intellectuals, artists, workers and students– met in a combative activity. There Dr. Alberto Breamauntz and Dr. Fausto Trejo addressed the participants. Poet Efraín Huerta with Margarita Paz and Laura Campos read poems as a tribute to Che.

In Prague, Latin American delegates attending the Women's World Democratic Federation Council meeting conveyed their condolences to the Cuban Embassy. The Slovak National Council kept a minute of silence. Foreign students in the capital of Czechoslovakia carried out mass demonstrations and raised a large sign bearing the words "To Victory Forever". Students from various countries took the floor. The World Federation of Trade Unions condemned the murder of Che.

In Naples, Italy, there were large demonstrations. In Florence a US flag was burned. In Rome thousands of people led by writer Cesare Zavattini and leaders from several leftist parties reached the US Embassy. Writer Alberto Moravia and film director Pier Paolo Passolini were arrested. Zavattini declared that the death of Commander Guevara affected all, like a family, the family of all men. Filmmaker Francesco Rosi stated his intention of making a movie dedicated to Che: singer Mina Mazzini declared that Commander Guevara had become a national hero in Italy.

In Vienna demonstrators took down the Bolivian flag from that country's embassy at the Austrian capital. In Sweden, Denmark and Holland there were also demonstrations condemning the murder. Bill Littlewood, a simple British worker, sent to Cuba his beautiful and deeply felt verses dedicated to Che Guevara. He wrote: "This is the only poetry I have ever written."

At the main lecture hall of the University of Madrid's Department of Philosophy and Letters, a commemorative event to the memory of the Heroic Guerrilla was held.

In a huge meeting held in Italy, María Teresa León, on behalf of her husband, famous poet Rafael Alberti, and other Spanish exiles, said:

"I bring the pain and the grief of Rafael Alberti, and with my own also the grief of all Spanish exiles, and the pain of all those that remained there with their eyes turned to freedom, the pain of the Spanish youth that do not bend their knees and that had looked on Che Guevara as the hero of the furious present time in our Latin America...

"He died in his law, next to the poorest of America, the most abandoned, stripped of everything but their hope. At the place where he was murdered two sources will emerge —one of freedom and one of justice. Bolivian Indians, the disinherited ones of a continent, will whisper his name, will say that he is alive, that he knocks on their doors because he is thirsty, and they will leave on their window sills pitchers of water so that Che can drink when he passes by. Because he will pass and will roam a whole continent and his name will be the strength of the future, the high star of the Southern Cross that will call on all the Americas to rise and fight for its political and economic independence against all foreign domination."

In Bulgaria the Communist Youth paid him homage; likewise students at the Central University of Bucharest, Rumania. The weekly Polish magazine *Politika* mentioned Che and his struggle in Bolivia. Meanwhile in the Soviet Union, Latin American students repudiated the crime perpetrated in Bolivia and condemned US imperialism.

Leaders of the party, the state and the government of the People's Popular Democratic Republic of Korea and also those of Vietnam visited the Cuban embassies in their respective capitals to express solidarity with the grief of the Cuban people and of all revolutionaries in the world.

Nguyen Thi Dinh, Deputy Commander in Chief of the Popular Armed Forces of Liberation in South Vietnam sent a message to Cuba.

Television networks and radio stations reported on the events in Bolivia and on Che's murder. The wave of protests covered the world. State dignitaries, secretaries of communist parties and of other leftist and progressive parties sent their condolences to the government and people of Cuba.

In New York a large crowd went through the streets of the city with bells, coffins, incense and flowers condemning the crime. At three o'clock they met at the door of the Bolivian Mission to the United Nations.

An attack by demonstrators was also reported on the US Embassy in London. From Washington, journalist George Weeks said on October 21: "International communist leader Ernesto Che Guevara was one of the heroes of the pacifist demonstration held here today.

"Thousand of pictures of the Argentine-Cuban killed in Bolivia were handed out among demonstrators when they reached the Abraham Lincoln Memorial to begin the 36-hour protest demonstration against the Vietnam War.

"A folk singer dedicated a song to him. One of the organizers asked for a minute of silence in his memory and many posters and signs paid him tribute.

"There was applause among the 25,000 demonstrators when a singer announced that he would dedicate his next song to 'one of the great revolutionaries of our time, who was murdered when he was participating in the Bolivian people's revolution' [...]"

US media were not able to remain indifferent to the Heroic Guerrilla. *Newsday* reported that Che had been "a magnificent guerrilla, a brave man." *The New York Post*: "He belongs to the romance of history." *The Christian Science Monitor:* "The main source of his strength was his attitude opposite the United States." *The Washington Post:* "He died in his life's work, toiling for the revolution."

In Bamako, Mali, journalist P. Haldare said that Che Guevara was convinced that to give up freedom was to relinquish man's condition.

The Cuban embassy in Algiers received the visit of European, African and Latin American residents who went to express their grief for the crime. The General Union of Algerian Workers called a meeting where Rachid Bennatig, leader of the organization, declared: "Che Guevara's death has caused in Algerian workers a moment of mourning filled with emotion and rage."

Students of Congo Kinshasa, Congo Brazzaville, Guinea, Mali, Guinea Bissau, Algeria, Morocco, Zimbabwe, Angola, Tanzania, Mozambique and Uganda condemned Che's murder.

At the Tanzanian capital the newspaper *The National List* reported that Che was the commander par excellence of all columns that fight imperialism on three continents.

Palestinian students residing in Cairo also condemned Che's death.

Presidents Houari Boumedienne of Algiers, and Sékou Touré of Guinea, sent their condolences to Cuba. Likewise, a message was received from the Liberation Front of Mozambique (FRELIMO).

The Bolivian government was praised and congratulated by the United States. In a speech, US Senator Howard Baker expressed his gratitude. Baker said that the events had a deep significance for his country, and that the $460.6 million dollars assigned to Bolivia was a small price for the victory –the cost of a week in the Vietnam War.

Bolivian journalist Jorge Rossa told that in Santa Cruz the city's mayor, Colonel Félix Moreno, summoned the people through local radio stations to participate in "the festival of rejoicing", organized to celebrate Che Guevara's death.

"The bonfire kindled on September 24 Square and guarded by soldiers", wrote Rossa, "seemed an act of the Inquisition. The cheerful music played by the Municipal Band became a funeral march. City employees officially summoned served in silence free glasses of cane spirits. Even the hundred or so 'representatives of the people', all volunteers —the 'cream' of this rotten society— stood silently around the bonfire. The most gruesome 'feast' that the perverse human mind has been able to conceive, became a grotesque but authentic wake."

Cochabamba university students called off the most important of their festivities. Every September 21 they celebrate the coming of spring and love, but on that year of 1967, due to the clashes with the police and the intense repression, they had postponed it for October. At the moment they were celebrating and were ready to choose their queen of the festival, the news of Che's murder arrived. Festivities were immediately suspended. Poet Ramiro Barrenechea   recalls the events:

"As leader of the CUB, but particularly as a poet, I was a member of the qualifying jury in order to prevent that chauvinism from the departments influenced the probity of the judges and caused esthetically regrettable results, as on other occasions.

"The feast was in its climax. There was one round to go for the final verdict, this time the contestants in bathing suits. Noise, multicolored petals, mixtures, balloons, and a cheerful band

143

playing taquiraris. Anxious and expectant faces. All ready to celebrate the triumph, and the closing of Students' Week, of spring.

"Suddenly, like a cold razor cutting my esthetic attention that already had a preference, a breathless, choking voice like a guttural sob speaks in my ear: 'Che is dead. The radio confirmed it a few minutes ago.'

"I snatched away from him the battery operated radio and heard: "Due to its importance we repeat: Near La Higuera...'

"There are some who remember everything, but I don't know what happened. I've even erased the time and the day. ¿Was it in the morning or in the afternoon? I did not wanted to confirm in historiography the precise information, because that moment has no time nor space. I remained suspended, alone, naked in my bones, without blood, air or tears.

"I don't know when, nor if I consulted with FUL members –it was their party—, but I grabbed the microphone and announced that as of that moment the festivity and the whole festival were suspended. We were in mourning, the young people, the country, humanity. Che was dead.

"Silence, a deep silence.

"I don't remember how we left the stadium, what we did, it was night, how we slept, if we slept.

"At the offices of FUL there was still a discussion, nor at all orderly, about the abrupt suspension of the festival. Angry mothers protested because of the queen's gown, its first wear twice postponed. However, most of the candidates understood the situation. I don't know what will become of them. Physical beauty is not a good companion of time and wrinkles."

University students and the great numbers of the dispossessed in Bolivia expressed their deep grief over the crime. The seven universities in the country held condemnation acts and showed their pain. At the University of Cochabamba a soccer game and several celebrations that had been programmed weeks before were suspended. Leaders from all universities in the country held a meeting and paid a posthumous homage. On Friday, October 13, after a mass meeting, student leaders headed by Eliodoro Alvarado, executive secretary of that university, and Ramiro Barrenechea, vice president of the Bolivian University Confederation signed a document. Both leaders described Che as a symbol of world youth, stressed his struggle for the people's liberation and declared him a "Bolivian citizen and patriot."

On the morning of the 14th, at the main lecture hall of the Law School, another great act was held in his remembrance. On this occasion. Alvarado spoke about the grief felt by the Bolivian people and compared Che with Simón Bolívar, Sucre and other Latin American patriots. Students demanded that he be granted the Bolivian citizenship post mortem, for having been a fighter for the liberation of Bolivia.

In Argentina students marched through the main avenues in several cities. In Rosario there were protests against the crime. The Peronista Youth disseminated a letter by Juan Domingo Perón as a tribute to Che and condemning his murder.

On that same day Father Hernán Benítez offered a funeral service for Che. Father Benítez said:

"Two thirds of the oppressed humanity has been shaken by his death. The other third, in the most secret place of their souls, does not ignore that the history of the future, if indeed we are on the road to a better world, belongs entirely to Che. One day, in the not too distant future, the victorious Third World will include his name in the martyrology of its heroes (...)"

At the beginning of the service, the priest said:

"He died with the characteristics of the legendary heroes, those who do not die in popular conscience. As the Jews in the Old Testament believed in prophet Elijah always alive, the Spaniards of medieval times in The Cid Campeador, and the Welsh in King Arthur, it is possible too that in the coming years the soldiers of the Third World will believe they sense the hallucinating presence of Che Guevara in the clamor of the guerrillas' struggles."

In another part of the service he expressed:

"Years ago he was already a legend. His enemies may blame him for whatever ideological deviation they think of. But no one in his senses will deny him passion, courage, heroism and a fully demonstrated perseverance in his vocation. The suffering of the masses hurt the bottom of his soul."

CIA agents against Regis Debray and Ciro Roberto Bustos

Repression unabated in Bolivia

In late October, a new wave of massive repression swept Bolivia. In La Paz, press reports revealed the arrest of more than thirty people, among them 10 prestigious medical doctors: René Flores Rodríguez, Javier Torres Goitía, Walter Parejas Fernández, Luis Ricardo Cano Zegada, Edmundo Ariñez, Guillermo Aponte, Miguel García, Clíver Herrera, Raúl Quiroga and Tomás Aramayo. In response to these events, Dr. Rolando Costa Arduz, Secretary for Relations of the Medical Association of Bolivia, summoned a press conference and stated that he had been unpleasantly surprised by the fact that the government had unleashed unduly violent repression against members of the medical organization. Dr. René Flores had been forcibly thrown into a police vehicle; the home of Dr. Walter Parejas had been raided and his medical library ransacked. Official behavior, he noted, had been guided by a campaign without precedent in the history of the country, and he notified that he had just wired the Pan American Medical Confederation, headquartered in Montevideo, to report the arrests.

Many other people were arrested in La Paz: Carlos Isaac Carvajal Nava, Jorge Rada Peredo, Eliseo Rocabado Terrazas, Darío Rueda Fernández, Napoleón Pacheco, Guido Fernández,

Zenón Arteaga, Ramiro Reinaga, Guido Perales, Cecilia Alcalá, Juan Silva, Felipe Herrera and Víctor Collazo, among others.

The examining magistrate of penal cases Olga Murillo de Velarde initiated proceedings against Pedro Aliaga Valverde, Mario Monje Molina, Víctor Andavares, Marcelino Zubieta, Antonio Quispe, Manuel Mamani, Luciano Heredia and others, charging them with publicizing pro-guerrilla warfare slogans, organizing groups of peasants to join the guerrillas and distributing large amounts of communist propaganda.

In Cochabamba, Gualberto Campos Alcalá and Amílcar Guzmán Vacaflor were arrested, allegedly for liaising with the guerrilla. At the same time, artist Mario Arrieta was detained in the capital as he was leaving the Municipal Theater where he was working; Remberto Echevarría Ampuero, newscaster in Radio Amauta, and José Ballón, the owner of Peña Naira, the most famous and authentic Bolivian nightclub that featured folk music and dances were also arrested.

Journalist Gonzalo López Muñoz, director of the Information Division of the Office of the President of the Republic, was also taken in for providing the guerrillas with blank credentials bearing his signature. The plan of the repressive forces was to put him in the same cell with common prisoners —hoodlums and murderers— with the aim of having him killed. For five days López Muñoz went without food and had to sleep on the cell floor.

Once again repression extended to the mines, although the authorities admitted to having only two detainees in their power —union leaders Juan Arce and Pacífico Medina. In Oruro, Encarnación Nieto, Berta Porcel and Clara Torrico were captured and, as was customary, their homes were raided.

In Beni, Roberto Soria and Noelí Saucedo, who owned a store and a boat in the area of Riberalta, were also the victims of repression.

Several students were arrested in Santa Cruz, among them María Esther Barrero, Virgilio Ludueña, Edgar Barbery and Bismarck Osinaga Toledo, the latter a university leader in Law School. The executive secretary of the University, Said Zetún, filed a habeas corpus on the grounds that those persons had been arbitrarily detained and indicated that they were preparing their defense against the abusive measures implemented by the government.

In Cochabamba, right in the middle of 14 de Septiembre Square in the presence of witnesses, DIC agents seized René Rocabado, former editor of the newspaper *Extra*.

In Potosí Professor Mamerto Álvarez, top leader of the Teachers´ Federation, was detained. The teachers´ union went on a general strike to protest the action.

Arrests continued unabated. Julio Dagnino Pacheco was captured; Rodolfo Saldaña shot his way out of a trap laid by members of the Ministry of the Interior; Humberto Rhea Clavijo managed to leave the country clandestinely; Luis Tellería and Félix Arancibia Barrera went into hiding; Drs. Hugo Bleischner Taboada and Hugo Lozano abandoned La Paz; Simón Reyes and Osvaldo Ucasqui Acosta went underground. All were accused of forming part of an urban support network.

Regis Debray and Ciro Roberto Bustos are sentenced

The Court Martial in Camiri decided to hand down their decision against Regis Debray and Ciro Roberto Bustos on November 17, 1967. The Court Martial was made up by Colonel Efraín Guachalla Ibáñez, president; Colonel Remberto Iriarte Paz, prosecutor; Colonel Remberto Torres Lazarte, clerk/rapporteur; Colonels Luis Nicolau Velasco and Mario Mercado Aguilar, members. The attorneys for the defense were Raúl Novillo for Regis Debray, and Jaime Mendizábal Moya for Ciro Roberto Bustos.

Many people arrived in Camiri, including Alain Badiou, professor of Philosophy from Reims, France; Roger M. Lallemand, a Belgian lawyer; French Consul in Bolivia Therese de Montléon; Cultural Attaché Gerard Barthelemy, and dozens of journalists and correspondents working for news agencies from abroad.

The interest of the international community was focused on the expectations generated by the trial against the French intellectual. A release that appeared in the La Paz newspaper *El Diario*, reported the following: "Since the beginning of the military proceedings against 2 foreigners and 4 Bolivian nationals, and up to the present, the 'Cable West Coast' telecommunications service has transmitted from here more than 400,000 words to national and foreign papers.

"According to estimates, from this date and until the day the sentence is to be handed down —some 9 days from now— the number of words sent out in press releases will have exceeded half a million.

"Arrivals here included local press people, particularly from La Paz, and even one from Pakistan, as well as representatives from the mainstream agencies such as UPI, AP, AFL, DPU, EFE, Reuter, Interpress and others.

"US, French and Spanish TV networks were also present. There were cameramen from Argentina, the University of Chile and the European circuit.

"Among the newcomers were reporters and photographers from practically every country in Latin America. France was represented (and still is) by correspondents from important dailies, widely-sold magazines, political weeklies and yellow rags." At one point there were over 50 journalists present. Considering the constant turnover, it is not hard to believe that the number of journalists that came to Camiri added up to more than 100."

Regarding the situation in Camiri, *El Diario*'s correspondent reported that several foreign journalists had been expelled. "At times, relations between the Chief of the Second Section (Intelligence) and some foreign journalists and certain Bolivian correspondents became tense."

During the trial, Regis Debray denounced the machinations of the CIA from the very first days of his detention. He denied the false charges the prosecutor was trying to saddle him with. He stated that he would not stand to be told that he would be condemned because he had come into the country on two occasions with the aim of spying, that he had delivered maps to Che, brought him money, formed part of guerrilla high command; that he had planned military operations, trained the guerrillas, that he had been a commissar and the mastermind of the subversion, and a combatant in ambush. He pointed out that "all these are tall tales, totally unfounded lies that can never be proven."

In connection with the presence of Cubans, Peruvians and Argentines in the guerrilla, he said, " For Che, the real difference, the true border is not the one that separates a Bolivian from a Peruvian, a Peruvian from an Argentine, an Argentine from a Cuban; it is the one that separates the Latin Americans from the Yankees. That is why Bolivians, Peruvians, Cubans, Argentines are all brothers in the struggle, and wherever the ones are fighting, the others must fight, too, because they have everything in common: the same history, the same language, the same forefathers, the same fate and even the same owner, the same exploiter, the same enemy that treats them all in the same way: Yankee imperialism."

Regis Debray declared that the CIA had orchestrated the trial after his refusal to accept its proposals and shady deals. He referred to his meeting with DIC thugs — overexcited agents more versed in punching and kicking than in questioning — led by a CIA agent – a Puerto Rican or Panamanian, purportedly named Doctor González:

"Never did the so-called Doctor González pretend to believe that I could be a guerrilla, much less a guerrilla leader. He was well aware of my background, the way I had been detained, and the manner in which guerrillas behaved. All this led him to believe that I had some political – confidential – mission assigned to me from abroad. The whole interrogation revolved not around the guerrilla but around data, organizations, names in France, Italy, Cuba, allegedly related with what he termed 'international communist espionage'. Naturally, there was great curiosity about Che. I also told him that, at that point in time, I also shared his curiosity, that I, like any other journalist, had hoped to find him, but that I had been wrong, that Inti was the main leader [[...]], that their information was false, but that they lacked eyewitnesses, material evidence to prove otherwise.

"González, based on a dossier written in English, asked me about my entire curriculum vitae, from my early childhood to the present [[...]]. In the name of the Bolivian government –despite the fact that he was not a Bolivian himself– he offered me protection and silence if I ever decided to cooperate with them. In the end, he proposed that I draft a public statement reneging 'my deeds, my ideas', denouncing Cuba, communism, etc. in exchange for my immediate and discreet liberation. As you can see, for the CIA there is no limit to their lack of conscience, no limit to their contempt for men [[...]]."

Debray said that early in July some Cuban agents from the CIA had gone to Camiri to question the prisoners once again, saying that they had been sent or that they were Dr. González's replacements.

"The one that questioned me," said Debray, "had a great virtue: he was candid and spoke directly to the point. He questioned me about my address book –luckily harmless—, which was taken from me in Muyupampa, and about other documents, such as the credential from Mr. Maspero, a card from the director of *Sucesos,* and other official French papers. This explains, by the way, why those documents could not be produced here, since this man had them in his briefcase and had to take them with him to Washington [[...]]; however, what is of interest here is this man's candidness.

"At the end he said: 'Everything depends on our reports. Your fate is in your hands. We are perfectly aware of the fact that you are not a guerrilla leader, but you must have some clandestine mission and we are interested in hearing about it. If you cooperate with us, if you answer my questions correctly, without trying to cheat on us, I assure you that all this machinery that has been set up against you will very soon disappear. Whatever has been set up we can dismantle in just a few days, you'll be relegated to an inside page, they will talk about you much as they talk about anybody else. No more statements, no more press campaigns, no more signs on the streets, no more demonstrations.'"

In reference to the demonstrations and acts of protest against Regis Debray, in his book *Ñacahuasú. Notes for a Military History of Bolivia,* Bolivian military Diego Martínez Estévez wrote: "His (Debray's) popularity became so great that the Division Command radioed an order aimed at preventing outsiders from attending the hearing in which the defense was to make their arguments. To that end, an altercation was orchestrated in which some cadets in street clothes were to participate. The judge ordered the court immediately cleared."

Regis Debray narrated that the CIA did not seem satisfied. The propaganda machinery kept operating at full blast. "Systematically," he said, "through all possible means, my name was linked with Che's, suggesting very subtly that thanks to my 'revelations' they had first learned of his presence here, when they had already been in the know since mid-March. My name was linked – as you have seen from the signs that cover the walls of this building – with Fidel Castro's, as if there could be any possible comparison between two historic heroes, between two leaders of the Americas, and a mere journalist, an obscure student of my times and my nationality.

"From Miami, from Washington, pamphlets hit the streets, published like serials by the big media, where I'm portrayed as a bloodthirsty maniac since early childhood, who enjoyed watching for breakfast in Havana a series of executions; who was captured here in Bolivia, in the heart of the jungle, shaking behind a tree, while fighting raged around me. When infamy breaks loose, there is no way to rein it in."

The prosecutor addressed Regis Debray and Ciro Roberto Bustos using insulting epithets; he labeled them as murderers, paid bandits, mercenaries in Cuba's payroll. The court sentenced them to 30 years in prison, the maximum sentence provided in the penal code. Bolivian analysts noted that 30 years is applicable only to individuals who have committed murders, parricide or treason against the country, and none of these crimes had been committed by the defendants. They had murdered no one, they had not murdered their parents, nor had they committed treason against their respective countries.

The role of the CIA and the United States in the trial against Debray and Bustos was exposed and the international media reported it. US officials declared that the State Department would not issue any official comment regarding the sentence imposed on Regis Debray by a Bolivian military court-martial and, without batting an eye stated: "After all, we are not involved."

In most of the world the Barrientos government was condemned for the arbitrariness and the judicial and procedural violations committed during the trial. Committees in solidarity with Debray were organized in several countries. In Santiago de Chile, 198 journalists decided to deliver a letter to the Bolivian consul in Santiago, Eduardo La Fuente, requesting that the prisoners be set free, but the consul returned it alleging that it contained pejorative language addressed to the President.

Prestigious intellectuals, among them Gabriel García Márquez (Colombia), Julio Cortázar (Argentina), Jean Paul Sartre (France) and several hundred writers and artists, demanded freedom for Debray and his comrades.

The CIA was not prepared to pardon Regis Debray and Ciro Roberto Bustos. There were news of a murder plot and, at the same time, an all-out slander campaign was organized against them, accusing them of having passed on the information that Che was in Bolivia. That is to say, they were trying to destroy them physically, politically and morally. Since then the Agency has not slackened in its attempts to bribe, compromise or, in some way, neutralize them.

Background information on two Cuban born mercenaries used by the CIA against Che's guerrilla

Dr. González or Eduardo González was the alias with which Gustavo Villoldo Sampera operated. Villoldo was born on January 21, 1936 in Havana. His father was a lawyer and president of General Auto Company, and also owned Villoldo Motors, a Pontiac and Cadillac dealership in Cuba, located at 59 Paseo del Prado until 1954, when it moved to Calzada and 12 in Vedado.

In his early years, Villoldo lived on Robau St., between Infanta and Panorama, Buen Retiro, in Marianao. He was later sent to study in the United States. In 1953 the family moved to 4608 1st. Ave. between 46th and 60th St., Miramar. On February 8, 1955, with great pomp and lavishness, he married Elia Nogués Espino; the ceremony was covered by the society sections of *Diario de la Marina* and *Información*. In 1957, his father committed suicide in the wake of a scandal that greatly undermined the family's moral standing in Havana's high society.

In 1958, when the struggle against the vicious tyranny of Fulgencio Batista took to the streets of Havana and hundreds of young people were brutally murdered, tortured or missing, Gustavo Villoldo established relations with notorious figures of the tyrannical regime. He became close with proven killers and was granted an identity card conferring him the rank of police captain *ad honorem*.

Late in 1959 he was accused of collaborating with the Batista police and of informing on young revolutionaries. He left the country for the United States and in 1960 was recruited by the CIA to work on terrorist plots against Cuba. Two years later, as an agent in charge working with infiltration and sabotage groups, he carried out several terrorist actions. He then attended Fort Benning, Georgia, where he received military training with other terrorists and CIA agents —Luis Posada Carriles, Félix Rodríguez, and Jorge Mas Canosa, all Cuban born. In 1967 he was sent to Bolivia to work on Che's guerrilla in the area of the 4th Division headquartered in Camiri. There he took part in the questioning and torture of the detainees. He bragged about kicking and slapping the corpse of Che and claimed to have made the decision to hack off his hands with the intent of taking them to Miami. After the guerrilla warfare was over, the CIA ordered Villoldo to go to Brazil.

In April 1971 he traveled to Mexico to coordinate attempts against the life of Cuban diplomats. Later he was sent to Vietnam where he was in charge of intelligence operations until the US troops were defeated.

On August 26, 1976 he allowed his name to be used for the purchase of the National Bank of South, in Hialeah, Florida — property of the CIA. According to people close to him, the FBI placed Villoldo under protection and armor-plated his car because, according to what he said to close friends, there was a plot to kill him.

On the evening of September 14, 1978, there was a meeting of the CIA with FBI representatives Harry Brandson and Joseph Dawson, in which both provided the Agency with arguments and evidence that Gustavo Villoldo Sampera was deeply involved in drug trafficking, that a small aircraft he owned had disappeared with two crew members of Cuban origin who were also taking part in that illegal activity. The CIA decided to protect Villoldo and rejected the evidence presented by the FBI.

On July 2, 1981 Villoldo traveled to Santo Domingo leading a CIA team comprising 12 agents. He returned to the United States in 1983, where he opened a fish and seafood shop on North River Drive and 8th Ave., next to the Miami River, where fishing boats are moored. Some people have insisted that the shop is a cover for his drug trafficking activities and his links with the mafia; however, he is still under CIA protection. Gustavo Villoldo was in Honduras in 1984 supporting the Nicaraguan counterrevolution. He now lives in Miami.

Among his friends he counts CIA agents Jesús Vázquez Barrero, the owner of Monaco Auto Salle, on 8 SW and 18th Ave., Miami, and Pedro García Mellano, residing in Puerto Rico, who owns the La Gran Vía pastry shop.

Félix Ramos, the other CIA agent

Who is Félix Ramos, Félix Medina or Félix Ramos Medina, as he called himself?

His full name is Félix Ismael Fernando José Rodríguez Mendigutía, as recorded in volume 136, page 189 of the births section of the Vedado Civil Registrar's Office, with the date of birth May 31, 1941, and a resident of 56, Independencia St., Sancti Spíritus, former province of Las Villas, by virtue of declarations by Dr. Fernando Mendigutía Silvera, uncle on the registered child's mother's side, and in the presence of witnesses Manuel Suárez Carreño, an engineer by trade, residing on 3023, Calzada St., Vedado, and Gerardo Ramón Rodríguez, a clerk, residing at 167, Cárcel St. Havana.

He was raised by his uncle, José Antonio Mendigutía Silvera, known as *Toto,* Minister of Public Works during the Fulgencio Batista dictatorship and a very close collaborator of the dictator.

When he turned ten, Rodríguez enrolled in the Havana Military Academy. After the victory of the Cuban Revolution, he left for the United States where the CIA recruited him. In 1960 he set off for the Panama Canal to undergo terrorist training. At the end of that year he submitted to the CIA a plot to murder Commander in Chief Fidel Castro. The plot was approved. After he finished training, he worked in groups to infiltrate Cuba and carried out his first action on February 14, 1961, when a CIA team aboard a speedboat approached an area near Arcos de Canasí, in the border between the provinces of Matanzas and Havana. There they unloaded two tons of equipment and explosives to be used in various sabotage actions and buried them in a hillock close to the coast. A few days later, Cuban State Security seized the cache, since one of men who helped Rodríguez was a Cuban Security agent.

Félix Rodríguez brought instructions from the CIA for the domestic counterrevolution to carry out sabotage activities that should coincide with the Bay of Pigs invasion, among them blowing up the Bacunayagua Bridge that links Havana with Matanzas on the very important Vía Blanca turnpike. When the invasion was crushed in less than 72 hours and with Cuban State Security in hot pursuit, he hid in the home of another counterrevolutionary, Patricio Nodal, until Alejandro Vergara Mauri, an official in the

Spanish Embassy in Cuba, was ordered by the CIA to pick him up in his car and take him home with him (5 Línea St., Apt. 2A, Vedado, telephone number 3 7058), where he was very well treated. Félix Rodríguez commented – this was later confirmed — that Vergara was a CIA agent. The aforementioned Spanish official introduced Félix Rodríguez to the Venezuelan Ambassador to Havana, H. E. José Nuceti Sardi, and it was through him that Rodríguez was given political asylum in the Embassy on May 3, 1961 until September 13 of that same year, when he left for Caracas.

After reaching the United States, he continued with his terrorist activities. He was sent to Fort Benning, Georgia, where he underwent training with Luis Posada Carriles, Gustavo Villoldo Sampera, Jorge Mas Canosa and other terrorists. On August 25, 1962 he married Cuban born Rosa Nodal, also a CIA member.

In 1963 he was assigned as part of a group of agents to a CIA base of operations in Nicaragua. From there and in reprisal against Spain for trading with Cuba, the group attacked the Spanish merchant ship *Sierra de Aránzazu*. The scandal acquired such dimensions that the Agency was forced to bring them home. From US territory, Rodríguez continued with his plots and terrorist activities.

When the US Intelligence Services learned of Che's presence in Bolivia, Rodríguez and several other Cuban-born agents were dispatched to Santa Cruz de la Sierra and later to Vallegrande. On October 9 he boarded a helicopter to La Higuera where he tried to forcefully question the Heroic Guerrilla. After Che was murdered, Rodríguez returned to Vallegrande; from there he traveled to Santa Cruz, then to Panama and subsequently to the United States.

A classified report, coded as "A C.O.D. 25", drafted by Félix Rodríguez for the CIA regarding the decision to murder Che — which was later published by journalist José Luis Morales, in the Spanish magazine *Interviú* on September 30, 1987— reads: "The decision to execute the subversive leader was conveyed directly to the Office of the President through our Embassy in La Paz." The journalist said that the same report spoke disparagingly of officers and noncoms of the Bolivian Army calling them "cowards and inept" and indicating that "despite indiscretions and paid leaks by Bolivian military units, we have succeeded in crushing the communist armed insurrection that threatened to spill over into other countries."

Félix Rodríguez himself stated, "Brutality was customary in the army and the savage treatment dispensed to prisoners was normal; frequently, the troops were ordered to take no prisoners [[...]] most of the Bolivian officers used different degrees of brutality in treating their own men [[...]]."

Journalist Claudio Gatti interviewed Rodríguez and published the story in the Spanish magazine *Cambio 16,* No. 942, December 18, 1989. When asked who had been in charge of executing Che, Rodríguez answered, "I went out and sent Terán to carry out the order. I told him to shoot him below the neck to make it look as if he had been killed in combat. Terán asked for a rifle and went into the room with a couple of soldiers [[...]] and I jotted down in my notebook: the time, 13:10, October 9, 1967."

In 1968 the CIA sent Rodríguez to Peru as an advisor on intelligence and long-range patrolling for the first paratroopers´ unit, known as Sinchís.

On February 24, 1969 he became a US citizen. He was immediately sent to South Vietnam. Rodríguez left for Saigon on March 13 of that year, as part of a group of 500 CIA agents stationed in that country. His job there was to torture and question prisoners and, in so doing, he also stole some of the prisoners´ belongings he still keeps as trophies. For his participation in the war he earned the US Government's recognition. In Saigon he was used by the Agency as interpreter to work with Argentine General Tomás Armando Sánchez de Bustamante. He prepared an itemized report for the CIA that reflected all the General's activities and opinions, as well as a personal characterization of the officer.

On April 20, 1976 he was pensioned and decorated by the CIA with the Intelligence Star for Valor. However, he continued working for the Agency.

Shortly after Zenteno Anaya was shot to death in 1976 in downtown Paris, Félix Rodríguez claimed he got a mysterious telephone call. The woman speaking asked for Félix Ramos —his alias in Bolivia— and then told him, "You're next." Rodríguez immediately asked the CIA for protection, convinced that some revolutionary group had discovered, identified and located him. The Agency installed a security system in his car and armor-plated it.

In 1979 he joined Ted Shackley, former CIA Chief of Station in Saigon, in arms trafficking to South America. Together with another

157

partner in the arms deals, Gerard Latchinian, he plotted a plan to murder former Honduran President Roberto Suazo Córdoba. Latchinian was sentenced to jail; however, Félix Rodríguez went free because all the compromising evidence against him had mysteriously disappeared.

During 1980 and 1981, Rodríguez carried out various CIA missions in Uruguay, Brazil, Costa Rica, Honduras, Guatemala and El Salvador. He also served in an advisory capacity with the Chilean Army on counter-insurgency tactics.

On June 7, 1981 Rodríguez had a bitter argument with a CIA official whom he attempted to blackmail, threatening to make public several terrorist plots against Nicaragua if he did not come through with a large sum of money. They reached an agreement in exchange for his silence.

On December 17, 1981 former CIA officer Karl Jenkins invited Rodríguez and other former members of the infiltration groups against Cuba to a meeting at a restaurant on 8th and 26th St. in Miami.

Around that time, Rodríguez organized terrorist plots against Cuban merchant ships carrying goods to Nicaragua. In 1982 he surfaced as an advisor to the Argentine Army, where he was known as El Gaucho.

The CIA sent him to San Salvador in 1984 to work in counterinsurgency activities and the delivery of arms and food supplies to the Nicaraguan "contras". For these operations he used Max Gómez as an alias. Before departing for El Salvador and through Donald Gregg, an advisor to George Bush, he met with the US President, who corroborated that he was the right man for the job.

Although he established his base of operations at the Ilopango airport in El Salvador, he traveled frequently to Honduras and Guatemala to coordinate the actions he intended to carry out. His assistant was Luis Posada Carriles, the perpetrator of the criminal bombing of the Cubana Airlines airplane where 73 people died on October 6, 1976, off the shores of Barbados.

Félix Rodríguez was linked to the big scandal in the United States known as Iran Contras. He was accused of arms and drug trafficking in collusion with the CIA and the Nicaraguan contras. All compromising evidence once again disappeared and a US Senate Subcommittee found him not guilty.

Rodríguez attended the inauguration of US President George Bush with his friend, General Rafael Bustillos, Chief of the Salvadoran Air Force.

The editor of Miami's *El Nuevo Herald,* Pedro Sevcec, recorded for his paper the following answer to one of the many questions he addressed to Rodríguez, which was published on October 16, 1989: "Sometimes when I'm alone, I sit here in the wee hours of the morning and go over the things I have done in my life. You get a feeling of satisfaction when you realize you've done your duty."

Félix Rodríguez lives in *Dade Country* in Florida. In his living room he has a museum of sorts which includes dozens of war mementos, documents, a grenade that according to him he carried in an incursion to Cuba, rifles and bayonets used against the Vietnamese, a defused bomb, pictures with US President George Bush, various objects seized from the guerrillas, among them a piece of underwear he claims belonged to Salvadoran combatant Nidia Díaz. His home is protected by electronic equipment and alarms to prevent access.

Che's *Diary* in Bolivia and the new CIA disinformation campaign

The CIA begins a new disinformation campaign

After the events at La Higuera and Che's assassination, the CIA intensified its disinformation campaign with the objective of distorting the truth about the guerrilla movement and to slander its main protagonists.

CIA experts prepared countless actions. One of them was designed to discredit the image of Tania the Guerrilla. For that purpose they planted an article in the press where they quoted a defector, an alleged former intelligence officer of the GDR named Günter Männel, who left for the Federal Republic of Germany where he spread slanderous rumors about her. The article fabricated by the CIA, was published on May 5, 1968 by the German daily *Welt Am Sonntag*.

In June of that year a CIA officer arrived in La Paz to "have a chat" with several previously selected journalists. The meeting was held at a house in 235, 14 St. in the residential neighborhood of Calacoto. Apparently the reason for the meeting was to show the article published in West Germany and exchange information about Tania in particular and the guerrilla movement in general.

A few days later the La Paz daily *El Diario* reprinted the article from the German newspaper and the Agency officer met again with the journalists. One of them told a friend that when the officer asked him his opinion on the article and encouraged him to write about what they had talked the previous time, he answered: "No one in Bolivia is going to believe those fantastic stories". He gave an explanation at length about his views, and mentioned several people that had known Tania and had a high opinion of her. He concluded that he could not accept a proposal of that nature, because no one in Bolivia would believe it, not even Barrientos.

The CIA officer answered that "Bolivians were unimportant. They are illiterate, can't read. What we care about are Europeans and Americans. There is a high percentage of them that will believe it, another percent will see fit to believe it, and we will make another percent believe it. The rest will be in doubt. Our success will depend on whether we can make adventurers of the guerrillas and a vulgar woman of Tania."

He was equally insistent about the capital importance of mass media in order to use them for that purpose, and offered him an important sum of money for the article. He made clear that Tania was not the objective, but Che; his was the image and influence in the revolutionary movement that should be affected, for the theory of armed struggle as the way for revolution had to be discredited. For that purpose it was necessary to create and generate distrust about the activity and effectiveness of his beliefs, as well as to take advantage of the events in Bolivia to promote the existing divisions and contradictions among leftists. With that purpose in mind they would spread the opinion that Che was wrong when he chose Bolivia, because in that country there were no conditions for the struggle; that he had acted in that manner because of contradictions with the Cuban leadership.

He pointed out the need of insisting that Bolivian miners, peasants and students were indifferent to the guerrillas, that all members of the Communist Party of Bolivia (PCB) betrayed them and were directly responsible for the failure, that Cuba abandoned them and did not assist them because of commitments with the Soviet Union.

He mentioned phrases that should be attributed to Che so that they were repeated constantly. The journalist remembered the following: "All Bolivian communists are pigs and bourgeois, and the revolution will sweep them away". "The peasants betrayed us; they are insensitive and act like stones." "I have failed." "It's all over." "Revolution can not be realized." "I have been defeated." "Don't shoot, I'm Che Guevara and I'm more valuable to you alive than dead." "I did not take the decision to come to Bolivia. Others took it for me."

As part of its campaign, the CIA began to prepare with the utmost care the alterations, omissions and addenda to Che's diary, in order to make it consistent with the distortions. For that purpose, expert forgers were at work on the last floor of the US embassy in La Paz. The campaign was not launched because of the publication of *Che's Diary in Bolivia* in Havana.

The CIA was preparing slanderous material against members of the Bolivian Communist Party and other leftist parties and organizations, members of the urban network and important figures that were sympathizers of the guerrilla movement. Likewise they prepared false declarations and commitments with the Bolivian intelligence agencies or the CIA by some of the people who had been arrested, with the intention of blackmailing them in order to keep them under control or recruit several of them.

Information obtained through other means were attributed to those people in order to discredit them before public opinion, while protecting those who were useful to the Agency or were potential assets.

Regarding Che's guerrilla movement in Bolivia and his figure, there was a systematic and well orchestrated propaganda campaign with books, pamphlets, newspaper and magazine articles, editorials, interviews. In all of them truth was distorted and manipulated. Writers close to the agency were used to spread false rumors.

The CIA, in spite of its hundreds of experts, its huge resources and its finely tuned plans, has been unable to deteriorate Che's and the guerrilla's image and prestige. As Abraham Lincoln said, "You can fool all the people some of the time, and some of the people all the time, but you cannot fool all the people all the time."

Negotiations to sell Che's *Diary*

While CIA experts were working to include or eliminate elements of interests in Che's Diary, the Bolivian high military command tried to market it.

Insistent rumors circulated in La Paz that the government had sold the copyright of Che's documents to *The New York Times* and a US television network. These rumors caused a bidding competition that started at $20,000 dollars and peaked at $400,000.

Since its arrival in La Paz, the original diary had been kept in a strongbox. All necessary precautions were taken for its protection, including frequent changes of the combination. When the diary had to be taken to the Military Geographic Institute in order to photograph some pages that would be used as evidence in Regis Debray's trial, it was done under strict security measures. Lieutenant Commander Moisés Vásquez Sempértegui and two other officers acted as permanent guards. Colonel Amadeo Saldías kept an eye on the photographer while he was working. When the diary was shown to representatives of the European company Magnum Publicity and to journalists Andrew Saint George and Juan de Onis, they were under the constant supervision of officers Moisés Vásquez Sempértegui and Ángel Vargas Tejada.

On November 3, 1967, Magnum offered $50,000 for Che's diary, and next day Barrientos announced the agreement. Ovando knew of the sale through the press and immediately voiced his disagreement and claimed he had a better offer. In private he said that Barrientos probably had secret dealings with Magnum to pocket part of the money. On November 7 Ovando said that the diary would be sold to the highest bidder, and that there was an offer of $100,000. These contradictions increased the already tense relationship between both generals and the differences of opinion among the military high command had to be discussed.

On November 17, 1967 there was a declaration that the decision on the sale of the diary would be the responsibility of the Armed Forces. Meanwhile, there was a leak that the delay was because CIA experts had not decided which aspects should be eliminated from or added to the original.

Magnum Publicity, *Paris Match*'s parent company, disavowed Michele Ray, its representative in La Paz, who offered $400,000 for the diary. On their part, military sources pointed out that Magnum had promised only $120,000, plus a 10 percent royalty.

On November 22 a Supreme Decree authorized the Armed Forces to dispose of all of Che's documents and belongings. Nevertheless, on December 1 Ovando said to the Brazilian daily

O Jornal that the diary would never leave Bolivia. However, on December 3 it was revealed in New York that Magnum Photos, Inc., an international corporation of graphic reporters, was negotiating with the Bolivian government and had offered $125,000.

Publishing corporation Doubleday and Co. abstained from negotiations for fear that Aleida March, Che Guevara's widow, could challenge the deal and file a legal claim.

On December 4 it was known that Time-Life, Inc. and *Paris Match* were in a bidding war for the publishing rights. The following day, Barrientos claimed that international communism was trying to disrupt the negotiations with Magnum for a total of $300,000 dollars. On December 15 it was informed that they had fell through.

After his commercial defeat, Barrientos asked Ovando for the diary and gave it to Captain Norberto *El Bubby* Salomón, a trusted aide, with the order of making a copy at the Ministry of the Interior.

Minister Antonio Arguedas convinced Salomón of going to dinner while the copy was made, a job entrusted to Ricardo Aneiva Torrico, head of the Technical Department, his aide Jaime Moreno Quintana, and photographer Fernando Manzaneda Mallea. Previously Arguedas had ordered Aneiva to make an extra copy. When Arguedas and *El Bubby* returned to the Ministry, the copy was ready. Captain Salomón took to Barrientos both the original and a copy.

Negotiations for the sale of Che's diary continued, but for one reason or another did not materialize. The CIA was not interested in the sale for the moment, because it had to finish the doctoring of the diary and establish certain commitments with the publisher.

Unease in the Bolivian Armed forces and escape of the surviving guerrillas

There were increasing contradictions and unease in the Bolivian Armed Forces. In early January 1968, the Colchani unit, stationed at the Chilean border, rose up in rebellion because the military high command had ordered the arrest of its commander, Captain Humberto Monterrey, for voicing strong criticisms against Barrientos

The rebels went to the Uyuni mines with the objective of proclaiming together with the miners their disobedience to the

164

President's authority and a call for an uprising in the whole country. In view of the situation, Barrientos ordered that the unit be subdued by force. There was a bloody clash and Captain Monterrey died in strange circumstances. Four of his aides were seriously wounded.

On February 15, 1968, an event related to the guerrilla movement hit the front pages: the surviving group of the guerrillas, after being surrounded several times by the army and escaping, reached the town of Sabaya, department of Oruro, near the Chilean border. In their march from the guerrilla area, more than 1,000 kilometers away, they had been aided and protected by a Bolivian Communist Party detachment and common people, collaborators that at the risk of their lives hid them at Cochabamba and La Paz until they were taken to the border. The Bolivian intelligence services and the CIA were unable to detect the guerrillas or suspect their movements.

When Barrientos discovered the whereabouts of the guerrillas, he ordered the deployment of the Ingavi Regiment from La Paz, the Camacho from Oruro, and the CITE assault troops and paratroopers stationed at Cochabamba. Colonel Manuel Cárdenas Mallo, chief of operations of the General Staff, was placed in command of the troops and received orders to track down the guerrillas, but on February 16 they crossed the border into Chilean territory. Members of the Chilean Communist Party were waiting for them.

The people of Chile welcomed them with open arms. President of the Senate Salvador Allende gave them the necessary assistance. He personally accompanied them to Tahiti, where the Cuban Ambassador to France, Baudilio Castellanos, was waiting for them.

Barrientos had to admit his failure. The military high command justified it with the following communiqué:

"The Cuban guerrilla group crossed the border into Chilean territory.

"The belated communications from Sabaya, due to the lack of transmission means, as well as to the bad weather at the area, was the reason that prevented the use of paratroopers, as it had been planned to cut their retreat route."

Outraged by his military failure, the discredit to his government, the warm welcome to the guerrillas by the Chilean

165

people, the Chilean government's denial to return the guerrillas, and Salvador Allende's personal protection, Barrientos adopted the ridiculous position of accusing Chile at the OAS of complicity with the guerrilla movement.

In mid June, 1968 there was a new military uprising. Troops trained by US advisors in anti-guerrilla warfare and that had participated in the combats at Quebrada del Yuro rebelled and threatened to kill their officers, for the President had promised to demobilize them once operations were over, but had forgotten his commitment. Instead, their superior officers hired them as cane cutters to a private company in the Santa Cruz department. Wages were paid to the officers who did not give a single cent to the soldiers. The situation created a deep sense of unease that culminated in the revolt. The troop took control of the weapons, arrested the officers, threatened them with lynching and prepared the defense of the Guabirá barracks, where they were stationed.

In relation to Barrientos' unkempt promise, Gary Prado wrote in his book *Power and Armed Forces* the following:

"Perhaps because of the way he acted, General Barrientos frequently made promises that afterwards were hard to keep or caused critical situations for his subordinates."

Renting Bolivian soldiers as slave labor to private construction or agricultural companies was common practice. Military officers exploited them mercilessly, physically punished them and gave them bad food: a corn flour soup known as "lagua". In his book Prado claimed that "Lack of sensitivity and of morals in some commanders made them exploit that labor for their own benefit."

After the combats at La Higuera and Quebrada del Yuro, soldiers considered they deserved a special treatment and recognition, but soon they understood that they simply had been instruments of a policy in which they only supplied the dead. Once the guerrillas were gone, they went back to be the same exploited, physically punished and badly fed soldiers.

Barrientos feared that the protest could spread to other units and ordered them bombed until surrender. Several Air Force planes flew low over the barracks, but soldiers fired their machine guns at them. Finally, Barrientos was forced to give in and authorize the discharge of the soldiers, besides promising in public that there would be no reprisals.

166

Che's Diary in Bolivia is distributed in Havana at no cost

On July 1, 1968, *Che's Diary in Bolivia* began to be distributed at no cost in Havana. It was also reported that it would soon be published by Punto Final in Chile; Maspero in France; Ruedo Ibérico in Spain; Feltrinelli in Italy; Trikont Verlag in West Germany; *Ramparts* magazine in the United States; Editorial Siglo XXI in Mexico, and in many other countries.

The news was a political earthquake that shook the foundations of the Bolivian government, the Armed Forces and its intelligence services, the United Status embassy and the CIA Station in that country.

Barrientos and Juan José Torres immediately denied its authenticity. In a press conference Torres said: "I believe it is sensationalism on the part of Castro. We have not given Guevara's diary to anyone."

Torres explained that "only a few pages had been photocopied to authenticate Guevara's handwriting", and finally said that "according to national law, the documents captured to the guerrillas are the property of the nation's Armed Forces, that the diary had been put away in a safe and secure place, and that only top military officers had had access to its content; that at no time copyright had been ceded for its publication neither domestically nor abroad, in spite of the many offers received."

Commander in Chief Fidel Castro, in a speech broadcast to the whole country by radio and TV, said: "(…) nobody in his right mind could conceive that someone would publish a false copy of a document whose original is in somebody else's hands, and that that somebody else is the enemy. The very idea that we would incur in such a mistake is preposterous –not only a mistake, but such immorality, that this revolution is not in the habit of doing.

"We received photostatic copies that were subjected to a careful study [...]

And there is not the slightest doubt that it is the authentic Diary."

News from Havana that *Che's Diary in Bolivia* was being distributed free of charge was transmitted all over the world, and the manner the secret of its publishing was handled caused a great impact on international public opinion. Newspapers and magazines

167

in Mexico, Santiago de Chile, Montevideo, Buenos Aires, Bogota, Rio de Janeiro, Lima, Quito, Caracas, Munich, Milan, Rome, Paris, Algiers, Madrid, Cairo, London, Brussels and New York headlined the news. On its part, Czechoslovak news agency CETEKA doubted the authenticity of the diary and the truth of the news from Havana.

The publication of *Che's Diary in Bolivia* was a huge failure for the CIA, and its libelous plans against Che and the Cuban revolution were dealt a serious blow.

An urgent meeting of the Bolivian High Command

Immediately after acknowledging the publication of *Che's Diary in Bolivia*, Barrientos convened an urgent meeting of the military high command with the purpose of discussing the situation and accountability for the leak. An important Bolivian source that had access to the meeting told:

"Barrientos did not make a direct accusation on Ovando, but through references and elements that he set out it was obvious he was referring to him and that Ovando would have to resign to save the government's prestige.

The President tried to take advantage of the publication of Che's diary to get rid of Ovando and all the members of the Armed Forces General Staff loyal to him. For a long time both generals had been trying to eliminate each other. Barrientos knew that Ovando had plotted against him and had made plans for a coup that included the possibility of his assassination. It was no secret that on several occasions Barrientos had tried to substitute Ovando, but had been unable to do so. On this occasion there was a possibility of success and he was ready to take it.

In the Armed Forces there was a balance of power, for Ovando had maneuvered quite skillfully and appointed trustworthy officers totally loyal to him as commanders of the country's most important regiments. For that reason he could not be replaced without convincing grounds; otherwise the measure could provoke a coup, for those commanders knew that Ovando's fall would mean their own, and that factor was an obstacle for Barrientos."

The source added that "since it now appeared that Ovando was responsible for the publication of Che's diary in Havana,

168

Barrientos could attain his goal of substituting him. Considering that the government of Bolivia, the Armed Forces and the intelligence services had been placed in a position of ridicule and national and international discredit, someone had to pay. That someone could not be other than Ovando, and Barrientos was not willing to pardon him.

"It was a stormy meeting", continued the source. "All agreed that Ovando's fate was cast; but when he spoke, he struck all those present speechless, including Barrientos himself. General Ovando, who had a calm and inexpressive character, was a man of great authority and very respected in the Armed Forces. He explained that he could prove that he had nothing to do with the leak, that he was innocent of everything the President accused him of. He also said that if the book published in Havana contained all the pages of Guevara's diary, he would accept responsibility, but if there were thirteen pages missing –and immediately he mentioned the page number of every one of them— the blame should be placed on the Ministry of the Interior. Ovando explained that when Barrientos asked him for the diary to have it photocopied at the Ministry of the Interior, before delivering it he kept those thirteen pages as a security measure. Ovando assured that it was easy to know if the source of the leak was the US Embassy or the CIA, because their copy had the image of a soldier's fingers on several pages. The meeting was adjourned until a copy of the Cuban edition could be obtained to collate it with the copies in Bolivia."

For several years it was believed that photographer Fernando Manzaneda had not photocopied the whole diary, because he had been pressed for time when they asked him to do the job. Allegedly that was the reason for the missing thirteen pages. But now the truth is known: Manzaneda did photocopy all that was given to him. He also made the two copies that Minister Arguedas asked him to.

On July 10 the La Paz newspaper *Presencia* published Che's diary and Ovando guaranteed its authenticity. He also announced that an investigation would be made in order to ferret out the guilty party.

Intrigue was the order of the day. Barrientos' closest collaborators spread rumors that Ovando was responsible of the leak, that he should be substituted and tried in court for any responsibility, for he was equally guilty whether he had leaked the document or allowed someone else to do it. The rumors caused in

Ovando a depression so deep that he told his family and closest friends that he would resign because of suspicions and treacherous comments, and although he was not guilty it was difficult to convince others that he had nothing to do with the issue.

Friends and collaborators began a series of urgent contacts to counter the smear campaign. On July 12 they managed to get the Bolivian Congress to demand a clarification from Barrientos, besides a complete investigation of the matter.

At the same time, Ovando had a secret meeting with the leader of the Bolivian Socialist Phalanx and told him that the one responsible for the delivery of Che's diary to Cuba was Minister of the Interior Antonio Arguedas, for when Ovando personally collated the original with the version printed in Havana, in the latter were missing the thirteen pages he had taken out. All of La Paz knew of the close friendship between Barrientos and Arguedas, so an attack against the latter was also an attack on the President, and the Phalanx, who considered both its enemies, would take advantage of the situation.

In relation to the friendship between Barrientos and Arguedas, Gary Prado wrote that the Minister was part of a very small group of members of the Armed Forces totally faithful to Barrientos, who had been extraordinarily favored by him, even beyond what was permitted by military regulations.

The Bolivian Socialist Phalanx presented Congress with a request that the Minister of National Defense General Enrique Gallardo Ballesteros answer in writing the following questions:

"Who were the officers that had the diary in their custody? How many photocopies were made of this document and where are they? Who ordered that copies of the diary were given or access to the original be granted to foreign journalists, and CIA and FBI personnel? Is that not considered interference of a foreign country in Bolivia's internal affairs? Did the Armed Forces and the government know that *The New York Times* had a copy of Che's diary? Why was not the publication of the diary speeded up in the country? Why Che's diary was not published in the care of the Armed Forces, if it was a matter of national interest and would mean a considerable income for the country? Why the government did not release the supreme decree of December 6, 1967, which disposed of Che's diary?"

The Bolivian Socialist Phalanx claimed in a press release that Barrientos gave Arguedas a copy of the diary without taking into account that he was under suspicion because of his fickle Marxist leanings. On his part, Ovando sent Barrientos a request in writing to investigate the Minister of the Interior, which read as follows:

"Mr. President,

The organizations of the Armed Forces in charge of the investigation about the manner in which the Diary of Ernesto "Che" Guevara left the country have established that said document, on the occasion that it was in the custody of the Ministry of Government, was handled with extreme indiscretion for a period of 24 hours.

Since we have serious evidence that the unusual carelessness of the highest security organization of the Executive Power could have been the source of the infiltration of said document, I respectfully request that Department 2 of the General Staff carry out the strictest investigation of that agency, beginning by the Minister of Government himself.

I have the utmost confidence that in this manner I will be able to prove to the Captain General and all the country that the Armed Forces did not neglect its sacred mission and its permanent duties to the security of the nation. The disloyal campaign launched against the Armed Forces can not reach any of its members, of whose moral and professional stature I vouch for."

The military proceedings on the leak of *Che's Diary* begins

On July 19, 1968 the military legal proceedings began at La Paz to determine the possible errors or crimes committed in the care of Che's documents. Questioning began under strict security measures. Joaquín Zenteno Anaya, Arnaldo Saucedo Parada, Andrés Sélich Shop, Herberto Olmos Rimbaut, Miguel Ayoroa Montaño, Moisés Vásquez Sempértegui, Mario Eduardo Huerta Lorenzetti, Ángel Vargas Tejada and Federico Arana Cerrudo were summoned. In their declarations, they were unable to conceal the interfering role of the CIA and the US Embassy against Che's guerrilla.

That evening Antonio Arguedas disappeared. The Bolivian government sealed the country's borders to prevent his escape. On its part, the CIA dismantled is Technical Department —all equipment and documents were transferred to a house at 235, 24th Street, on the Calacoto neighborhood, property of Gerardo Vargas, which had been rented for some time by CIA officer Hugo Murray.

Documents and equipment, which were moved in through the back door very late at night, were received by a US embassy official that drove a station wagon with diplomatic license plate 326.

During the move, several file drawers containing recorded tapes, agent payrolls, photos of security houses and other important documents were lost. The drawers were found by revolutionaries, who jealously guarded them for several years.

Revelations of Bolivia's former Minister of the Interior Antonio Arguedas about the CIA's interference in his country's internal Affairs

Antonio Arguedas reveals how he was recruited by the CIA

In one of his many press conferences at that time in Lima, Peru, Antonio Arguedas revealed his links with the CIA. He told journalists that in 1964, when he was appointed as Assistant Secretary of the Interior Ministry, he received the visit of Colonel Edward Fox who told him that if he remained in his post the United States would suspend its economic aid to Bolivia and would take the most drastic sanctions and pressures against the Bolivian government. Arguedas said that in order to avoid such measures he submitted his resignation; but some twenty days later, Colonel Fox told him that his situation could be arranged if he was willing to talk with a US diplomat. He then introduced Larry Sternfield, the CIA Chief of Station in Bolivia, who suggested a trip to Lima.

At the Peruvian capital he was escorted by CIA officer Nicolás Leondiris to an apartment located on Piérola Avenue, where two Americans questioned him for four days. Arguedas said that on the first day they asked who his friends were, his relations, what had been his links to the Bolivian Communist Party, which leftist leaders he knew, what conversations he had with them. On the second day he answered a questionnaire on his life. On the third he was submitted to a polygraph test, and they put wires to his hands, heart and head. On the last day he was drugged. When he came to, the interrogation was over.

After his return to Bolivia, the possibility of being appointed Minister of the Interior came up. The Americans promised him they would praise him and lobby for him in all the Bolivian capital's circles as the proper man for the post. He traveled to Washington invited by the US government, and there an official gave him an explanation on each and every Latin American government. An expert on Cuba told him terrible things about the Cuban revolution.

He returned to Bolivia and was appointed Minister of the Interior. He confessed that he lived in a permanent dilemma. It was then that the guerrilla made its appearance. The CIA Chief of Station told him that he would send him some advisors, because the security agents he had were no good at all. In that manner Cuban born CIA agents came to Bolivia. Arguedas told the press that in the beginning those agents worked under his orders, but at some moment they began to act with total independence. He was outraged by this situation, because Bolivian citizens denounced interrogations and tortures by people who had a foreign accent. He notified that it could not go on, but they did not heed his warning. Arguedas told the conference that Cuban born CIA agent Julio Gabriel García had a Bolivian mistress to whom he told all the secrets of the State's security service.

Among the discrepancies with the Americans, he told that as a result of a lawsuit of COMIBOL and Lipez Mining, a US company, the CIA pressured him to use his influence so that the court would rule in favor of the US party. Since the trial went according to the law, the Americans thought that Arguedas was getting out of control.

Another addition to his bad relations with the CIA was that on June 13, 1968, the date of his birthday, CIA Station head Thomas Hazlett sent for him to give him a present. Upset because of the American's arrogance he did not go. The next day CIA officer Hugo Murray told him that the Chief was angry, because he had a present for him that had been sent from the US. Arguedas said that in the name of good relations he went to Hazlett's home, located on 7 St., at the Obrajes neighborhood. The present was a pistol with a belt and an empty magazine that had a photograph of Fidel Castro, Che Guevara and Raúl Castro. Right away he thought it was the beginning of blackmail; that is, the CIA was hinting that if he did not act unconditionally at their service he would be denounced as a Castroite. At that moment he remembered that he had the negatives of Che's diary in a drawer in his desk. When he returned to his office he wrote a note to Commander Fidel Castro, took out the negatives and sent them to Havana.

The next day he called the CIA Station Chief and asked for an explanation on the present. Hazlett told him that it was a joke by Tilton, the former Station head, and that probably the photos of the Cuban leaders were to be used for target practice.

Antonio Arguedas, Minister of the interior of Bolivia, evades the CIA

The scandal of the Bolivian Minister of the Interior's escape involved the US Embassy in La Paz, the CIA Station, the top Bolivian military, its intelligence services, and particularly Barrientos. The President's enemies took advantage of the event and prepared a demonstration calling for his resignation. It was such a discredit that the Cabinet in full resigned. In this circumstance Barrientos was forced to appoint new ministers among his military allies, because the contacted civilians did not accept. Observers underscored the fact that at the swearing in of the new Cabinet there were neither members of the military high command nor the leaders of the parties in power. Barrientos' isolation was increasingly obvious.

According to Bolivian sources, the Minister fled because he had been timely informed that the CIA had discovered that he had sent Che's diary to Cuba. Considering him a double agent, they were preparing his assassination. Arguedas had valuable information on many CIA covert operations in Bolivia and other Latin American countries. He also was familiar with the names of agents infiltrated in the media, the Armed Forces, political parties, labor unions, ministries and institutions. Arguedas knew about security houses, telephone tapping and mail surveillance by officers and members of the CIA Station in Bolivia. For those reasons it was extremely embarrassing his being alive. If he talked, the work of many years in Bolivia would be significantly compromised. Considering that possibility, the decision was to terminate him.

On July 19, when the Minister received an invitation from agent Julio Gabriel García to meet with him at 19:30 at a certain place to discuss a serious matter, he was certain that the information about the assassination was real.

To reach the meeting place he had to cross the Florida Bridge, that links downtown La Paz with the residential neighborhood of Calacoto. Two men were waiting for him with the order to kill him. The crime was calculated so that suspicions fell on leftist groups or the offended military for his having delivered Che's diary to Cuba. But at ten o'clock Arguedas, instead of going to the meeting, decided to leave on that very same night for Chile. He was accompanied by his driver José Matías Valencia, his brother Jaime Arguedas and one of the latter's aides, a man by the name of Crespo. After crossing the border, he went with his brother to the control post on the Chilean town of Colchani, where they asked for political asylum. Their other two companions returned to La Paz. From Colchani the Arguedas brothers were taken to Iquique to await the decision from the Chilean capital.

The CIA Station in Santiago made its moves through every possible channel to isolate and silence him. A CIA officer, together with Eduardo Zúñiga Pacheco, deputy director of investigations of the police, flew to Iquique in a Chilean Air Force airplane. He submitted Arguedas to a thorough search and questioning that lasted between two to three hours. Following instructions, Zúñiga offered him a personal fortune and new documents so that he could travel to any European country, in exchange of accusing General Ovando or General Barrientos of delivering Che's diary to Cuba for a large sum of money. Zúñiga promised to release him for few days and when Arguedas had evidence that the money had been deposited in a European bank, a press conference would be set up so that he could make the accusation.

"You'll have to finger one or the other", Zúñiga told him. "The Americans are not going to be the losers (...) nor Chile, nor you. The losers must be the individuals in your country that at this moment are trying to eliminate you."

Antonio Arguedas declared that when he refused the proposal, there were attempts to blackmail him, pressures and threats. Likewise they wanted to make him say that the Socialist Party of Chile was linked to the Bolivian guerrillas. From Iquique he was taken to Santiago and held incommunicado.

The CIA appointed officer Nicolás Leondiris to personally attend to Arguedas, for they knew each other well from working together since 1964.

In Santiago de Chile, the CIA pressured him again with the intention of making him sign a document asking to return to Bolivia. Simultaneously they published a press release in his name that explained that he was not asking for political asylum, but rather wanted to return to Bolivia as soon as possible. The Agency's plan was to deliver him to the government so that Bolivians could be blamed for Arguedas' murder in case they were unable to reach an agreement with the former Interior Minister.

US Ambassador Edward Korry met several times with Arguedas trying to convince him. On his part, CIA officer Nicolas Leondiris told him: "Everything is arranged, Don Antonio. We are going to take every measure so that you can get out, but we maintain our initial offer. You know that Marcos Vásquez (Sempértegui) wants to put you up against the wall in Bolivia, so don't say that General Barrientos or General Ovando were the perpetrators. Why don't you say it was Marcos Vásquez who obtained the copy and sold it, and that you, in order to save national dignity, are giving yourself up? All you have to do, if saying it embarrasses you, is to write down a figure, and I'll see to it you get paid in my country."

Arguedas did not accept the offer and Leondiris made a new business proposal: go to Cuba, say that he was in favor of the Cuban revolution, get in touch with as many people as he could and communicate all the information that he obtained. He promised Arguedas that in that case he could get anything he wanted. Arguedas explained that he did not take part in such dealings. This caused him that during the time he was in Chile he was detained, put in solitary confinement, and strictly controlled by the CIA. Meanwhile, the agency launched an extensive disinformation campaign in order to neutralize him.

Some newspaper headlines in right wing media might give an idea of this campaign. Some of them are the following:

"Arguedas wants to return to Bolivia." "He is sorry for what he has done." "When he knew of reproaches from Barrientos, he cried." "Arguedas was Chile's public Enemy Number one in Bolivia." "He organized anti-chilean Demonstrations in La Paz." "His escape is an intrigue against Chile by the Bolivian Government." "Arguedas was the man of the military and he escaped with Ovando's help." "The objective was to overthrow Barrientos and use Chile as a sounding board." "He sold Che's Diary.".

In order to counter this colossal propaganda, some journalists demanded that the right of political asylum be respected. The staff of *Punto Final* magazine hired lawyer Jaime Faivovich to represent Arguedas. Faivovich filed a writ of *habeas corpus* at the Appeals Court. The court immediately requested a report from the Police's Department of Investigations. Meanwhile in La Paz, Barrientos made threatening declarations against Arguedas, which the new Bolivian consul in Santiago de Chile, Alfredo Galindo, leaked to the local press, a fact that irritated the US Embassy.

The following day, in a 180 degrees turnabout, Barrientos urged Arguedas to return to Bolivia and give himself up to the civil or military authorities. He would have full guarantees, for he would not be charged with treason.

Cuba's Foreign Relations Minister Raúl Roa García declared that his government would grant him political asylum if Chilean authorities denied it. In view of the situation, Chile had no alternative, but on the condition that he immediately left the country.

Just before he left, Arguedas gave an interview where he explained that he had sent a copy of Che's diary to Fidel Castro because US imperialism was trying to use it in a provocation against the Cuban government.

Arguedas Leaves for London

Antonio Arguedas boarded a British United Airways flight on July 26, 1968, at 17:00 hours, that would take him to London with stopovers at Buenos Aires, Sao Paulo, Rio de Janeiro, Las Palmas and Madrid. His escort was CIA officer Nicolás Leondiris and

Chilean police officer Oscar Pizarro Barrios. The plane arrived to Ezeiza International Airport in Buenos Aires at 18:40, where a group of journalists was expecting him, some looking for news, others as a measure of solidarity, in order to prevent an attempt against him. One hour later he resumed his trip.

When Arguedas' plane landed at Barajas Airport in the Spanish capital, two Cuban embassy officials, Héctor Gallo Portieles and Guillermo Ruiz, were expecting him. Security measures had been tightened and airport facilities were under strict surveillance by Spanish security services. Cubana Airlines executive Pablo Fernández was able to reach the plane's steps dressed as a mechanic and give Arguedas a written message. The presence of another Cuban on the plane surprised him.

In the airport's cafeteria there was a private conversation between Arguedas and Cuban diplomat Héctor Gallo Portieles. The Cuban mission in the UK received a message that the former Interior Minister was aboard British United Airways flight 662 bound for London. Cuban Ambassador Alba Griñán Núñez ordered Second Secretary Guido Sánchez Robert to go to the airport and give him any assistance he needed, but British immigration authorities did not allow him access to Arguedas.

At a room in Gatwick Airport, Arguedas was questioned and held for four hours until the CIA obtained that a British official allowed him to enter the country. However, Arguedas was warned that his entry was illegal, his name was not on the passenger list and that he could stay in the UK for just three days.

The CIA took him to the Apollo Hotel, then to the Richmond Hill. At both lodgings he was registered under an assumed name. Officially he never traveled to London or registered at any hotel.

The British press published the arrival of Arguedas. However, a Home Office officer declared that they did not know his whereabouts, while the Foreign Office said that he was under the protection of the Home Office.

A Cuban official received confidential information that the CIA was exerting pressure on their British counterparts to find an adequate way to eliminate Arguedas.

A very prestigious British lawyer, Geoffrey Bing, suggested the Cuban Embassy to contact MPs Lord Brockwey and Arthur Stanley Newens to inform them on the serious situation that the former

Minister could be in. Newens was the chairman of a movement against colonization and he also was very influential and respected in Parliament. He was very receptive and promised to look into the matter. Newens wrote a letter to Arguedas, care of the Home Office, in which he asked him to write or telephone him.

Cuban ambassador Ms Griñán asked the Foreign Office for an interview with the purpose of communicating her concerns in view of the apparent contradiction between the Foreign Office's declarations and what had been published in *The Guardian* that the Home Office did not know of Arguedas' whereabouts. Ambassador Griñán also requested a meeting with Arguedas.

The interview was granted and on July 30 she met with Lord Chalfont (Alun Arthur Gwynne Jones Hardman), Minister of State for Foreign Relations, who kindly assured her of his full disposition to help her. Likewise he revealed that the Foreign Office knew of Arguedas' whereabouts, and that she could meet with him at any moment. Ambassador Griñán thanked him for the information and answered to the proposal: "As soon as possible, any time, any place."

On that same day immigration authorities told Arguedas that there was pressure from several members of Parliament that demanded his freedom, and for that reason he was given new warranties. He was allowed to speak in Spanish with Foreign Office officials and with the Bolivian Ambassador in the United Kingdom, Roberto Querejazú Calvo.

On July 31 the Cuban Ambassador went to the Foreign Office where she would meet with Arguedas at five p.m. Several officials were waiting with the intention of being present at the meeting, but she kindly declined and indicated that she would see Arguedas in private. The meeting lasted about one hour and Ambassador Griñán repeated the Cuban government's offer of granting him political asylum. Before leaving, the Cuban Ambassador requested protection from British officials for former Bolivian Minister of the Interior, since they were in charge of his personal well being, so that he could go to lunch, together with Chilean lawyer Jaime Faivovich, at her residence on Wilton Crescent St. and return safely to the hotel. Ambassador Griñán wanted to avoid a CIA assassination attempt disguised as an accident during the trip to her residence and back. The request was granted. The lunch was held on August 1, 1968.

Faivovich's presence in London was because publishing houses Punto Final (Chile), Maspero (France), and Feltrinelli (Italy) had decided to pay for the lawyer's trip to Europe so that he could give all possible assistance to Arguedas. Faivovich was closely watched by US intelligence services: his room at the Hilton was raided and thoroughly searched. The searches were reported in the press and forced the Home Office Secretary David Ennales to declare in Parliament that British authorities and the hotel management knew nothing of the matter. To public opinion it was obvious that there were parties that could act above the law in London.

Meanwhile, on July 30, UPI reported from Bolivia that "Alleged activities of the US Central Intelligence Agency in this country have provoked the reaction of university students who are calling for an investigation about the doings of that agency here. In a public document that was published today in local papers, the Student Center of the San Andrés Greater University's Law School asked for the creation of a committee formed by journalists and students to investigate the CIA's activities in Bolivia, which they deem are 'an attempt against the country's sovereignty.'

"The demand of an investigation of CIA agents' activity in Bolivia is based on three cases in which they interfered in domestic issues. The first agent mentioned is (Julio) Gabriel García, a participant in antiguerrilla warfare and organizer of complete files on the private lives of the country's most important citizens and public figures. Another is Jorge González, identified as the man who headed the creation of a huge telephone network for the surveillance of the private lives of the country's citizens. Finally Miguel Nápoles is charged of being the head censor of all mail coming to Bolivia from abroad."

On August 2, 1968, Arguedas flew from London to New York for a five day stopover, and continuing travel on to Lima and later to La Paz. His case became so notorious that it was very difficult for the CIA to eliminate him in the United States.

The trip to New York caused a wave of rumors and raised important questions. State Department spokesman Carl Bartch declared that Arguedas had asked for a tourist visa, for he wanted to stay in the US for a "brief period" before continuing on to another destination.

Some news agencies pointed out that Arguedas traveled to New York after agreeing on several issues with the CIA in Bolivia –not to mention the names of CIA agents in Bolivia, some of who were top military officers, government ministers, officials, diplomats, journalists, and party and labor union leaders; keep silent about the CIA's actions in Chile and Peru; and delivery of a recorded tape in which officer Mario Terán explained the manner and circumstances in which Che was murdered.

Observers indicated that if there had not been an agreement, it would have been practically impossible for him to obtain a visa at the US Consulate in London, nor would he have been allowed in that country in transit or as a visitor, as informed by State Department's spokesperson Carl Bartch. Besides, it was said that he left London under an assumed name and accompanied by two CIA agents.

Sources that checked the passenger lists of all flights arriving from London to New York in early August, 1968, reported that his name was not in any of them.

Arguedas stayed for five days in the United States. On August 7 he left for Lima. He said to the press that CIA agents questioned him in a safe house that the agency had in Richmond Hill, London. *The Times*, one of Britain's most influential newspapers, published those serious accusations, which caused criticism in many sector of the country

Labor MP Stanley Newens declared to the press that it was unacceptable that someone on British territory had been submitted unfairly and unreasonably to an interrogatory by agents of a foreign power, and asked that Prime Minister Harold Wilson find out the truth about those versions that claimed that former Bolivian minister Arguedas had been interrogated by CIA agents during his London sojourn. The question was presented in Parliament.

In La Paz, US Ambassador Douglas Henderson informed the Bolivian Foreign Ministry on August 6 that he would leave the country on account of his wife's health. The next day he left for the United States.

Arguedas: New York Lima La Paz

Arguedas arrived in the Peruvian capital on August 7, 1968 and from there he sent the following cable to London:
EMBACUBA PHA 163
CUBANEX LDNV

HERE TELEX CALL TO ALBA GRIÑAN TLX 261094 CUBANEZ LONDON

BEING UNABLE UNITED STATES CENTRAL INTELLIGENCE AGENCY (CIA) TO ELIMINATE ME, IT HAS DECREED MY CHARACTER ASSASSINATION BY SPREADING INTRIGUES AND SLANDERS IN ORDER TO SUPPLANT MY REVOLUTIONARY POSITION.

CHILEAN GOVERNMENT HAS GRANTED ASYLUM WITH THE CONDITION OF LEAVING CHILE ON FIRST AVAILABLE PLANE. I WAS INSISTENTLY PRESSURED TO GO TO CUBA THROUGH ANY EUROPEAN COUNTRY. I WAS ONLY FREE FOR TEN MINUTES IN SANTIAGO.

CHILEAN POLICE AGENT OSCAR PIZARRO BARRIOS AND US CIA AGENT NICOLÁS LEONDIRIS ESCORTED ME FROM SANTIAGO TO LONDON. BOTH AGENTS TOOK ME TO APOLLO HOTEL AND REGISTERED ME WITH MY MOTHER'S LAST NAME (MENDIETA), THEN TOOK ME TO RICHMOND HILL WHERE I WAS REGISTERED AS PÉREZ. CHILEAN IDENTITY DOCUMENTS WERE SEIZED FROM ME BY AGENT LEONDIRIS.

UNDER THREAT OF DEATH TO MY FAMILY AND OF A COUP IN BOLIVIA CIA PERMITTED ME TO TALK WITH BRITISH OFFICIALS AND CUBAN AMBASADOR, TO WHOM I DECLARED BY POSITION AS A NATIONAL LEFTIST MARXIST AND MY DESIRE OF RETURNING IMMEDIATELY TO MY COUNTRY.

SINCE I WAS PHOTOGRAPHED IN IQUIQUE (CHILE), I DECLARED THAT MY LIFE WAS THREATENED BY THE US INTELLIGENCE SERVICE, WHOSE ACTIVITIES IN LATIN AMERICA AND IN BOLIVIA I WOULD DENOUNCE IN A PRESS CONFERENCE, WHICH WAS THE REASON I REQUESTED ASYLUM.

CHILEAN POLICE KEPT ME IINCOMMUNICADO AND SUBJECT TO INTENSE QUESTIONING, WHICH I REFUSED TO ANSWER FOR EIGHT DAYS. ONLY WHEN I AGREED NOT TO REVEAL CIA ACTIVITIES AND THE CORRESPONDING GUARANTEES WERE ESTABLISHED, I WAS GRANTED THE PRESS CONFERENCE.

I NEVER HAD PERSONAL RELATIONS WITH CUBAN CIA AGENT GABRIEL GARCÍA, WHOSE CRIMES I WILL MAKE PUBLIC.

I HAVE AN ENTRY VISA FOR BOLIVIA AND WILL ARRVE IN LA PAZ ON SATURDAY, AUGUST 17 ON A BRANIFF FLIGHT.

I APPEAL TO THE PATRIOTISM OF ALL BOLIVIANS SO THAT MY RETUNS DOES NOT JUSTIFY A COUP OR SUBVERSIVE AGITATION. I DO NOT PRETEND TO JUSTIFY GOVERNMENT'S ERRORS.

I ASSUME RESPONSIBILITY. I WILL ONLY TELL THE TRUTH AND HOPE FOR JUSTICE.

ANTONIO ARGUEDAS

CALL ENDED.

At the Peruvian capital he denounced activities against his country by the CIA and the US Embassy. Arguedas explained that a triumphant revolution in Bolivia should not end in the taking over of the Quemado Palace, but with the expulsion of the US Ambassador, and that when violent struggle was victorious, the Americans' seat should be destroyed and Americans swept off the streets where they walk as conquerors. He said that he was returning to Bolivia to unmask the CIA, which operates in the whole world, and particularly is destroying the national independence of several Latin American countries.

Outrage in the Bolivian Armed Forces with Barrientos for having authorized the return of Arguedas was obvious. For that reason they decided to call off the traditional parade on August 7, 1968, held every year in commemoration of Bolivia's independence. Barrientos learned of the suspension of the parade through the radio.

A week later, and without previously consulting Ovando, Barrientos removed from their posts Chief of General Staff Juan José Torres and Army Chief of Staff Marcos Vásquez Sempértegui. The decision caused new contradictions, for it was obvious that Barrientos had taken a serious step and begun to oust officers loyal to Ovando. Additionally, Juan José Torres was rapidly adopting more radical nationalist positions and had a very critical attitude regarding the policy of submission of Barrientos toward the CIA, the United States and its embassy in La Paz. Torres had said to close friends that it was necessary to immediately stop the arrogance and interference of the Americans in Bolivia's internal affairs. pOther officers who shared those positions were also substituted, such as Colonel Manuel Cárdenas Mallo, Chief of Operations.

Bolivian sources explained that Barrientos authorized Arguedas' return to Bolivia and at all times maintained a benevolent attitude towards him because the former Interior Minister knew many dark aspects of Barrientos' political and private life that if revealed would mean the end of his government. For example:

—He knew that since 1960 Barrientos was a CIA agent, recruited by US Colonel Edward Fox after a proposal by also CIA agent Julio Sanjinés Goytía, whom Barrientos had appointed as ambassador in Washington.

—Every week Barrientos met secretly in La Paz with the CIA Chief of Station who paid the president for his services through a bank account in the United States.

—CIA officer Nicolás Leondiris gave Barrientos an important sum of money in an apartment that the agency had right across the dental office of Dr. Oscar Serrano to finance his presidential campaign and destabilize Victor Paz Extensor's government.

—Barrientos bribed certain military officers, politicians, officials, journalists and labor leaders by giving them money, bestowing personal favors or appointing relatives or friends to government posts and in the Diplomatic Corps.

For those powerful reasons, Arguedas was able to return to La Paz on August 17, 1968. And in a press conference, he denounced the penetration of his country by the CIA and the US Embassy.

Arguedas declared that when he was investigating the presence of a guerrilla group, it was discovered that in a house near the Mexican Embassy an alleged press information service was operating telegraphic equipment and means for tapping telephone conversations. When he was preparing a press conference to announce that the intelligence network of the guerrilla had fallen in the hands of the state security forces, to his surprise CIA officer Hugo Murray told him that the equipment was his. Arguedas pointed out that the CIA, in spite of its great influence in the Ministry of the Interior, had organized its own network.

He also denounced that the CIA was preparing a kardex where a great number of Bolivians would appear, that it was trying to take control of the State's intelligence service, distort information, infiltrate its agents in some political parties and collaborate with people in whose military or political careers they were interested.

Arguedas explained that the CIA recruited two kinds of agents in political parties: the first, those charged with revealing to them all party plans and the list of members, and second, those who would adapt the party line to the agency's interests. He claimed that on many opportunities political agents achieved success and even became leaders of those infiltrated parties.

In relation to the CIA's infiltration in Bolivian media, he said that there were two types: direct agents, such as Hugo Alfonso Salmón, and those in charge of spreading certain news through national channels. On other occasions there would be witnesses or article writers trained abroad who were in charge of intriguing in the country itself.

All this work was made by a group of writers of the Agency. He recounted the manner in which the operation against Tania had been planned, for he found out the way in which the article against her had been planted, delivered by the chief of the CIA. Later it was published in *El Diario,* saying that it had been sent from the Federal Republic of Germany.

Revelations by Arguedas were the cause of combative demonstrations that accused the government of complicity with the US Embassy and the CIA. Demonstrators demanded the expulsion of the US ambassador as well as of CIA officers and agents.

On August 17 at Santa Cruz there were several dynamite attacks. The first one was against the Cruz del Sur bookshop, owned by the city mayor, Lieutenant Colonel Félix Moreno, when a bomb destroyed the shop windows and a large number of books. The home of prosecutor Mariano Saucedo was shot and the Center of Petrochemical Studies was bombed. Unknown persons shot the chief of the Department of Criminal Investigations (DIC) Guillermo Millet, and the exclusive club Círculo de Amigos was also shot.

The following day the commander of the 8th Division, General Remberto Iriarte, declared that the Armed Forces had taken control of the city and gave orders to shoot the perpetrators on sight. On that same day DIC agents arrested Jorge Chávez, Executive

Secretary of the High School Confederation of Bolivia. and held him incommunicado, a fact that caused angry protests and demonstrations.

At Potosí the local DIC headquarters was bombed. Agents from that agency raided the university campus and students called for a march of protest that filled the city's main avenues.

Several students were arrested in the universities of Oruro and Cochabamba. The rest reacted calling for a strike in defense of their colleagues. They were repressed by the police.

Posters were put at San Andrés Greater University in La Paz that accused the CIA and the US Embassy of interference in Bolivia's internal affairs. Students Adolfo Quiroga and Horacio Rueda, together with some of their colleagues, signaled Barrientos as the one responsible for allowing US blatant interference. Several demonstrations were organized where slogans were chanted against the United States, the CIA and the US ambassador, such as "Death to Henderson!", and "Down with US imperialism!"

Police raided the university and arrested several professors and students, among others Jaime Rubín de Celis, a leader of the University Federation of La Paz. In reprisal, the students held DIC agents Hugo Aranda Farfán, Alejandro Ochoa and Augusto Roque Lara. They demanded the liberation of their arrested comrades in exchange for the agents in their power.

On August 18, the newspaper *Presencia* reported that at 22:00 hours there was in suburban areas of La Paz a student demonstration that demanded the liberation of their arrested comrades in Cochabamba, Oruro and La Paz. Additionally they criticized the government for their raids on the universities and condemned the Armed Forces as the ones responsible. The paper reported that among the slogans one of them was "Glory to Che Guevara!"

The police blocked every access and broke up the demonstration with tear gas. Repression was intensified at all universities, but students kept retaliating.

On the walls of universities and of the surrounding streets graffiti against the United States, Henderson and Barrientos began to appear. There was a call to set up a tribunal to try them and sentence them to death.

The press reported that on August 22, 1968, several CIA officers left Bolivia in a special plane. Even CIA Station Chief Thomas

Hazlett left the country. Some left, but others had been sent, because on August 2 of that year John Ronan Higgins had arrived in Bolivia as the new Station Chief. Other officers had arrived on previous dates –Richard Olson on January 4, Arthur Porn on the 5th and William Boner on June 4.

The delivery of Che's diary to Cuba and its subsequent consequences was a hard blow for the US intelligence services and the US Embassy in Bolivia.

The United States repudiated. American Ambassador in Bolivia substituted

Criticism against the interfering role of Douglas Henderson was widespread. The US Embassy in La Paz and its officials received constant death threats and anonymous calls. In the city's walls people wrote insults against the ambassador and urged his elimination. Even the ambassador's wife received death threats. The US ambassador was well known in the country for calling Bolivians the worst names –corrupt, people of the worst kind, lazy, thieves, slackers, indolent, liars, and not to be trusted.

He complained that the State Department had sent him to a "filthy and dirty place" that ruined his diplomatic career. He repeated over and over that he did not want to return ever to this country of coca eating Indians.

In Bolivia there was much talk that at a reception just before he left Henderson refused to shake hands with Barrientos and mumbled in English the word "pig". Barrientos, who learned the language during his stay at a US military base, answered him, which caused a row between the two. When the Bolivian president walked away, Henderson kept insulting him: never in his life had he met a dumber and more vulgar fellow; that because the poverty and the little economic and cultural development of Bolivia, any ignorant person could be president, but Barrientos was the bottom of the barrel.

Protests against the US ambassador came from all sectors of the country. Death threats increased. Henderson commented that Barrientos was behind it, but Mrs. Henderson claimed that it came from some of the embassy's officials, because she knew how they envied and hated him.

Anti-US feelings in Latin America grew at the period. In Puerto Rico there were demonstrations against the visit of US President Lyndon B. Johnson and a bomb exploded at National Guard headquarters. In El Salvador eggs and paint cans were thrown against the US president's automobile. Similar scenes happened in other Central American capitals. In Cali, Colombia, 3,000 university students burned a US flag and protested against the presence of the US Peace Corps. In Ecuador there were great protest marches in the cities of Machala and Santa Rosa, with much shouting against the United States. Police repression caused five deaths. In Brazil, Venezuela, Peru, Argentina and Uruguay there were also demonstrations that ended with dozens of dead and wounded.

In Guatemala, Colonel John Webber, head of the US military mission; US Navy Commander Ernest Monroe; NCO Harry Green; and Ambassador John Gordon Mein were shot to death. In Sao Paulo, Brazil, Charles E. Chandier, a military officer, was machine-gunned down.

The US government, concerned over so many protests and aggressions against its representatives, plus the threats against its officials in Bolivia, decided to replace Ambassador Henderson. The State Department appointed a man that could erase Henderson's arrogance and contempt toward Bolivians. The responsibility was given to Raúl H. Castro, born in Mexico and with a law degree from the University of Arizona in 1949. US authorities believed that because of his Latino origin he would make Bolivians forget their many grievances.

Castro had begun his career in 1941 in the State Department as an assistant at the US Consulate in Aguas Prietas, Mexico. In October, 1964 he was appointed ambassador to El Salvador, a post he held until August, 1968, when he was reassigned to Bolivia.

At La Paz there were rumors that the State Department had appointed Raúl H. Castro to Bolivia with the hope that in street demonstrations slogans would not chanted against the ambassador, or that in university and street walls offensive graffiti with his name would not written, because the State Department and the CIA were convinced that the Bolivians respected and loved both those name and surname.

Among Ambassador Castro's activities in the Bolivian capital to erase his predecessor's bad image was his attendance in 1969 to the Entrance of the Great Power, an important festivity held every year in one of the most popular La Paz neighborhoods, accompanied by a kind of carnival where important folk groups performed.

Henderson's substitute was very active socially: he showed special interest in Bolivian painters, bought their works with autochthonous subjects, and flattered them. He also showed interests in literature and writers and met with some of them. Castro congratulated poets and artists, promised trips and scholarships, talked about Bolivian culture with admiration and respect. But most of his interlocutors did not trust him.

One evening the ambassador went to Peña Naira, a well known center of folk music and dances. All had been set up so that his journalist friends reported the extraordinary fact of the attendance of the American ambassador to the famous folk club. Several songs were dedicated to him and he applauded enthusiastically, until one of the performers, who some assure it was Benjo Cruz, considered the most popular and talented folk singer/songwriter of the moment, apologized on behalf of all the artists for their mistake, because they had thought that the Raúl Castro present was the one from Cuba, and that all the songs had been dedicated to that Raúl and to none other. His words were greeted with an ovation. The US ambassador and his entourage stomped angrily out of the club.

New scandal in La Paz alter Arguedas' revelations

On September 3 independent members of parliament: Marcelo Quiroga Santa Cruz and José Ortiz Mercado requested from Congress that clarifications be made about the CIA's interference in Bolivia. Members of the government coalition, following orders from the president, prevented Congress from convening and initiating a process of impeachment against Barrientos.

Three days later Congress ratified the state of siege after a violent session that ended in the small hours of the morning. As a protest, congressmen of the opposition abandoned the building.

On September 1, Chilean journalist Diego Santos Almeida from the magazine *Punto Final* reported from La Paz that Antonio Arguedas confirmed his serious accusations against the CIA that compromised not only Bolivia, but also Chile, Peru and other Latin American countries, for that secret US agency acted in connivance with the respective governments or with national officials.

Demonstrations in La Paz were held one after the other by different sectors of the country and at the same time demanded clarification on all issues denounced by Arguedas. On September 21 Barrientos declared without turning a hair that the CIA had not been active in Bolivia, and that he had no knowledge of such an organization.

The leader of the Christian Democratic Party Remo di Natale asked the government and the Armed Forces to explain CIA activities in Bolivia. The answer was to arrest him and throw him into prison.

Workers, peasants, intellectuals and students demanded energetically that all Arguedas' accusations be elucidated. Barrientos had no choice but accepting that the House of Representatives name a commission to investigate all accusations by the former Interior Minister.

The commission began its hearings on October 7, 1968. Several persons linked to the events were summoned: Lieutenant Colonel Hugo Rocha Patiño, chief of Section B, Army Department of Intelligence; Major Rubén Peña Lino, Intelligence service; Lieutenant Colonel Hugo Echavarría Tardío, chief of Intelligence, 4th Division; Colonel Federico Arana Cerrudo, Chief of Military Intelligence; Lieutenant Colonel Andrés Sélich Shop, Chief of Staff of Tactical Group No. 3; José Matías Valencia, Arguedas' driver; Lieutenant Colonel Roberto "Toto" Quintanilla, deputy chief, Ministry of the Interior's Department of Intelligence; Ricardo Aneiva Torrico, chief of Technical Department, Ministry of the Interior, and his assistant Jaime Moreno Quintana; and Julio Durán Arce and Fernando Manzaneda Mallea, photographers.

On October 8 students from the University of La Paz paid homage to the Heroic Guerrilla. Fiery speeches were made and revolutionary slogans were chanted. A particularly emotional speech was made by Father Mauricio Lefebre. Large posters with Che's image were placed on the University's walls, and a great student march was prepared. Meanwhile, the army and the police blocked the Prado Promenade and were ready with tear gas, attack dogs and fire trucks. But the students, unlike other times, apparently

191

decided to disperse and not face the repressive forces. They went by Landaeta Street to Buenos Aires Avenue, an important throughway that separates the Tembladerani, Tacagua and Chujini workers' neighborhoods. At important points of the route they organized rallies, so the march began to grow with workers, students from other educational centers and neighbors. Speakers were student leaders Jorge Ríos Dalence, Ramiro Barrenechea, Raúl Ibarguen, Juan José Saavedra and Eusebio Gironda. They made clear references to Che and mentioned the revolutionary struggle. Some of those present raised ELN flags and displayed photos of the Heroic Guerrilla; others came with torches.

Such was the revolutionary fervor that the crowd began chanting "Glory to Che." At 3 am the city was still occupied by the military placed at strategic points, although on this occasion they did not dare to act because of the magnitude of the demonstration. Barrientos answer was to close down the academic year.

At Bolivia's mines, the anniversary of Che's assassination was also commemorated. Before beginning their working day miners kept a minute of silence. From that moment on, a new tradition was born in Bolivia that years later found its way to Parliament. In some poor La Paz neighborhoods the first spiritualist centers sprang up, for Bolivian believers thought that the soul of the Heroic Guerrilla can work miracles. People with asthma and respiratory diseases flock to those places in search of cure. They make vows, light candles, pray to him and ask him fervently for help to leave behind their misfortune.

Photos of Che with flowers and lit candles began to appear in the humble pahuichis of the Guaraní, in adobe or mud houses of the Quechuas and Aymaras, in miners' homes, in huts of La Paz' high hills, even in residences of luxurious neighborhoods. At the hamlet where he was murdered he is known now as Saint Ernest of La Higuera.

Bolivian peasants ask the Heroic Guerrilla to give them rain, the cure of a sick cow or a dying son, a good crop, protection against all evils.

At the Alasitas Fair, every January 24 the image of Che appears, even carved in seeds. That day Aymara Indians take to the fair miniatures of everything they want to have in abundance. They hope that their god Ekeko will bless their miniatures and then a time of plenty will arrive.

Why Bolivian peasants place stones

At places where guerrillas died or were murdered peasants placed stones. When they pass by, they kneel and pray for assistance, once in a while candles and flowers appear.

Many peasants believe that life came from the stones. An ancient Bolivian legend claims that from the depths of Lake Titicaca was born Viracocha, the eighth Inca, who on seeing that the world was dark created the moon, the sun, the stars and gave light to the world. Then he went to Cuzco, capital of the Incas. But 18 leagues away, in a place called Cacha, men who did not know who Viracocha and his brave warriors were, or the good he had done to the world and what he wanted to do for them, tried to murder them. Viracocha and his warriors turned to stone again in order to await the moment of continuing the struggle.

The legend says that men are born and die, plants dry up, snow melts, water transforms, the wind comes, passes by and leaves, but stones are eternal, not even fire can destroy them.

Bolivian writer Guillermo Francovich, who has been a professor and rector of the University of Sucre, has held important diplomatic posts, was director of UNESCO Regional Center and is a member of the Bolivian Academy of the Language, wrote in his book *Bolivia's Profound Myths*: "The oldest myth is of Indian origin. The primitive and still little known dwellers of Kollasuyo created the primordial myth of our culture. The strength, the immensity, the grandeur of the mountain ranges in which they lived led them to the sacralization of stones and mountains. To them they were animated. In them they found their own origin and the people's fate was linked to them (...)"

Francovich quotes researcher Paredes, who in 1920 wrote in his work *Myths, Superstitions and Survivals in Bolivia*: "(...) the cult of mountains, of caves, of rivers, and above all of stones is still vital. 'The cult of stones is general among Indians (...) They believe they are the base of their world and the efficient principle of life's phenomena.' Indians particularly venerate isolated stones, because when there is a war they become warriors and after fighting go back to its rocky condition (...)

"Paredes writes: 'Indians feel predilection for crags or certain rocks that have the figure of people or animals'."

Fernando Diez de Medina, a controversial Bolivian politician and diplomat and an important writer, novelist, poet and researcher, a lover of myths and legends of his country, says in his book *Nayjama* that man comes from the stone, the stone is man. And stone and being transmute so much that they become one. Souls of granite. Granites of soul. And if man has the hardness and the daring of basalt and quartz, the rock stands and is moved with fury, with pain, with the passion of man.

And Francovich points out: "The stone myth not only configured the religiosity of the Kollas and manifestations of their art. It gave sense to their lives and was present in their social and political organization. We have seen, as Bachelard says, that men find a challenge in the stone. The stone, with its hardness, its resistance to manipulation, provokes the will of men and breeds attitudes and feelings in them that are shaped into their behavior and even in their institutions.

"Kollas are conscious of the permanence, stability, solidity of things that surround them. Rocks and mountains are silhouetted in their firm and precise girth, remain impassive to elements like wind or water that roll over them (...)"

One understands then why there are stones at the place where Commander Ernesto Che Guevara and his comrades were murdered. From Ñacahuasú to La Higuera, the guerrilla presence survives in the stones, and Che lives on.

Contradictions between Barrientos and Ovando

Expectations around Arguedas' trial were a real disaster for the US Embassy, the CIA Station in La Paz and Barrientos. They decided that a military court should try Arguedas with the deliberate purpose of silencing his testimony, censor witnesses, compromise the Armed Forces, minimize its political importance and belittle its results Several congressmen protested the arbitrary decision claiming that Arguedas as Minister of the Interior was a public servant, and as such had to be tried, and that there were no legal reasons to try the case in a military court. Nevertheless, maneuvers and pressures on the part of the Americans, plus Barrientos interests, prevailed. On September 17 at 13:45 hours the trial began under the strictest security measures. The court decided to hear the case *in camera*. During the proceedings, the press revealed the existence of a secret US base in an area near the La Paz international airport. Neighbors called the base "Guantanamito" (Little Guantánamo), alluding the naval base that the US illegally occupies in Cuba. The base had an area of 14 hectares and was some 15 kilometers from the Bolivian capital. It was also used for radioelectronic communications between La Paz, the Panama Canal and Washington. The US Embassy could not deny the information and new elements of US interference in Bolivia were unmasked.

The trial continued in the midst of protests by congressmen and Arguedas himself, who refused to testify claiming that it was a farce orchestrated by the CIA and the US embassy.

Through Bolivian sources it was known that the editor of the daily *Jornada* Jorge Suárez, in a private conversation with Ovando, had told him that if the trail continued Arguedas was going to reveal many secrets he knew about Ovando and other top military officers, that his silence up to the moment could not be interpreted as permanent. On November 6 the Military Court ruled it had no jurisdiction on the matter. After consultation with the Supreme Court, the case was placed at the disposal of ordinary justice, Arguedas was released on parole.

The scandal even reached the British Parliament, where MP Stan Newens denounced CIA's acts against Arguedas in London.

Stan Newens' Speech in Parliament

Former Cuban Ambassador in the UK Alba Griñán Núñez carefully translated the minutes of the session of the British Parliament with the discussions on Arguedas' accusations and the CIA's participation in London.

Stan Newtens' words are taken from these minutes.

"November 19, 1968

"Mr. Stan Newens: The question I wish to pose is not a trivial

195

matter of purely local importance, but one that has important implications of both national and international character. It has to do with the visit to this country from July 27 to August 2 of Mr. Antonio Arguedas, who up to a month before had been Minister of the Interior in General Barrientos' administration.

"Mr. Arguedas was dismissed from office when it transpired that he had sent to President Castro of Cuba photostatic copies of the campaign diary kept by Commander Ernesto Guevara, the socialist revolutionary and leader of the guerrilla, who apparently was murdered in cold blood in a remote place in Bolivia after his capture on October 7, 1967. When Mr. Arguedas' action transpired, a government crisis broke out in Bolivia and he fled to Chile, where he was granted temporary asylum.

"Apparently negotiations were held with Argentina and other Latin American countries considered as havens, but they all failed.

"Finally it was determined that Mr. Arguedas would go to New York by way of London and he traveled in a B.U.A flight that arrived at Gatwick Airport on the afternoon of Saturday, July 27.

"In the flight Mr. Arguedas was accompanied with two escorts, a Chilean by the name of Mr. Pizarro Barrios and an employee of the United States Central Intelligence Agency, Mr. Nicolás Leondiris.

"When the plane landed in Madrid, it seems that Mr. Arguedas managed to contact the Cuban chargé d'affaires, who informed him of the offering of asylum made by Fidel Castro. However, Mr. Arguedas was anxious to go to New York, but agreed to discuss certain matters with the Cubans in London.

"Nevertheless, the Cuban representative was unable to get a seat on the plane and arranged by telephone that a representative of the Cuban embassy in London would go to Gatwick with the purpose of meeting Mr. Arguedas on his arrival. He did just that, but when Mr. Arguedas arrived he was taken to an office while the question of his admittance to Britain was discussed.

"Although the Cuban representative made his best efforts to see him he was unable to do it. Nobody has satisfactorily explained why the change of idea about this meeting between Madrid and London, and the deduction is obvious. My understanding is that at the airport all negotiations in his name were made, in fact, by his escorts and he was not directly interviewed at all by British officials. He would have preferred to continue voyage to New York without this stay.

"Alter leaving the airport, Mr. Arguedas went to the Apollo Hotel, where he was registered by his escort under his mother's name, Mendieta.

"I personally took an interest on the matter on July 29, in my capacity as President of the Movement for Colonial Freedom, which follows events in the majority of the developing countries. I made inquiries at the Home Office and was informed that Mr. Arguedas address could not reasonably be given to me, but the Home Office agreed to forward him a letter, which I wrote and gave him information that would allow him to contact me. On the following day, Mr. Faivovich, who was Mr. Arguedas' attorney, arrived in Gatwick, and again inquiries were made at the Home Office with a similar answer. Mr. Faivovich was advised to contact the Department of Immigration at the Home Office on the following morning.

"On Wednesday, July 31, once again I contacted the Home Office and inquired if a meeting could be arranged in the presence of Home Office officials, without revealing Mr. Arguedas' hotel. I was told that it would be consulted with the predecessor of my distinguished friend, the Undersecretary of State, who would be out all day. However, on August 1 I was informed that Mr. Arguedas had met the previous day with the ambassadors of Bolivia and Cuba. On August 3 I received a letter from my distinguished friend accompanying my letter to Mr. Arguedas, in which he had written that his life was not in danger, but denouncing United States imperialism.

"I was naturally concerned with the difficulties presented in my way and I wished to assure myself that Mr. Arguedas was not acting under duress. I was not entirely surprised when in an interview after his return to La Paz, Mr. Arguedas made declarations indicating that he had been prevented from communicating freely with other people, that he had been under threat and moral pressure, and that he had been asked for guarantees before communicating with Home Office officials and with the ambassadors of Bolivia and Cuba in London.

"Later on it was made clear that Mr. Arguedas was taken from Apollo Hotel to a facility on Richmond Hill, which I later managed to identify as the Richmond Hotel. There he was registered under the assumed name of Antonio Pérez, the passport number that was offered in a question made by the distinguished member from Richmond Surrey (Mr. A. Royle). Apparently two gentlemen that escorted him were registered as Petrelli Suárez and Mr. Stead.

"I wish to ask my distinguished friend, was the Home Office informed of all these facts then, and what investigations have been made about these registers under assumed name and about the passport numbers that were used? Will my distinguished friend explain the reasons why that action was admitted? Having considered those facts, would anyone in his sane mind deny that the information that has been presented to the House justified a complete and appropriate investigation in order to determine what truly happened, particularly in view of the disseminated knowledge of CIA implication, which has been added by the information given by Mr. Arguedas since the events to which I have referred? I recognize that the declarations he made could all have contained falsehoods. Yet, I have checked them in a number of points and my investigations have totally proved the truth in the allegation on those points. For example, on the question of the Richmond Hill Hotel, Mr. Arguedas did not give that name, but investigations found that what he said agrees with the facts.

If we were treating with an organization such as the Girl Guides and not the CIA, it very well could be argued that the idea of questioning people under moral pressure was absurd, but the CIA has never been famous for its high standards of veracity. For years denials after denials have been published about the use of money by the CIA to subsidize or infiltrate groups of students, workers and culture, but in 1967 the whole story broke loose, and Mr. Thomas Braden, a California newspaper editor, in fact is demanding credit for it. At another time reports were denied that the general strike that took place in Guyana in 1963 against Dr. Cheddi Jagan was financed by the CIA, but later they were proven true and it was also shown that the money had been channeled through Public Services International , which has its offices in London.

"Considering the obvious CIA's displeasure at being identified in the practice of its operations in Britain, there is cause here for great concern. Every person that is familiar with developing countries knows that CIA interference is enormous. Fortunately, the organization is not always successful, but there is always the truth that many of the coups and coup attempts that have taken place in the developing countries during the last 10 or 15 years have involved the CIA.

"Mr. Speaker: Order. The distinguished gentleman, sir, must return to ministerial responsibility.

"Mr. Newens: Yes, Mr. Speaker. I was just trying hard to show that it would not be strange to find out that the CIA was interested in a gentleman that has held a high post in a developing country. It is clear that the interference of the CIA in Bolivia when this gentleman came was considerable.

"No British government would allow foreign agents, be they Russian, Americans or any other, to perform their services in British soil. In the case of Mr. Arguedas there is overwhelming evidence that this happened. If the Home Office did not know what was happening then, when the former Interior Minister of Bolivia was in the country, and considered that my doubts had been satisfactorily treated through the taken action, it is clear that a serious revision is required of the manner in which cases of this kind are handled. If Mr. Arguedas was treated in this manner, if the facts that I have presented this evening before the House are correct, there may be other persons that perhaps never will be noted by Parliament that could be submitted to similar or worse treatment. There have been many cases of this kind that are on record as having happened in other countries.

"We in the House have the right to be satisfied on these matters. It is difficult to imagine that USSR agents, for example, in an equivalent position to that of the CIA agents, would bring their victims to this country. But if they did, which is extremely doubtful, one expects that they be allowed to conduct themselves in the manner that Mr. Arguedas' escorts did. In circumstances such as those, we in Britain should insist on the same treatment for the agents of a foreign power that endeavor to operate on British soil.

"From my point of view, the facts that I have presented today to the House are sufficiently important to justify a complete investigation of all the questions raised.

"Distinguished members, I have the right to be assured that the British government will not permit that agents of any foreign power operate on British soil. Without that assurance, a serious concern would be felt in many sectors of our population.

"I do not apologize for bringing this case to the House and I await (…) for what my distinguished friend has to say.

"10:15 p.m."

Contradictions at top government level and the Bolivian Armed Forces. Permanent interference of the United States

A toast for Che Guevara

Dr. Alfonso Camacho Peña, former Minister of Education and Culture of Bolivia, recalled that the arrival of the New Year 1969 was feted at several military regiments. At Roboré, the seat of the 5th Regiment, it had a special connotation because in the midst of toasts and greetings to the New Year, Colonel Antonio Prado Prado raised his glass and said for all to hear:

"I toast a man loyal and consistent with his ideals. I toast a man that although is on the opposite side, died as a man for defending his ideas. I toast Commander Ernesto Che Guevara, whom we have fought, but who deserves our admiration and respect.

"To him, comrades!"

Some of the present raised their glasses timidly; others remained silent, confused. There were murmurs. The Roboré regiment's commander put his hands to his head, for Colonel Prado was a much respected officer. He was considered an honest, highly moral man, a very cultivated person. Before joining the army he had done six years of medical school and was considered a great reader, with an ample knowledge of world history.

The former minister pointed out that Colonel Prado was considered a highly intelligent officer with a privileged memory. In many circles he was considered an intellectual.

For his honest words he was arrested and a few days later brought before an honor military court.

Those who had to judge him told him to take back his words and declare that he had done it under the effect of alcohol, that he had been completely drunk on New Year's Eve,

When the officer corps was gathered, Colonel Prado declared that he would take the opportunity to accuse the Honor Court of pressuring him to lie. He told of the proposition that had been made to him and subsequently said that when he had toasted Commander Ernesto Che Guevara he was not drunk, nor was he drunk at the present moment. He spoke of universal history to show how troops had acknowledged the courage and valor of their enemies, and mentioned several examples. He said that those officers and soldiers were brave enough and had the courage and the valor of admiring and respecting their enemies, and that was the case of Commander Ernesto Che Guevara, who deserved respect and admiration.

The court adjourned, claiming that Colonel Antonio Prado Prado was insane. For that reason they suggested that he be discharged from the Bolivian Armed Forces, which was made effective. However, several officers backed him. Fifty days later, after a hard fought trial, he was reinstated.

Colonel Prado's attitude began a trend in the Bolivian Armed Forces that has increased through the years. In 1987, on the occasion of the 20th anniversary of Che's fall, several commemorations were organized in the country. The events were harshly criticized by a reactionary congressman. A retired Navy officer, Lieutenant Commander Jaime Paredes Sempértegui, identity card 2015115 L. P., after considering Che a hero, asked the Congressman:

"1. Did you know that in the Chaco campaign, after the siege of Boquerón our "Paraguayan enemies" received General Marzana and the few men who resisted the siege as heroes? Some of them are still alive. Ask them if we, in their own country, treated them in the same manner.

"2. Do you know who delivered to us the urn with the ashes of Col. Eduardo Abaroa that at present rest in the Church of St.

Francis? None other than our "Chilean enemies", with the following bronze inscription:

"Homage of the Army of Chile to the Hero of Calama, Eduardo Abaroa."

"Honorable Congressman: For these historic deeds and acts, both enemy and friendly forces pay tribute and respect to heroes when they are considered as such.

"Finally you must know that war is not only a prerogative of the military. All through history war has always affected civilian life, and in modern times the supreme direction of the war has become the responsibility of politicians, who are civilians and not part of the military. On the other hand, in total war, civilian industries and energies are absorbed by the war effort.

"For these reasons, military history is inseparable of the general historic context, and it is convenient that all, both civilians as well as members of the Armed Forces, study the history of war.

"Based on these simple considerations, I personally believe that Che deserves respect as the 'Commander of the Americas' [...]"

New revelations in La Paz

In the first days of 1969 raids and repression were intensified. Unease against Barrientos' government extended to large sectors of the country, including the Armed Forces and Congress. In February Senator Raúl Lema Peláez, National Prize of Literature winner Augusto Céspedes, and journalist José María Centellas were arrested. These events increased the protests against the Bolivian president. In early April, 1969, the newspaper *Presencia* reported declarations of military officers that testified against Antonio Arguedas, in which they admitted the predominant role of the CIA and the US Embassy in the struggle against Che's guerrilla movement. Joaquín Zenteno Anaya's revelations made a particular impact, because in his testimony he pointed out that Barrientos personally authorized the participation of CIA agents and ordered that they were given access to all information.

Among other things, Zenteno Anaya said: "Ramos and Captain Eduardo González, both Cuban born, had access to our investigation results [...] according to a personal recommendation sent to my command by H.E. the President of the Republic [...]"

When he was asked by the court he was more categorical: "On August 8 I received a request for a meeting from Mr. William Culleghan, the coordinator of the US Intelligence Service, who put Captains Félix Ramos and Eduardo González under my command, provided with documents of recommendation from the Constitutional President [...]" He added that Dr. González and Julio Gabriel García presumably belonged to the CIA.

When these declarations reached public opinion a new political storm brewed: the interfering role of the CIA was too obvious. On this occasion it was not Arguedas the accusing party, but the military themselves who admitted the fact. Initially Barrientos and Ovando tried to deny everything that journalists were revealing, but the evidence submitted were too obvious, so then they began to blame each other for the responsibility of the authorization.

Ovando declared to the press that he completely ignored the presence of those agents among the US military advisors. With these declarations he hinted that someone above him had authorized it; that someone could be no other than Barrientos.

Immediately the President answered that he did not know the existence of such secret agents, whom he supposed were military officers who had come to Bolivia to train units in counterinsurgency. When they introduced the CIA agents to him they had said they were US Army officers, so he had been deceived. Barrientos tried to put the blame on someone else and in that manner free himself of the responsibility. Yet his arguments were so vague that could be interpreted in two ways: he was either duped by the Americans or by the Armed Forces of his own country.

In the middle of the dispute, Ovando introduced a new element when he said that neither he nor the Bolivian Armed Forces had authorized the CIA agents.

With those words he not only was shedding personal accountability, but also responsibility of the institution he commanded. The guilty party would have to be found among the Americans or in Barrientos himself.

The accusations that the CIA agents had had a free hand against the guerrilla in Bolivia and even above the Bolivian military had no further need of clarification. It had been proven. What should be cleared up was who had authorized it and given them access to secret documents.

As the discussion between both generals had become public, a new element was added when Barrientos' private secretary Daniel Salamanca summoned a press conference. He had in his power several documents –which he showed—that CIA agent Julio Gabriel García had sent to the Presidential Palace for the President, as well as that agent's intention of trying to suppress some opposition media. Salamanca claimed that García had asked for a meeting with Barrientos to propose a plan of action to halt the opposition's antigovernment campaign. Comments, reactions and astonishment in view of Salamanca's revelations seemed to have no limit, but Barrientos' private secretary showed them an organization chart made by the CIA and presented by García for the setting up of a radio station, a newspaper plus the organization of a cadre of officials that would infiltrate public institutions and universities. This cost him that Barrientos dismissed him from the Palace and from his position.

The US Embassy and the CIA Station did their utmost to silence the new scandal, but information was leaked one way or the other. These circumstances affected the Americans, who barely could reconcile interests and contradictions among the military.

Salamanca's actions were considered very strange. Some say that he tried to help Barrientos, but made such a mess of things that forced him into serious contradictions. Others claim that he was part of a conspiracy and his declarations were timed to deal Barrientos a demolishing blow, "for he was neither naïve nor a fool, nor was he insane or drugged that he would reveal such secrets at so delicate and difficult time." He was also described as a very opportunistic person, for when he realized that Barrientos was nearing his end, he took advantage of the controversial situation to make it up to whoever would replace him, so that he could claim some merit in Barrientos' overthrow.

Barrientos' loss of prestige was complete. The only alternative he considered feasible was maintaining that he had been misled. Meanwhile, congressmen of the Bolivian Socialist Phalanx challenged him to answer why he left himself be fooled, who fooled him, plus a number of questions that once more put him in a difficult situation. Among the many questions were the following:

"What domestic or foreign authorities gave him false information and biased versions on the alleged military condition of the CIA agents?

"What did the government do to verify the alleged military condition of those agents?

"Is it possible to accept CIA agents as US Army personnel without being verified?

"In what measure is the President responsible for this charade and in what measure the Commander in Chief of the Nation's Armed Forces?

This incisive questioning had on the part of Barrientos a single answer: that there was a campaign by the opposition against the Armed Forces, which was an evident contradiction for it was precisely members of the Armed Forces who with their declarations had shown the interference in Bolivia's internal affairs and against Che's guerrilla on the part of the CIA and the US Embassy. The situation was getting out of hands for the Americans. Considering the real danger of Barrientos' fall and the seriousness of the situation, they pressured Zenteno Anaya to take back his accusations.

The US Ambassador met with Barrientos and Zenteno Anaya. The following day, the Presidency's Secretary of Information met with Zenteno, who was staying at the Sucre Hotel, and prepared with him a press conference in which he would make "sensational revelations". Following the President's orders, the Secretary of Information visited Father José Gramunt, a close friend of Barrientos who was director of Fides, a Catholic radio station very popular in Bolivia, with the order to broadcast Zenteno's declaration.

As planned, Zenteno held the press conference and declared that in his deposition in court at no time had he used the word CIA, but SIE (Spanish acronym for US Army Intelligence Service). The skeptic journalists reminded him that in court he had distinctly said CIA. He then answered that the judges allowed to be persuaded with false reasons. They insisted that at the end of his declaration he read them according to the law, but he responded that all was due to a phonetic confusion that he was not able to correct. Subsequently he claimed that Ramos and González were SIE —not CIA— agents.

Bolivian analysts considered that Zenteno's argumentation was weak, because it is well known that in a military court the deponent must know the literal transcription made by the court's stenographer, subsequently hear it read and finally sign it. Zenteno followed all those steps, which means that without any doubt he spoke of the CIA, and not the SIE, as he later pretended.

206

Journalists indicated that the rest of the officers also spoke of the CIA in their depositions.

On June 12, 1969, the press reported that "General Zenteno Anaya's declaration in a press conference has caused a stir, astonishment, and widespread skepticism."

Barrientos declared that he was completely satisfied with Zenteno's correction and that should be the end of that. In private he held that Zenteno, Ovando, Salamanca, Juan José Torres, Marcos Vásquez Sempértegui, congressmen and journalists that accused him would pay with their lives.

However, a new element would be added to the scandal when the La Paz daily *Jornada* reported that the SIE acronym did not exist in the US Army, proving Zenteno a liar. The newspaper claimed that the declaration was the result of pressures by the US Embassy and the CIA Station, and that Barrientos had promised Zenteno to appoint him Ambassador to Peru.

On April 24 Barrientos invited a small group of close friends and trusted military officers to his private residence at 8409, Man Céspedes St., at the residential neighborhood of La Florida. The gathering lasted late into the night with a discussion on the internal situation of the country, the Armed Forces, the accusations against the President and the disloyalty of many officers. Barrientos pointed out his contradictions with Ovando, Torres and Vásquez Sempértegui, and expressed very vulgar words about Cárdenas Mallo, Salamanca and Zenteno. Barrientos' friends proposed several options: that he declare himself a dictator and abolish the Constitution and Congress; to eliminate a number of his opponents and send the rest into exile. Together with those propositions a plan sprang up that was codenamed May Plan, because it would be launched on May 1. Subsequently it was known that the plan had been presented by the CIA's Head of Station in Bolivia and endorsed by Barrientos. The purpose of the meeting had been to implicate all those presenting in its execution.

Perspectiva magazine questioned that after the guerrilla, power sectors and the vital forces of the nation asked themselves what had happened.

"Then the crisis deepened, the status quo began to fall apart. The first institution to suffer it were the Armed forces, which had acted in unitary manner during the anti guerrilla campaign; but young officers felt the impact, not only that they were forced to accept advise from CIA agents and Green Berets, but because they wondered about the guerrillas' actions. Unwittingly, they discovered that it was simply the effect of something with more depth: underdevelopment and dependency."

The magazine pointed out that from that moment on, the national trend was strengthened among the military. This influenced the church, from whose rank and file emerged the third-world priests with a Gospel at the service of the poor. In some political parties, such as Christian Democrats, radical and revolutionary factions appeared advocating socialism and the need of a left leaning process in Bolivia. The magazine also said that imperialism, conscious that the situation was becoming uncontrollable, decided through the CIA to implement a plan to eliminate the nationalistic trend by terminating political leaders, military officers, labor union leaders and others that had shown revolutionary fickleness, and that an operation in the style of the Night of the Long Knives should be capped by a proclamation with which Barrientos would become dictator.

As part of the plan, Barrientos would visit regiments and other important military units, so that his image could gain authority and prestige, and at the same time neutralize Ovando's influence. On April 25 he visited the Colorado Regiment, stationed near the capital, but he did not attain the expected receptivity, because the military knew that Barrientos was promoting a paramilitary force known as FURMOD, trained by US advisors, which he was planning to use in secret if he did not get support from the Armed Forces.

On April 1969, the President flew to the town of Arque in a helicopter presented to him by the head of the US military mission. He was planning to proceed later to Tacopaya, also in the department of Cochabamba, and subsequently continue visiting the country's main regiments.

Death of General René Barrientos Ortuño

President of Bolivia René Barrientos, accompanied by his aide Captain Leovigildo Orellana, and his pilot Lieutenant Carlos Rafael Estívariz, landed on April 27, 1969, at 11:30 a.m., on the town of Arque, some 60 kilometers southeast of Cochabamba, in order to inaugurate a school named after John F. Kennedy.

The H 23 helicopter, register number FAB-602 of the Bolivian Air Force, settled softly on the soccer field of the small town. A welcoming committee of local authorities and Father Lucio Paredes, the town's priest, was waiting. At two o'clock Barrientos was due in Tacopaya, but Arque's authorities had prepared lunch, so take off was delayed for an hour.

A few minutes past the planned take off time, Barrientos climbed aboard the helicopter and while the craft was climbing and in front of the curious peasants, it exploded in mid air and crashed down in flames. Press reports informed of "a clear day, cloudless sky and no wind."

Father Lucio Paredes said that there was a loud report; then he saw a great flare up and dust, "as the smoke of a deafening storm." He also pointed out that at the site where the burning helicopter crashed everything was white hot, and trapped in it were the three victims. Later he added: "We wanted to extract first the General. Our humanitarian effort was totally useless. His body was completely burned [...] the other two victims, aide and pilot, were in the same condition [...]"

"After the destroyed helicopter cooled down, we proceeded to take out the General and the officers; they were trapped in the twisted metal, totally burned."

Bolivian military sources claimed that it had been an attack by rival political groups bent on assassinating him to raise Ovando to power. Those partial to that opinion indicated that there is evidence and witness accounts that four people stationed along the route that the helicopter would follow shot at the craft, which caused the explosion and subsequently the fire. However, official reports claimed that the accident happened because the helicopter hit a high tension wire of the power grid, although in the vicinity of the crash there was only a very thin old telephone wire a few meters above the ground.

Whatever the cause, the fact is that he burned to death, just as he had declared that he had done with Che. From that moment a new legend emerged in Bolivia: "Che executed him and condemned him to die by fire."

209

Other Bolivian military sources claimed that the assassination was carried out on April 27 because the May Plan had been discovered, which had the intention of dissolving Congress and unleashing a brutal repression that would eliminate dozens of civilians and members of the military in the following twenty four hours.

Barrientos intended to crush all opposition to his government and its inner contradictions, because both "did not permit him to govern." Others pointed out that since 1967, in the midst of counterguerrilla operations, the assassination attempt had already been planned and counted with Ovando's approval. The occasion would be one of Barrientos' helicopter trips, but the plan had not been carried out for different reasons.

Those sources pointed out that Ovando ordered the assassination attempt be made after he had left for the United States on an official visit, so that he could deny any attempt to blame him, and at the same time calm down the Americans and give them guarantees.

Barrientos' trip to Arque was on the presidential schedule, not at all a secret. On April 27, very early in the morning, four military officers dressed in civilian clothes, all of them faithful to Ovando, arrived in town. According to the same sources, the four positioned themselves on a side of the Arque valley, by a narrow ravine that the helicopter had to overfly. When the presidential craft was climbing, they fired. Some peasants later said that they had heard two bursts of machine gun fire coming from one side; then the helicopter lurched erratically and finally went down in flames.

Uruguayan journalist Carlos María Gutiérrez reported that the father of Barrientos' aide, Leovigildo Orellana, claimed that his son's body had bullet wounds. Likewise the corpse of pilot Carlos Rafael Estívariz —who dropped peasants and guerrilla Jorge Vázquez Viaña over the jungle from a helicopter—, when he was exhumed, the new autopsy revealed a bullet entry wound in the kidney area. Mario Bolívar, a lieutenant with the Traffic Police who was in Arque on that day, declared that when the helicopter crashed he saw three men run to the site, examine it and then flee to the mountains. Bolívar added that at the time he had been pressured by his superiors not to reveal what he had seen.

Those who are convinced it was an assassination have more elements. For example, at the time of the take off from Arque, before the helicopter had crashed, El Cóndor Radio station in Oruro, linked to Altiplano Radio in La Paz, flashed the news of Barrientos' death, even before the competent authorities had heard of it. This event caused confusion and disbelief due to the lack of communications and its distance from Oruro, a fact that provoked an immediate denial by Illimani Official Radio, a rather significant fact.

According to observers, the US Embassy was not oblivious to the assassination plan. They knew of it in detail, but did nothing to prevent it. The Bolivian president was a discredited figure and no longer served US interests, particularly because he knew too much. He was better off dead. Observers noted that at the embassy the news was received with complete calmness, and even with open satisfaction.

Those sources indicated that Generals Juan José Torres and César Ruiz met right away and summoned an urgent meeting at the Miraflores Great Barracks. From there they called Ovando, who coincidentally was at the moment at the Bolivian embassy in Washington, although it was a Sunday afternoon.

Another attention grabber by observers was the speed and efficiency shown by Colonel Reque Terán, commander of the Military College, located at the opposite side of the Bolivian capital, who at three o'clock in the afternoon had already occupied the Presidential Palace, blocked all doors, and denied access to ministers and government officials.

A few minutes after three Rosemary Galindo de Ugarte, Barrientos' wife, arrived to the Palace to confirm her husband's death and also to collect some of his valuable possessions. According to military sources, Reque Terán behaved very rudely, a fact condemned by informants, because up to the moment he had being respectful to the Barrientos family. Besides, Rosemary was a distinguished lady from a prestigious and respected family. Her brother Marcelo Galindo was Minister of the Presidency, and her father, Walter Galindo Quiroga, had been rector of the University of Cochabamba.

The sources pointed out that Reque Terán told her that since two o'clock she had ceased to be the First Lady of the Republic, therefore she could not go into Barrientos' office. After she left, Reque Terán guffawed and said that there would be no more celebrations of Rosemary's birthday at the Palace. According to informants, he was referring to the fact that every May 3 she celebrated at the Hall of Mirrors, following a strict schedule for receiving congratulations and presents, according to invitations and the protocol set out by the Presidency's National Direction of Information.

Something that also called the attention of observers was the speed with which the three generals agreed to give their support to Vice President Luis Adolfo Siles Salinas as new president and the terms of the communiqué that they released at 15:45 hours; that is, less than two hours after Barrientos' death, and in spite of the fact that two of the generals were in La Paz and the third in Washington.

The text of the communiqué is the following:

"Considering the sad news of the death of His Excellency the President of the Republic and Captain General of the Armed Forces of the Nation, the Commander in Chief communicates to public opinion that the Constitutional Vice President Dr. Luis Adolfo Siles has taken charge of the Presidency, according to the Political Constitution of the State.

"The Commander in Chief and the Armed Forces of the Nation comply with, and will give its support to, the legally constituted government, and proclaim that they will drastically repress any attempt of subversion against the legally constituted order.

"We exhort every citizen to maintain the utmost calmness and prudence at the time that the Motherland lives hours of mourning and national misfortune."

In relation to Barrientos' death, Bolivian believers have given a mystical interpretation and justify it as God's punishment for him having ordered Che Guevara's assassination.

After the Heroic Guerilla's death there was an intense drought in several regions of the country, and because of it in April a wave of large winged and dark colored insects known as "taparacos" – Quechua for night butterfly—invaded streetlamps in plazas, parks, light bulbs at homes, kitchen corners, kerosene lamps or candles, and flew around constantly. There were so many that they had to be swept away. Some people were terrorized, because according to popular belief taparacos are the bearers of punishment, bad luck, death and evil omen for everyone that has acted wrongly in life and with family. According to the custom, they made the sign of the cross and repeated a litany to drive the curse away.

Alter Barrientos' death the taparacos disappeared. The fact affirmed the belief that they had come to punish him. Consistent with this belief, a chain letter began to circulate among the Bolivian military and their families, which said that Barrientos' death was the punishment of God and that all that were guilty of Che's assassination had a serious misfortune in store. In order to save themselves they had to say three Lord's Prayers and three Hail Marys. Then they had to make nine copies of the letter and send them to nine different persons.

The people that received the letter added new events about personal or family misfortunes that had fallen on those related to the crime, which gave credibility to the letter. The correspondence reached the whole country, reinforcing the legend that in Bolivia is called "Che's curse."

A new president is sworn in and murder is attempted on Antonio Arguedas

At four in the afternoon –hardly two hours after Barrientos death—, Vice President Luis Adolfo Siles Salinas arrived to the Palace of Government. Twenty two minutes later he was sworn in as Constitutional President of the Republic of Bolivia, with the apparent support of the Armed Forces and the US Ambassador's enthusiasm. The inauguration was held in a tense atmosphere of division and insecurity, for the Armed Forces considered that the new president should not be a civilian.

Siles Salinas went alone to the Presidential Palace. Thus he evaded the strict vigilance that Reque Terán had placed around his residence, which remained surrounded by soldiers to prevent him from reaching the seat of government. The maneuver would allow Ovando to return from the US in time to take over the presidency, considering the apparent irresponsibility and absence of the Vice President. However, Siles Salinas left his home by an alternate route and arrived to the Presidential Palace, thus surprising Reque Terán and the rest of the officers present.

The US Embassy showed his satisfaction with the new president. Siles Salinas was very familiar to them since he had held the position of president of the Bolivian-American Center, where he played an important role promoting friendship and US culture, way of life and ideology.

At the Palace of Government political bustle was centered on the appointment of new ministers and readjustment of persons close to the new president. Siles Salinas accepted conditions imposed by Ovando –confirmed the High Command in whole and appointed as ministers of Defense and of the Interior men totally loyal to the Commander in Chief.

New information about Arguedas complicated the situation. On May 8, 1969 his residence was the target of a brutal terrorist attack when a grenade and a dynamite bomb were thrown inside the house. There was considerable damage. Arguedas blamed CIA agents John H. Corr y Alberto Garza as the ones who masterminded the attack and a secret military lodge called Group of Honor as the perpetrators. On that same day, as he was walking by the Torino Hotel in La Paz with Spanish journalist Pedro Sánchez Quierolo, unknown persons shot him with a burst of machine gun fire from a passing car. He was rushed to the Isabel la Católica Clinic, where a few hours later his condition was reported as serious due to loss of blood. The Spanish journalist was unharmed.

At that moment Siles Salinas began to face serious difficulties. Ambitions, infighting and settling of scores among rival groups were the order of the day. The attempt on Arguedas life would be one of many during that era of Bolivian politics. Shortly after the home of Roberto Jordán Pando, a leader of the MNR and a permanent critic of Ovando, was also targeted for a terrorist attack. Unknown persons threw an incendiary grenade that exploded in the garage seriously putting at risk the lives of the Bolivian politician and of his family. The grenade was of Bolivian army issue. Jordán Pando publicly accused Ovando and his followers as the guilty parties.

While Arguedas was recovering at the hospital he received death threats, as well as his family. For that reason, when on July 8, 1969 he left the hospital, Arguedas released a declaration to the press, went to the Mexican embassy in La Paz and requested political asylum. The press printed his declarations, which in part said that "unfortunately, US power has shown all the contempt that it feels for our country and has ordered its services the execution of a series of outrages against me, outrages that range from open violations of the Constitution and the law to the perpetration of destructive terrorist acts."

The declaration went on to explain that in the area of propaganda paid for by the Yankee embassy, "all resources have been used to minimize my denunciation, and venal publicists have been paid for all kinds of tejida against me. In spite of abundant evidence of US interference, none of the so called law enforcement agencies has taken any measure for at least questioning any of the many persons whose full names are on the proceedings of the makeshift trial against me."

When Arguedas request for political asylum became public, the Bolivian Foreign Ministry declared that he was an ordinary criminal and was not entitled to the appropriate safe-conduct. This attitude caused a dispute with the Mexican authorities, particularly with Mexican ambassador in La Paz Pedro González Lugo.

Interpress Service news agency reported that Bolivian Undersecretary of Foreign Relations Franz Ruck Uriburu had revealed that the Mexican government had delivered through its embassy in La Paz a declaration that considered as political the diplomatic asylum requested by Arguedas, and also that it qualified under the asylum convention of 1954. The Mexican Ambassador insisted that if by September 15 Bolivian authorities had not granted Arguedas the safe-conduct, compliance of diplomatic asylum signed by Mexico and Bolivia could be affected. The embassy would also cancel the reception to the diplomatic corps for the commemoration of Mexico's Independence Day.

President Siles Salinas agreed to the political asylum request, but the decision increased the contradictions and problems between the Bolivian government and the Armed Forces, which were reluctant to support such a decision.

Execution of Honorato Rojas. Repression in Cochabamba

On July 15, President Adolfo Siles Salinas announced to the country that Honorato Rojas, the peasant that on August 31, 1967, had guided the guerrilla rearguard to the ambush at Port Mauricio, on the Grande River, had been shot to death.

Barrientos had rewarded Rojas' treason with a five hectare plot about six kilometers from the city of Santa Cruz, were he lived in

215

hiding. A commando of the National Liberation Army of Bolivia had approached his house and executed him. The event created panic among those implicated in the murder of Che and other guerrillas, for they understood the execution as a clear warning that the ELN would settle the score to all the guilty parties.

On July 19 a message by Inti Peredo was made public –"We Will Return to the Mountains". The communiqué announced that the blood of Che and his combatants shed in the fields of Bolivia would germinate the seed of liberation. The ELN considered itself the heir of the teachings and the example of Che, the new Bolívar of Latin America. Those who had cowardly murdered him would never kill his thinking and his example. The message concluded asking all to raise Che's flag.

Peredo's announcement shook the country and repression was brutally intensified. Many persons were arrested and tortured, among them several ELN members.

With the help of many revolutionaries, particularly Chilean Beatriz Allende, Inti Peredo made his secret entry in Bolivia. At Cochabamba, where he was suspected of being in hiding, the repressive apparatus took extreme security measures and Ministry of the Interior's chief of intelligence Toto Quintanilla traveled to that city to head the repressive operations.

Through a CIA agent by the name of José Gamarra Quiroga who had penetrated the ELN's leadership, the repressive agencies raided several safehouses. One of them, located at Pacieri and Lanza streets, was surrounded by agents of the Ministry of the Interior in plainclothes. One of the agents hid inside the house. When ELN members Rita Valdivia Rivera, codename *Maya*, and Enrique Ortega, codename *Víctor*, entered the house together with Chilean Raúl Zapata, the hidden agent fired his gun and ran away. Immediately the men outside opened fire against the house from all directions.

The three revolutionaries put up a fierce resistance for over an hour and the police was unable to take the house. Shooting subsided and the attackers called for reinforcements. *Maya* and *Víctor* decided that Raúl Zapata should leave and inform Inti Peredo of the situation. Some time later a truckful of soldiers arrived and the battle raged on. Considering the large number of attackers, their volume of fire and the fact that they were running out of ammunition, Maya and Víctor decided to take their own lives. When resistance ceased, police went in and found Maya dead and Víctor dying. Bolivian writer Jesús Lara narrates that a "brave" goon kicked Víctor in the face.

Sometime later, the CIA agent that fingered the house and gave information on the ELN was executed.

Repression continued all through August, 1969. On the fist day of the month the new Minister of the Interior, Eufronio Padilla, announced the discovery of three weapon deposits of the National Liberation Army of Bolivia.

Radio stations in Bolivia broadcast a new message by Inti Peredo

On September 4 radio stations transmitted a new communiqué by Inti Peredo in which he explained the need to liberate Bolivia from the oppression and dominance of US imperialism.

The message had an extraordinary impact in all the country, and it was picked up by newspapers and radio stations, while important figures commented on it. Meanwhile, Inti Peredo went secretly from Cochabamba to La Paz, where he stayed at a house on 584, Santa Cruz St., the property of Fernando Martínez, known as *Tesorito* (Little Treasure). At dawn, on September 9, over 150 policemen surrounded the house. Police opened fire. Inti resisted for an hour, until a hand grenade thrown through a window caused him several wounds. After the explosion a police assault team battered down the door and went into the house. Peredo was seriously wounded in a leg and an arm, but did not receive medical attention. He was taken to prison, where he was tortured, and Toto Quintanilla hit him on the head several times with a rifle butt. Two hours later he was still alive and Dr. Hebert Miranda Pereira was ordered to administer him a lethal injection.

Official reports said that Peredo died by the explosion of a grenade at a house the police had raided. At 22:20 hours the body was exposed to the press. It showed evident signs of violence and torture.

The next day relatives asked for the body. The Ministry of the Interior assured them that it had been cremated due to decomposition. But since Peredo's family did not accept the excuse, on September 11 they delivered the corpse with the expressed prohibition of performing an autopsy. They were also ordered to take the body directly to La Paz airport and from there fly it to Beni, the Peredo family's hometown. The coffin was closely guarded by the police and several of them traveled with the relatives.

Later it was known that the autopsy found cranial and encephalic trauma, fracture of the temporal and parietal cranial bones, cerebral lesions and hemorrhage.

The death of the Bolivian guerrilla was a deep shock for ample sectors of the country. Repression grew. The authorities feared that after the impact caused by Inti's death disturbances and demonstrations would break out.

The ELN sentenced Dr. Hebert Miranda Pereira and Toto Quintanilla to death.

Repression against the family of guerrilla Benjamín Coronado

After Inti Peredo's murder, a brutal repression swept over revolutionary and progressive sectors in the country. Among the many persons that were controlled by the Bolivian secret services and the CIA, as well as arrested and charged as the main guerrilla liaisons, were several women —Elsa Zapata, Tota Arce, Elba Figueroa, Mirna del Río, Marta Espinosa, Delfina Burgoa, Catalina Quispe and Josefina Farjat.

The home of guerrilla Benjamín Coronado's parents, located on 777 Lucas Jaime St. in the Miraflores neighborhood, was raided by the military. Coronado's father, Benigno, was arrested. From that moment on, the house was under surveillance from the fifth floor of the Workers' Hospital, right across the street. On several occasions Coronado Sr. was tortured, even shooting him in the mouth, which prevented him from speaking for a long time. The authorities reported that he had tried to kill himself.

Geraldine Córdova de Coronado, Benjamín's mother, was also arrested. Toto Quintanilla and over 50 plainclothes soldiers armed to the teeth, surrounded the house and raided it as if it were a military fortress. Subsequently they took valuable objects, the family's meager savings, ripped the floor up looking for weapons and only left when the house was virtually destroyed.

Taken from prison to prison, Mrs. Coronado was tortured and kept in solitary confinement until she was transferred to a women's prison on 7th St in the Obrajes neighborhood. Due to her delicate state of health, the nuns that ran the prison interceded on her behalf with the authorities to have her sent to the Saint Martin of Porras Clinic, on Ecuador Avenue. She was permanently guarded by a member of the repressive services. Once in the clinic, a group of students disarmed the policeman and liberated her.

Harassment against the family continued. Raquel, one of Benjamín's sisters, was walking through La Paz when she was kidnapped and disappeared for several days, until relatives found out that she was being held in a safe house of the Interior Ministry located on Busch Avenue on Haiti St., where she was tortured. Rachel's son, Carlos Álvarez Córdova, a boy eleven years old, was left alone in their home, watched by the police while all the family was in prison.

In spite of torture, Geraldine continued to struggle for the humble people of her country. She died on April 26, 1988, at 77 years of age. She was shrouded in the flag of the National Liberation Army, as had been her wish. Her funeral was attended by members of all Bolivian parties of the left, who accompanied her to the resting place of her combative remains

The ending of Luis Adolfo Siles Salinas' government

On September 19, 1969, Congressman Ambrosio García made a serious charge in Parliament. According to García, General Alfredo Ovando had received $600,000 dollars from two US enterprises —the Bolivian Gulf Oil Company and Williams Brothers—, to finance the presidential electoral campaign, in exchange for important concessions to US oil and steel corporations.

The *ovandistas* (Ovando's followers) congressmen reacted violently and said the denouncement was an infamous libel, which

219

caused a serious disorder. According to witnesses, the *ovandistas* insulted Congressman García and demanded evidence. All spoke at once. Some considered President Siles was responsible for the mud slinging against Ovando. Others thought it credible, claiming that Ovando had limitless ambitions, and that in his sickly obsession for the presidency he was capable of anything.

In view of the accusation, Ovando declared that it was evidence of the reach of the great imperialist interests and their fear of losing everything with the coming of a firm position for re-establishing political and economic sovereignty in Bolivia. When journalists asked him which imperialism he meant, he answered: "Yankee imperialism". Ovando added that imperialism was the promoter of a monstrous blackmail with the purpose of quashing the ways for independence and progress in Bolivia.

The press insisted that in US circles there was concern that Ovando's words meant more than the usual electoral rhetoric used by many Bolivian politicians and signified a nationalistic posture.

Ovando knew what he was talking about when he accused US imperialism of blackmail. A few days before the US Ambassador had told the general that he backed President Siles Salinas without reservations and that the United States would not support nor recognize any government in Bolivia imposed by a military coup. The ambassador made it very clear, so that there were no doubts.

Ovando told him that he could not interfere in Bolivia's inner affairs, but the ambassador answered that he had documentary evidence that top Bolivian Army officers had received funding from several private companies to finance his presidential campaign. Outraged, Ovando left. When Representative Ambrosio García accused him in Congress, Ovando knew that the ambassador was behind it.

But as the scandal continued, Ovando was forced to resign as Commander in Chief until the charge was investigated.

A few days later Ambrosio García received a visit at home. Masked men that said they were members of the Legion of the Blue Leopards gave him a thorough beating and threatened to kill him unless he withdrew his accusations. Early next morning, García declared to the press that he had no evidence to prove his accusations and that he had based it on an article by journalist Justiniano Canedo. Canedo protested and denied the accusation, outraged for having been dragged into an issue he was not aware of. The Legion of the Blue Leopards was never mentioned again.

A short time later, it was publicly known that Representative Ambrosio García was a CIA agent.

Military coup against President Luis Adolfo Siles Salinas

After the accusation by Ambrosio García, events rushed in. Nationalistic military officers declared they were fed up with CIA and US Embassy interference in Bolivia's internal affairs. They claimed that although the US Department changed ambassadors, they were all the same.

On September 26, 1969, a junta of Armed Forces commanders completed a coup d'etat and released a document titled "Revolutionary Mandate of the Armed Forces." The document explained that they had decided to assume the responsibility of constructing a national and revolutionary power that would defend social justice, the greatness of the Motherland and a true national independence that was in danger of failing due to subjugation from abroad.

The document pointed out the need of making a speedy and profound transformation of economic, social, political and cultural structures to combat poverty; organize a revolutionary government conformed by civilians and the military in search of national unity; demand the recovery of natural wealth; face the problem of unemployment; build housing and establish the most scrupulous administrative honesty.

Concerning foreign relations, it declared that it was indispensable to adopt an independent foreign policy based on the unrenounceable right of the Bolivian state to freely determine its own foreign policy; establish diplomatic and economic relations with socialist countries; make a contribution to the political an economic unity of Latin America; and sustain the sacred right of maritime reintegration. The document also summoned the country to the struggle against illiteracy, the defense of popular culture, of Indian and mestizo traditions.

Finally, the Revolutionary Junta appointed Ovando as President of the Republic and Juan José Torres as Commander in Chief of the Armed Forces.

The population was skeptic of such a revolutionary mandate. After all, it was the 185th military coup in 144 years of the republic's turbulent history.

Journalist and researcher Lupe Cajías wrote that very few people knew about the coup, for practically everybody was listening to Radio Altiplano and its constant interruptions with news flashes about the Bolivian Airlines crash in which many people died, among them the soccer team Strongest. It should be noted that Cajías was referring to the importance of the radio as a source of news, for in 1969 television was a newcomer to the Bolivian capital.

In relation to the coup d'etat and the Revolutionary Junta, Juan Lechín the powerful leader of the COB declared:

"Unfortunately for the country and particularly for the working people, the whole High Command, including General Ovando, is responsible of the bloody events on May and September, 1965. Therefore, it is useless to try to convince the sensible people of this country who have a memory that by magic the enemies of yesterday will become the friends of that same people through a dictate of that Military High Command."

Lupe Cajías pointed out that Lechín was one of the few that said that Ovando and his followers took over power to check a revolutionary movement that was building up clandestinely throughout the country, and that included armed struggle in its actions as never before. She also claimed that the guerrillas had not been finished on October 8, 1967, and that its influence reached two pillars of reaction: the Armed Forces and the Church.

The Revolutionary Junta set up a civilian-military cabinet with personages of nationalistic, progressive, rightist and fascist positions. In its 344th edition of October 3, *Oiga* magazine reported that in Ovando's government "there are historically conservative and pro US men, half-hearted figures that are willing to modernize only certain aspects of reality, and openly nationalistic and even leftist sectors, aside from young nationalistic officers that are not members of the cabinet, but who exist, act and pressure."

Fifteen days later Ovando's government was recognized by Peru –at that time headed by General Juan Velasco Alvarado, who had nationalized US oil companies and maintained nationalistic and progressive policies. Relations between both countries grew significantly. It was then that Ovando declared that he was thinking of establishing an ideological confederation with Peru.

In the midst of that convulsive situation, the date of October 8, 1968 arrived. At several locations in La Paz sprang up large posters with the image of Che and signs that said "Long Live the ELN and Inti Peredo."

Bolivian intellectuals Silvia Ávila and Guido Oria wrote that the hill slopes that surround La Paz were illuminated with torches forming the words "Long Live Che." They could be seen from all parts of the city and remained lit until dawn.

According to press reports, students from the Greater San Andrés University took to the streets on October 9. In the front ranks marched arm in arm Adolfo Quiroga Bonadona, president of the University Confederation, Mario Suárez Moreno, Hugo Rodríguez Román, Horacio Rueda Peña, Norberto Rodríguez Silva, Juan José Saavedra, Ricardo Justiniano Roca and many others. Demonstrators shouted "Death to Imperialism!" and their slogans shook the streets of the Bolivian capital; simultaneously they demanded the nationalization of US companies Gulf Oil and Power. That day stones rained on the US Embassy building.

On October 17, 1969 the Bolivian government nationalized the Bolivian Gulf Oil Company, a US property, and declared a Day of National Dignity. The army occupied all the facilities. The United States threatened Bolivia with sanctions to all bilateral programs unless it received rapid, adequate and effective compensation.

On October 20, there was in La Paz a huge popular demonstration supporting the measure and condemning US threats. Witness told that the crowd was in frenzy. From the Presidential Palace's balconies Ovando said: "Bolivians are at war against imperialism to conquer their dignity."

Another source said that a group of foreign journalists could not believe their eyes. One of them asked himself: This same Ovando that speaks today against US imperialism, is he the same man that made war with US assistance against the guerrilla in which Che Guevara died? Is he the same one that commanded the Armed Forces when the bloody repression against these workers, Indians and miners that cheer him today? What is happening in Bolivia?

The answer perhaps could be found in the declaration signed by Jorge Rosales on behalf of the Nationalistic Revolutionary Left

Movement; Guillermo Aponte Burela for the Revolutionary Party of the Revolutionary Left; Hugo Montoya and Walter Vázquez Michel for Leftist Bolivian Socialist Phalanx; and Jorge Ríos Dalence for the Revolutionary Christian Democratic Party, which expressed that the supreme decree that returned to the state the oil concessions granted to Bolivian Gulf, as well as the nationalization of its assets, is an anti-imperialist and revolutionary measure that because of its importance deserves the support of all leftist political forces, and in particular of those that have permanently struggled to achieve that popular yearning.

That was precisely what the demonstrators were cheering. The Bolivians are a noble and dignified people. They harbor a deep feeling of hate and disdain for those who exploit, besmirch and insult them. It has deep anti-US feelings with a good measure of rancor. They were cheering the move against US imperialism.

Bolivian analysts pointed out that Ovando needed a propaganda effect in order to win the credibility of the people, and to show that the Armed Forces was no longer the institution that had been sustained by bayonets and had drowned in blood the demands made by miners, peasants and students, but that now it was the one that should move forward the changes that Bolivia demanded to throw off the imperialist yoke imposed by previous governments. That had been the true reason for nationalizing the Bolivian Gulf Oil Company.

On the 31st, the government ordered the Army to withdraw from the mines that had been occupied since the massacre of the Night of San Juan. The measure was greeted with shows of sympathy.

In his book *Power and Armed Forces,* Gary Prado mentioned Juan José Torres' position on the speech he made on the occasion of a visit to Bolivia by the Inter American Defense Board. Torres lashed against the prevailing system and the old military mentality in Latin American armies that frequently were the armed guardians of unfair social systems. He pointed out that the most serious and brutal enemy of democracy was within the borders of the continent, spread along a geography of hunger, unemployment and destitution. According to Torres, the peoples of the continent had no way out but violence and uncontrollable revolution to bring about the changes for constitute a world of social justice. Torres also assured that the armed forces of all the countries and the Inter American Defense Board itself should be willing and efficient agents of the battle against underdevelopment, instead of exclusively identifying themselves as repressors of international communism.

The US mission in Bolivia believed that Torres led an important sector of the Bolivian Armed Forces that was adopting excessively nationalistic positions. His declarations were considered a challenge by the Americans.

Subsequently Torres attended a forum at the University of Cochabamba called "The Roads of Revolution." This time he expressed the need of a class alliance for obtaining the great structural transformations required by the country. If the revolutionary forces, he said, do not strive for a liaison with the army, imperialism would use the institution to block for a long time the progressive perspective of the country.

The Revolutionary Junta took new measures consistent with its program. Against the open opposition of the Americans they began with the installation of smelting furnaces to process tin; appropriated part of the army's budget to finance a literacy campaign, re-established diplomatic relations with the Soviet Union, intensified their bonds of friendship and exchange with the nationalist governments of Peru and Panama. Ovando declared in a press conference that Cuba should be readmitted into the Organization of American States (OAS) and be allowed the free exercise of its privileges as a sovereign sister nation. There was an announcement that the government was discussing the possibility of freeing Regis Debray and other prisoners in Camiri.

When the US Ambassador knew that Ovando had met in secret with Debray's wife and that he was willing to set him free, he remarked indignantly: "All we need is that they shoot those who killed Che Guevara."

Other measures of great importance were: abolition of the State Security Law, passed immediately after the appearance of the guerrillas, designed to legalize all out repression, and also the so called anti-labor union law to obtain government control of the labor movement. Lastly, he promised full labor and political freedoms.

On November 17, Deputy Secretary of Foreign Relations Edgar Camacho Omiste informed about the possibility of solving the issue of Arguedas political asylum in a few days.

Camacho kept his word: Arguedas left for Mexico and shortly after received the visit of Marino Chang Navarro, brother of Juan Pablo (*el Chino*), the Peruvian that was murdered together with Che at La Higuera's school. Marino wanted to know where his brother had been buried and the circumstances of his death. After the meeting, the young Peruvian took a bus of the Ticabús line to travel to Lima. When he reached the border town of Chinamas between El Salvador and Guatemala, he was taken prisoner and disappeared forever. Another still unsolved crime.

A new Ambassador in Bolivia

As soon as General Alfredo Ovando was sworn in as president, US Ambassador Raúl H. Castro was substituted. Their relation had soured since Castro had tried to blackmail Ovando through Representative Ambrosio García.

The new ambassador was Ernest Víctor Siracusa, who arrived in La Paz on November, 1969. Born in Coalinga, California, on November 20, 1918, he studied in Fullerton College. In 1940 he got his BA at Stanford University and in 1950 he received a rigorous CIA training at the Massachusetts Institute of Technology. Siracusa worked for private companies, and in 1941 became a member of the US Diplomatic Corps. His assignments included the following posts: third secretary and vice consul in Mexico City and La Ceiba, Honduras; second secretary and consul in Guatemala; in charge of Central American and Panamanian affairs in the State Department; first secretary in Buenos Aires; in charge of Brazilian affairs in the State Department; director of the Office of West Coast Affairs in the State Department. He was also first secretary at the US Embassy in Rome, counselor to the US Mission at the UN, and counselor to the US Ambassador in Lima, Peru. In 1960, he was appointed ambassador in Bolivia.

Siracusa's mission was to quash nationalist tendencies in Bolivia and collaborate with the same intention in Peru. In December, 1969 he was appointed as coordinator of operations against communism in the region of South America.

Reaction in the US Embassy at La Paz

Indignation was rampant at the US Embassy because the Bolivian military were going too far. Due to this disobedience, there was an increase in the plan of economic and political pressures, as well as blackmail for destabilizing the country. They decreed an economic blockade, paralyzed all projects with external financing, threatened to flood the market with the US' strategic tin reserves, which would cause in Bolivia an economic crisis of inestimable consequences. They prompted their stalwarts to confront nationalists in the military and the political and mass movements that supported them. They financed press campaigns. Immediately Bolivian rightist newspapers began to attack Juan José Torres, the Revolutionary Junta, the Bolivian Workers' Central, universities, and everything that had a whiff of nationalism.

According to later investigations, the CIA established a plan to promote social tensions, stimulate ambitions of power among the military, assassinate people of different ideologies, and sow division among sectors, besides chaos and mistrust. The CIA designed a plan to stimulate regional feelings, ethnic conflicts and even separatism. The plan had as its goal the division of Bolivia into two separate countries, a trend that found fertile soil in Santa Cruz and El Beni departments.

The CIA was positive that the economic blockade, press campaigns and social insecurity were the main actions that would sweep nationalist officers away. Later on it was known that the Agency was persuaded that an important group of the Bolivian military had a clear inclination to nationalist extreme leftist or even communist position. The US magazine *Business Week* reported that Bolivia was becoming a mini Cuba.

The Gulf Oil Company prevented oil exports and blocked the arrival of materials for the construction of a gas pipeline to Argentina. The Williams Brothers construction company abandoned the project and put the Bolivian government in danger of not meeting the deadline agreed upon with the government of Argentina. It also blocked the $23 million dollars granted by the World Bank for the financing and fired 1,600 workers.

From Washington, the new US ambassador to La Paz said that perhaps at some time Bolivia could have been a proud nation, but at the moment it was a professional beggar; therefore, it had to respect those that gave the money or would have to go without it. Subsequently the 1285th edition of the US magazine *Hanson's Latin American Letter* published on November 1, 1969 the declarations, although it was careful not to quote the ambassador directly.

Those words caused indignation in large sectors of the country, including among the military. Journalist René Rocabado Alcácer answered those serious insults in the magazine *Letras Bolivianas*.

"We Bolivians", Rocabado wrote, "have never been, are not, nor will ever be 'professional beggars', because we have always paid the Great Usurer in national currency more than the established world prices for what they sold us. Beggars, people without dignity, those who use the names of 'Ed', 'Al', 'Jim' and think in English even if they have copper colored skin, have been many of the rulers that, precisely to preserve the interests of the Great Usurer, charged to the credits even the import of tear gas, half the cost of which was paid by the local US embassy."

To all these US pressures were added those by the military governments of Argentina and Brazil, which were alarmed by the revolutionary turn of their Peruvian and Bolivian neighbors.

The CIA and the US Military Mission in La Paz regrouped the rightist, reactionary, anti communists and pro US Bolivian military to unite them around some figure that at the moment they were still evaluating, with the purpose of countering the left and nationalist leaning military, so that later they could be neutralized and finally defeated.

In Bolivia there was a process of transformations. Nationalist, anti-imperialist and anti US feelings were increasingly growing. Bolivian analysts have claimed that Che was the catalyst of Bolivian nationality that made an impact in all sectors of the country, particularly in the Armed Forces. Even after death he had achieved a political victory.

Colonel Rubén Sánchez Valdivia, who had been a prisoner of the guerrillas, said: "From my conversation with the guerrillas I understood that they were fighting for the poor, and I asked myself: Why were we fighting? What were we defending? Whom were we defending? At least they –the guerrillas— defended the poor. I understood that completely." Sánchez claimed that Che's presence had its effects and found receptive ears not only in a civilian environment, particularly among workers, popular sectors, leftist politicians, peasants, students and intellectuals, but also among the military, who from then on felt a greater concern for the situation of workers and peasants, the most impoverished sectors of the country. Likewise, he said that "If we analyze the origin of this situation, the greatest drive, the greatest ideological and political impulse in Bolivia stems from the presence and death of Che."

The CIA's plan against Ovando's and Juan José Torres' government

Crimes in Bolivia

US intelligence services, concerned over events in Bolivia and the radicalization of many military sectors in the nationalist process, launched its destabilizing plan in collaboration with rightist groups in the army and the police. The May Plan, designed for the assassination of the main political and nationalist military figures, had only to be updated.

In late 1969, Senator Jorge Soliz Román, an enemy of Ovando and leader of a peasant association set up by Barrientos, was shot to death by unknown killers who intercepted his car four kilometers from Cochabamba. Soliz was shot eighteen times. Many people in Bolivia are certain that the crime was instigated by the CIA in order to unite Barrientos' followers among the military and the peasant leaders against Ovando.

Bolivian Military Intelligence raided a house in the Sopocachi neighborhood where the CIA had set up a new telephone bugging facility. The finding was cause for a new scandal about US interference in Bolivian internal affairs. Ovando declared that the Agency and bad Bolivians were acting against the country. He expelled five US officials linked to that agency.

On December 31, members of the Ministry of the Interior located a house where some ELN members were in hiding, among them David Adriazola Veizaga, codename *Darío* in Che's guerrilla.

Bolivian journalist and researcher Lupe Cajías, a witness to this event, wrote: "It was New Year's Eve and we were sent to buy liquor at the corner store when suddenly the shooting began and we saw the jeeps and people running (...) They threw us out of the store and closed the door, and we did not know what to do, and we felt sorry for the guerrillas and the police, and we saw how they killed the one that tried to escape by the 'corte-camino'. Perhaps it was Darío, the last Bolivian survivor of Che's guerrilla. We hurried home to tell Dad the news so that *Presencia* could scoop the rest and we became heroes for several hours, telling and giving details of the slaughter."

Lupe's father is Huascar Cajías, an important Bolivian journalist and diplomat who at the time and for many years was the editor in chief of the newspaper *Presencia*. In 1988 he was in Rome as the Bolivian Ambassador to the Vatican.

In February, 1970, Bolivian journalist and intellectual Jaime Otero Calderón was found strangled to death in the premises of Editorial Artística, a publishing house he owned. The perpetrators were never found, but people linked his death to a piece that Otero published in his newsletter *Servicio Informativo Confidencial* (SIC), a denunciation of serious cases of corruption during the Barrientos government. Otero had promised greater revelations in the following edition. The charge affected CIA plans and those of the military that plotted with the Agency. Some claim that the CIA perpetrated the crime, and others that it had been Barrientos' military followers, although there was not much difference, for they both had the same interests and both would be affected by what had been published.

Jaime Otero Calderón, together with other prestigious Bolivian intellectuals, was sympathetic to Che Guevara. He collaborated with foreign journalists that traveled to Bolivia to report the trial against Regis Debray and the guerrilla related events. Otero was one of the twelve intellectuals who founded the National Coordination for the Resistance that released a manifesto to the nation calling for the struggle against US occupation. He was also a national leader of the Nationalist Revolutionary Movement, a former congressman and former minister secretary of the presidency during the Víctor Paz Estenssoro government.

On March 13, 1970 US envoy Charles Meyer arrived in La Paz. Journalist and researcher Lupe Cajías narrated that protest demonstrations reached the house where Inti Peredo had been murdered, where Father Mauricio Lefebre made a speech. The demonstrators shouted: "We'll avenge you! We'll avenge you!" Students from the poor neighborhoods of El Alto, where La Paz's international airport is located, put up barricades to block the passage of the US envoy.

On its part, the March 20, 1970 issue of *Oiga* magazine reported: "Saturday 14. - La Paz woke up in a calm atmosphere after a quite agitated day for Air Force, police and civilian security agent detachments that clashed with large crowds of demonstrators expressing their protest for the visit of Assistant Secretary of State for Inter-American Affairs Charles Meyer. But at 8:50 a.m. a violent explosion a few blocks from the US Embassy, where Meyer was at the moment, shook the people of La Paz from their lethargy."

Another political crime rocked the citizenry: journalist and former ambassador to Spain Alfredo Alexander Jordán, and his wife Marta Dupleych had been murdered. The proprietors of the important newspapers *Última Hora* and *Hoy*, they lived in the exclusive residential August 6 Avenue, where a young messenger delivered a gift wrapped package. When they opened it, a powerful bomb exploded and killed them both.

Alfredo Alexander wrote for his newspaper under the pen name of Erasmo and had frequent clashes with Ovando. He and his followers would be immediately suspected of the crime. This is seen as a typical political crime in the CIA's strategy.

Crimes continued. In early June the bodies of a young couple turned up in the outskirts of Cochabamba. They were later identified as Elmo José Catalán Avilés, a Chilean, and Bolivian Jenny Koeller. Elmo had worked in Santiago de Chile as a journalist for *Última Hora, El Siglo,* and the weekly magazine *Vistazo.* He had written two books on Chile's basic wealth, had been a union leader and was press secretary in Salvador Allende's first presidential campaign. In Chile he led the support network for Che's guerrillas.

Jenny Koeller was an architect, administrative secretary of the Cochabamba University Federation's Executive Committee and a prominent leader with a great deal of influence in the Bolivian student movement. Both were members of the National Liberation Army of Bolivia and were investigating the CIA's participation in

Che's murder, as well as the espionage agency's interference in Bolivia's internal affairs and other aspects denounced by former Minister of the Interior Antonio Arguedas. Catalán and Koeller were preparing a book that Feltrinelli would publish in Italy.

The press published a communiqué allegedly released by the National Liberation Army of Bolivia that claimed that one of its members was responsible for the crime due to rivalry and jealousy, but the ELN denied it.

The murders caused deep consternation and a wave of protests in all the country. During the funeral, student leaders openly accused the CIA and the Bolivian Armed Forces as the perpetrators.

For some Bolivian sources, Ovando's government wanted to avoid a confrontation with the students and deployed hundreds of police officers and army troops to maintain order. But fascist groups took advantage of the situation and opened fire on the demonstrators. The students retaliated and there was an indeterminate number of dead, although the government admitted only two and several wounded. However, eyewitnesses claimed there were dozens.

The fierce repression unleashed a wave of protests in the country's main cities. The army and the police suppressed them in a savage manner. Labor unions and students turned streets, squares, plazas, parks and avenues into true battlefields. The streets of Cochabamba were taken by students for six hours and in that time they put up barricades, set fire to vehicles, tossed bombs and Molotov cocktails.

The CIA used the murders of the young couple to create serious problems to the government of Ovando and nationalist officers, particularly to Juan José Torres. The Agency thought that the unity between forces of the left and the nationalist military for the struggle against imperialism had been definitely disrupted.

Another political assassination attempt in La Paz

On the night of August 20, 1970, several unknown persons surrounded the home of Congressman Zacarías Plaza. One of them entered the house wearing a mask and emptied his gun on

Plaza. He survived, but almost died from wounds to the liver and the intestines. One of his daughters was also wounded. The guilty parties were never found, but this was thought to be part of the CIA's plans and of the right to destabilize Ovando's government. Congressman Zacarías Plaza was a much hated man with enemies everywhere. He was known as *Bullet Shooting*. His worst enemies were the miners, for he was one of the leaders of the massacres at the mines –the best known had been on the Night of St. John, on June 24, 1967. Rightist sectors and the CIA thought that an intense repression would be unleashed on the miners, a fact that would affect the credibility of Ovando and the nationalist military, who were trying to win their trust.

After the failed attempt, Zacarías Plaza declared that those who had tried to kill him were members of a gang of murderers and hired killers.

Assassination plan against Juan José Torres

The repressive climate in Bolivia was so intense that the figure of Ovando was deteriorating. Reactionaries and rightist groups inside the Armed Forces, the police and the political sectors were gaining strength. Each day they became stronger and made demands in a threatening manner. Due to the crisis and the reactionary pressures, Ovando gave up ground until he adopted a position of abandonment. He replaced some of the progressive and revolutionary ministers, such as Marcelo Quiroga Santa Cruz, a fact that caused angry protests and a greater loss of his prestige. His political enemies, while pressuring him, spread rumors of all kinds –that he had cancer; that he only had a few weeks left; that his government was plagued with communists, ambitious and corrupt people.

The Armed Forces were divided in three sectors: extreme rightists –fascists and pro-US— on one side, against leftists and nationalists on the other; in the middle, a heterogeneous group that advocated the unity of the Armed Forces, notwithstanding the political or ideological positions, and who insisted on avoiding a military showdown between the two or, even worse, civil war.

The Revolutionary Junta that put Ovando in power was also divided. A group defended Juan José Torres' more radical ideas. They believed that they had to stand up to US pressures and local followers; crush those followers once and for all, and radicalize the revolutionary process. This group maintained that Ovando was kowtowing to the rightists and would end up being their ally, and above all he was giving ground to pressures from the US Ambassador. If he persisted on his ways, the group thought, the best thing would be to get him out of the way so Torres could assume power.

The other group advocated an understanding with rightist sectors and the Americans.

In parallel with these divisions there were scattered groups that had their own plans. They benefited from these contradictions in their purpose to attain leadership. One of those groups was headed by Colonel Andrés Sélich, the same that had attempted to use violence to interrogate Che in La Higuera. Sélich met secretly with several officers from the former Ranger units, trained by US military advisors, in order to plan an assassination attempt against Juan José Torres, for they believed he was changing the Bolivian tricolor flag for a red one with the sickle and hammer. Sélich had always maintained close relations with CIA officers, and according to Bolivian sources the assassination was approved by the Agency. The plan not only envisaged Torres' termination, but also killing other nationalist military, progressive priests, leftist journalists and intellectuals, student leaders, congressmen, labor and peasant leaders.

One of those present at the meeting was Mario Eduardo Huerta Lorenzetti, the young officer who in the school at La Higuera had given Che a blanket and a cigarette; the same one that had stood up to Félix Ramos when the CIA agent had tried to use violence on Che.

Murder on the road to Oruro

Huerta refused to participate in the assassination plans against Juan José Torres because he believed that the general was right in defending Bolivia from US penetration and CIA interference. From that moment on Sélich began to mock the young officer, accusing him of cowardice and threatening to kill him if he revealed what had been said in the meeting. Sélich also reproached him that at the first trial on the issue of Che's diary, Huerta had given information that compromised officers of the Bolivian Armed Forces.

Indeed, on that trial held on July 19, 1968, Huerta testified that on the morning of October 9, 1967 they took another wounded guerrilla from Quebrada del Yuro to the La Higuera school, an event that the military had not officially admitted. He also testified on how Che had been assassinated and that one of the guilty parties had been CIA agent Félix Ramos. At the time Huerta's testimony had been censored, but it was of no consequence. He also mentioned that he intended to write a book about what had happened at La Higuera.

Huerta was an exceptional witness, because he saw who murdered Che, Peruvian Juan Pablo Chang-Navarro and Bolivian Willy Cuba. He also knew the circumstances of the death of Alberto Fernández Montes de Oca (*Pacho*), and could tell the whole story of everything that happened at La Higuera, particularly the role of the CIA agent and the Bolivian military involved in the events.

On October 9, 1970, Huerta's body was found beheaded on the La Paz-Oruro highway. His death was reported by the local press as an unfortunate accident, when en route from Oruro to La Paz his car crashed against the rear of a parked truck with no lights.

According to Bolivian sources, the murder was ordered by Sélich with the backing of the CIA to avoid the discovery of the assassination plan against Torres, and also because of what Huerta knew about what had happened at La Higuera. The perpetrators chose the date of October 9 –anniversary of Che's assassination—in order to throw the police off course if the family did not accept the version of the automobile accident as the cause of death and insisted on an investigation. In that sense, members of the ELN would be suspected, which would justify the intense repression that would follow.

The circumstances of the crime were never investigated.

General Ovando knuckles under US Embassy pressures and dismisses General Juan José Torres

In the midst of deeply rooted divisions in the Bolivian Armed Forces, the possibilities of a military coup increased day by day.

On July 9, 1970, under pressure from the right, Ovando decided to dismiss Juan José Torres, who was increasingly growing in prestige, trust and authority among large sectors of the country. His substitution was one of the conditions demanded by US authorities to begin negotiations with Ovando and reach some agreements.

Torres' ouster triggered a greater distrust of Ovando. To many it was clear that rightist sectors were gaining fast and that finally they would finish off Ovando together with the allies in the Revolutionary Junta that still stood by him.

The National Liberation Army of Bolivia releases its communiqué "We are back in the mountains"

On July 20 a group or brave young men led by Osvaldo Pereda Leigue –Coco's and Inti's youngest brother— decided that the only way for Bolivia's definite liberation was armed struggle. Based on that decision they took up arms and went back to the mountains, where they occupied the facilities of the US company South H. American Placers, which exploited Bolivian gold, and took as hostages two German employees, Eugene Schulhauseb and Gunther Lerch. In exchange they demanded the liberation of ten ELN members who had been arrested since the events at Ñacahuasú.

German chancellor Willy Brandt interceded for the German citizens through his ambassador in La Paz, Karl Alexander Hampe.

As an answer to the demand, Ovando ordered that the prisoners be taken to Chile on a special flight. In that manner ELN members Loyola Guzmán, Rodolfo Saldaña, Gerardo Bermúdez, Félix Melgar, Oscar Bush, Víctor Córdova, Roberto Moreira, Juan Sánchez, Benigno Coronado and Enrique Ortega were liberated. The guerrillas soon freed the hostages.

Subsequently the ELN guerrilla marched to the Teoponte mountains and announced the restart of the struggle. They also released the communiqué "We Are Back in the Mountains". Ovando exhorted the guerrillas to lay down their arms and promised full guarantees for their lives.

The first eight young guerrillas that gave themselves up after believing in Ovando's promises were murdered. Simultaneously, the army napalmed the area. Meanwhile, requests were made to the United States asking for the return of US advisors and Green Berets.

On July 25 a Hercules cargo plane landed at La Paz international airport with a shipment of weapons that was immediately transported on Bolivian army trucks

Ovando's Minister of Information Alberto Bailey Gutiérrez, who together with Marcelo Quiroga Santa Cruz were considered the two most lucid civilians in the cabinet, denounced that one of the worst political crimes in national history was being committed by trying to cause a breakup between the people and the Bolivian Armed Forces. Subsequently he made an accusation that shook the country when he denounced that commanders in the Armed Forces were plotting to overthrow Ovando, deliver the country to the appetite of imperialists and bring to a standstill the process begun on September 26.

Immediately generals Roberto Miranda (Army), Fernando Sattori Rivera (Air Force), and Rear Admiral Alberto Albarracín (Naval Force), denied any coup attempts and demanded that Ovando declared himself on the matter.

When Bolivians knew of the murder of the eight youngsters, there was a great commotion in all sectors of society, for among the guerrillas were university student leaders, sons of wealthy families, middle class, petit bourgeoisie, the military, peasants, workers, religious people and the most popular Bolivian singer/songwriter, Benjo Cruz, whose real name was Benjamín Inda Cordeiro.

Before joining the guerrillas, Benjo Cruz recorded several songs. On one of them he sang: "I'm going to trade my guitar for a rifle to justify my singing." This was the same young artist that at the Peña Naira had dedicated several songs to Cuban General Raúl Castro —and not to US ambassador Raúl H. Castro, as the American diplomat, himself present at the nightclub, had initially believed.

The relatives of the murdered guerrillas began a hunger strike demanding that the army deliver the bodies. The first strikers were María Luisa Bonadona de Quiroga, Nelly Alborta, Tatiana de Saavedra and María Quiroga Bonadona. Other persons joined them: priests José Prats, Pedro Negre, Federico Aguilé, Roberto

Melchor, Gregorio Iriarte, Juan Bernardo Duannel, Pedro Ribols, and Mauricio Lefebre; Begoña Landaburo, a nun; Bishop Aníbal Guzmán, of the Methodist Church of Bolivia; student leaders and workers; friends of the victims and people in general.

Heading the strike was María Luisa Bonadona, mother of Adolfo, Emilio and Eduardo Quiroga Bonadona, three prominent university students who died in the Teoponte guerrilla. She bravely declared her support for her three sons' decision that followed the example of the great Che Guevara and the dream of a Latin American homeland. She publicly denounced that one of her sons had been executed, and immediately asked for justice and that the guilty parties were condemned,

In declarations to the press the father of the Quiroga brothers, General René Quiroga Paz Soldán, said that it was up to the Armed Forces to make the official announcement about the deaths in the armed action. "I was in the Chaco War for three years, and now the only thing that I ask of General Ovando and the unified command is that they give me my son's body."

At the time that General Quiroga made this request, only one of his sons' death was known. Subsequently the other two were confirmed.

The act of rebellion by the Bolivian revolutionaries caused a deep feeling of popular sympathy. Masses of students in all the cities of Bolivia proclaimed their solidarity. The Greater University of San Andrés in La Paz paid homage and called them "Martyrs of National Liberation." There was an impressive march of women dressed in black asking for the bodies. Violence rocked the cities once more. In La Paz nine bombs exploded; in Cochabamba the police prevented the university students from marching. They arrested several priests, among them Luis Espinal and Mauricio Lefebre, and charged them of links with the ELN. In La Paz and Oruro students blocked the streets and the police brutally repressed them, killing one and arresting 40 others.

Minister of the Interior Colonel Juan Ayoroa raided the university campuses looking "for terrorists", as he himself declared, but these measures caused the unanimous condemnation of the students.

The Bolivian Workers' Central described Ovando as a dictator. In retaliation, the Minister of the Interior raided COB's leader Juan Lechín Oquendo's home.

New conflicts were created. Through the Interior Minister, the right was ruling the country and did what was convenient to its purposes.

On August 7 it was known that the US Navy ship *Woolworth City*, with 30 tons of arms and ammunition for Bolivia, was arriving to the Peruvian port of Matarani. The local press reported that Bolivian Army trucks were waiting for the ship to dock and later transported the military supplies to La Paz by the Matarani-Arequipa-Puno-Desaguadero-La Paz route.

The plane in which Ovando would have traveled mysteriously blew up in midair

In the midst of this serious crisis, the plane in which General Ovando would have flown exploded in midair and crashed on one of Lake Titicaca's islands. The cause of the accident was never sufficiently explained, but Bolivian sources claimed that a group of the military followers of Barrientos prepared the sabotage when they knew that Ovando had planned to fly that day. At the last minute he decided against it and his son Marcelo flew in his place.

The death of his son was a severe blow to the President, for according to every known source he was a good father and his son a young man of talent, about to graduate from a US university, The General was very proud of him.

Other Bolivian sources informed that the sabotage had being prepared since April 27, 1970. That was the date of the first anniversary of Barrientos' death, which was commemorated with two masses at the same time in two different churches. Ovando and the military High Command attended one at the Cathedral of La Paz –considered by Barrientos' family and followers as an insult to his memory. Barrientos loyalists offered another mass at a different church. There, a small group of the attendees agreed to attempt against Ovando's life in the same manner that they thought he had ordered Barrientos' death.

The family of the deceased president did not attend any of the two ceremonies, but celebrated a funeral service in Cochabamba. No government authorities were invited.

240

A Cry of
Victory

October, 1987

Photographs donated to the authors by Bolivian journalist Rodolfo Saldaña.

Latin American youngsters entering La Higuera on the First Latin American March in Homage to Che and his comrades. October 8, 1987.

At La Higuera there is sun, but the weather is cold and dry at 2,000 meters above sea level.

Facing the former little school at La Higuera, where Commander Guevara, Bolivian Simeón Cuba and Peruvian Juan Pablo Chang-Navarro were assassinated on October 9, 1967. In the background the heights of Abra del Picacho.

With children from La Higuera and the surroundings, to whom they gave toys, books and other school utensils. October 8, 1987.

Children from La Higuera and the surroundings sing to Che.
October 8, 1987.

A La Higuera girl is interviewed. October 8, 1987.

Latin American youngsters with La Higuera and Pucará residents.

At La Higuera during the cultural event on the 20th Anniversary.

A peasant from the area is interviewed. In the background the image of Commander Guevara. October 8, 1987.

Latin American youngsters before the pedestal where Che's bust is placed by the Bolivian flag.

Facing Che's monument before its unveiling.

First Bolivian monument to Che at La Higuera, unveiled on October 8, 1987, at 11:30 a.m.

A toast with *agüita de quirusilla*. To your health, Guevara.

Youngsters from Argentina at the Latin American March in homage to Che and his comrades.

Latin American youngsters on a pilgrimage from Pucará to La Higuera.

Latin American youngsters in Pucará.

The
Will
to Win
1996-1997

Photographs donated to the authors by Bolivian journalist Ronald Méndez.

Alto Yuro, the place where Che waged his last combat.

Pucará, the nearest town to La Higuera. In Quechua, Pucará means "fortress".

The town of Pucará, some five kilometers from La Higuera, in the days of the search for the remains of Che and his comrades.

Bolivian recruits in the search for the remains at Vallegrande.

Bolivian recruits clear the ground for the digging in search of the remains. In the background, journalists and the Vallegrande Cemetery.

Experts and Bolivian personnel during the arduous work of digging at Vallegrande.

Journalists, technical personnel, and Argentinean and Cuban experts during the digging at Vallegrande.

A moment of consultation and exchange during the work at Vallegrande.

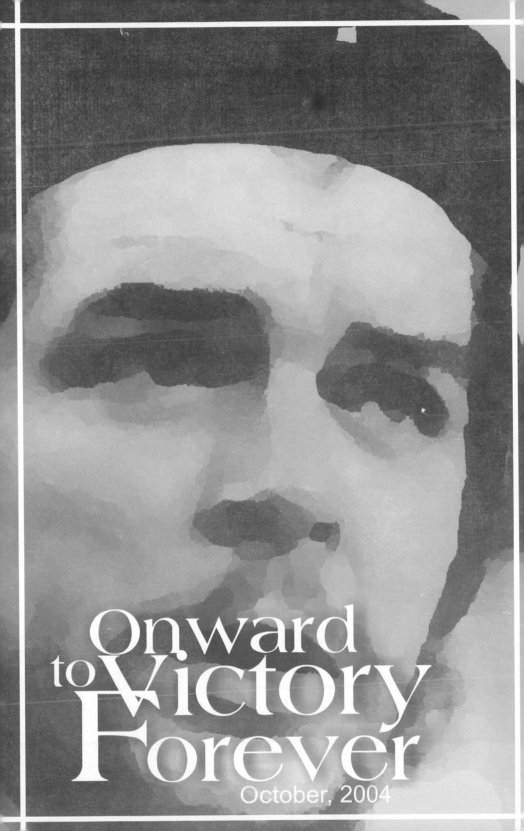

Onward to Victory Forever

October, 2004

Photographs donated to the authors by Dr. Juan Fernández (Argentine).

Outside view of the Vallegrande Cemetery.

In the background the roof of the Historical Site built at Vallegrande on the place where Che and his comrades were buried.

Historical Site built at Vallegrande at the exact place where the remains were found: Commander Ernesto Guevara; Cuban guerrillas Alberto Fernández Montes de Oca (Pacho), René Martínez Tamayo (Arturo), Orlando Pantoja Tamayo (Antonio); Bolivians Aniceto Reinaga (Aniceto) and Simeón Cuba (Willy); and Peruvian Juan Pablo Chang-Navarro (El Chino).

A mural with the image of Che and two Bolivian children.

Interior of the Historical Site, where homage of remembrance is paid to Commander Guevara and his comrades.

The grave where the remains were found on June and July, 1997. The stones bear the names of the guerrillas buried with Commander Guevara.

The grave where the remains were found on June and July, 1997. The stones bear the names of the guerrillas buried with Commander Guevara.

The laundry at the hospital, where the bodies were taken on October 9, 1967.

Lord of Malta Hospital at Vallegrande, the historical place where autopsy was performed on Commander Guevara.

The interior of the laundry and the former washtub, from where the body was taken on the early morning of October 11, 1967, to be buried in the common grave.

The entrance to the school at La Higuera.

The little school at La Higuera, where Che was assassinated on October 8, 1967. At present rebuilt.

Interior of the La Higuera school.

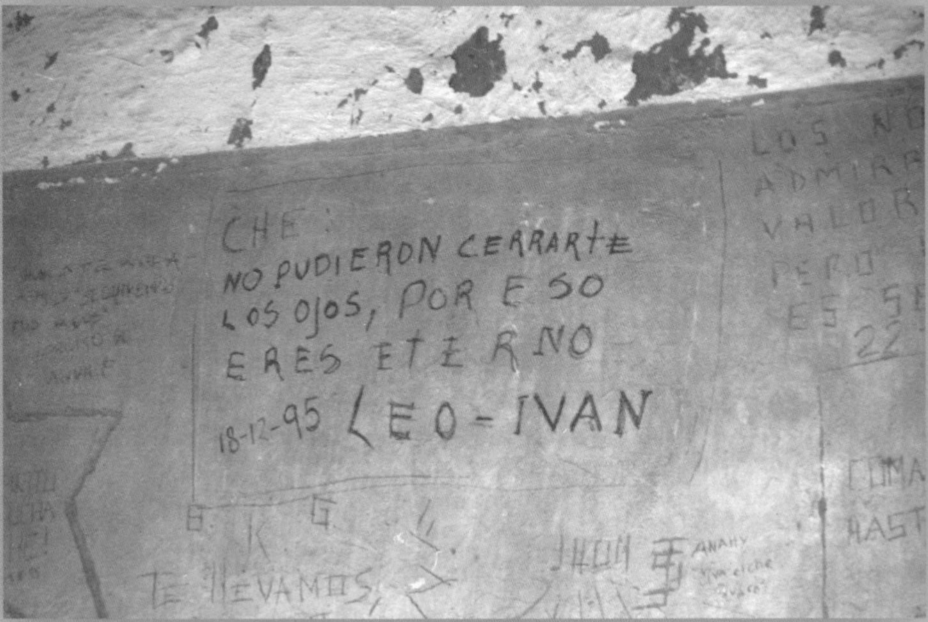

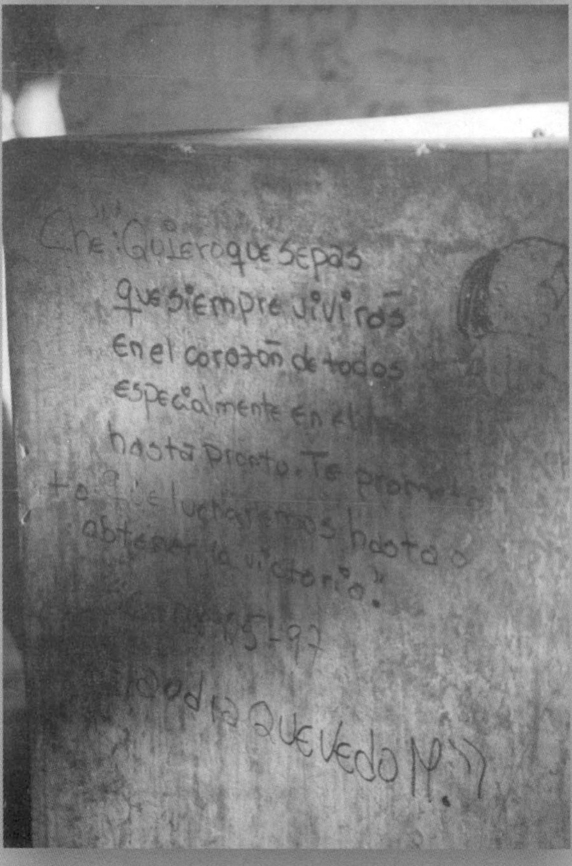

A wall of the laundry at the Lord of Malta Hospital.

Graciela Rodríguez, a washerwoman at the Vallegrande Hospital. She helped nurse Susana Osinagas to dress Che's lifeless body.

Susana Osinagas, the nurse that participated in the preparation of Che's body. She undressed him and bathed him on October 9, the day of his death.

Susana Osinagas, the nurse that participated in the preparation of Che's body.

Élida Hidalgo, the teacher, together with Eugenio Rosell and Dr. Gerardo Muñoz. To the left, Pucará's former mayor.

President of Bolivia Evo Morales, Cuban Ambassador Rafael Daussá Céspedes, and other important figures at the inauguration of a medical station at La Higuera. June 14, 2006.

Act of remembrance on Che's date of birth. La Higuera, June 14, 2006.

Homage to Che at La Higuera.

Participants in the act of June 14, 2006.

Fall of General Alfredo Ovando

The splits in the Armed Forces were known by all sectors of the Bolivian capital.

On September 27, 1970, the day before the first anniversary of the coup that brought him to power, Ovando decided to put at the disposal of the Armed Forces his post as President of the Republic. Once more the General's decision created deep divisions.

On October 3, 1970, groups of students, workers, peasants, professionals, journalists, progressive priests and young officers of the Armed Forces, offered Ovando their full support on the condition that he dismiss the three pro-coup commanders and the rightist military infiltrated in the government.

According to these sources, US Ambassador Ernest Siracusa damned the Bolivians and said that the country was the most inflammable nation in Latin America, and if the fire was not put out soon, the flames would be visible from Washington.

But events stepped up their pace when Minister of the Interior Juan Ayoroa ordered the arrest of General Juan José Torres on charges of conspiracy. Popular pressure against the order forced the Council of Ministers to resign. Yet when everyone thought that the new cabinet would reflect a return of Ovando to the nationalist positions proclaimed on September 26 and the radicalization of the process, what happened was quite the contrary.

The right strengthened its positions, Ovando promised the return to constitutionality and of foreign capital.

Minister of Interior Ayoroa reemerged with new force. He accused international communism of fomenting the urban guerrilla, closed down the weekly *Prensa*, published by the journalist's labor union, and which supported the nationalist process, and ordered the arrest of its editor, Andrés Solis Rada, who a few days before had alerted the country about a counterrevolutionary plot headed by the Minister of the Interior himself.

Ovando decided to pay the Bolivian Gulf Oil Company the sum of $71 million dollars as compensation. He promised to indict those who denounced alleged subversive plans, including his former minister Marcelo Quiroga Santa Cruz, who claimed that a coup had been organized and that the plotters were free.

Ovando's promises caused a wave of protests, for Quiroga was the most prestigious, radical and nationalist of his former ministers.

The same sources point out that Minister of the Interior Ayoroa declared: "Everybody knows about the coup, and the only one that seems to ignore is Ovando himself."

On the morning of October 4, Commander of the Army General Rogelio Miranda, communicated to the country from the Great Miraflores Barracks the end of the political mandate of the Armed Forces and of General Alfredo Ovando. In his place he proclaimed himself President of the Republic. All that day radio stations repeated the communiqué informing of the coup d'etat. However, General Miranda did not risk leaving the Miraflores Barracks.

Immediately General Juan José Torres headed to El Alto Air Force Base to resist the rightist coup, together with a group of civilians and of the military. Two poles of power had been created –rightists at the Miraflores Barracks, and nationalists at the air base.

An important factor was added to the events. At the Greater University of San Andrés in La Paz, the Political Command of the COB was installed, thanks to the initiative of the university rector, Pablo Ramos, who with several professors and political leaders invited Juan Lechín Oquendo and the COB's Executive Committee to a meeting. At the deliberations the idea of the Political Command emerged, formed by the Executive Committee of the COB, university authorities and representatives of the six parties of the left: Jorge Kolle Cueto for the Communist Party, Professor Raúl Ruiz González for the Marxist-Leninist Communist Party, Guillermo Lora for the Revolutionary Workers' Party, Dr. Hernán Siles Zuazo for the Revolutionary Nationalist Movement, Antonio Aranibar and Alfonso Camacho for the Revolutionary Christian Democratic Party, Dulfredo Rua Bejerano for the Spartacus Revolutionary Movement. Víctor López and Filemón Escóbar were also attending on behalf of the Miners' Labor Union Federation.

On October 6, Juan Lechín Oquendo and Antonio Aranibar were appointed to meet with General Torres. This decision was the determining factor in favor of the existing correlation of forces.

Journalists in radio stations and newspapers played a decisive role urging the population to resist the coup and to back General Torres and the COB. Of particular importance was the work by Jorge Mancilla Torres, Coco *Manto,* Clovis Díaz, Andrés Solis Rada and the journalists' labor union; likewise prominent religious figures, including evangelicals, Methodists and lay persons. Father José Prats declared that the coup was inspired and led by the Devil.

On October 6 Ovando requested political asylum in the Argentine Embassy. There were serious disagreements in the high command about who should be the new president. Due to irreconcilable divisions, a triumvirate was formed by General Efraín Guachilla, representing the Army; General Fernando Sattori Rivera, on behalf of the Air Force; and Rear Admiral Alberto Albarracín, for the Naval Force.

On that same day, before the swearing ceremony that would take place at 16:30 hours, the Air Force began its attack on the Miraflores Barracks. The ceremony was postponed until 21:00 hours.

In many political and social circles of the Bolivian capital it was claimed that CIA officer John Maisto was the organizer of the coup.

However, the US Embassy, the CIA Station and the coup plotters had not counted on the Bolivian people. The Political Command called for a general strike, and the occupation of factories and work centers until the triumvirate was expelled. Students occupied the universities, peasants blocked roads and highways. The popular forces took to the streets, plazas and avenues. In Oruro, the population forced the retreat of 2nd Division troops marching to the capital in support of the rightist coup.

The nationalist military resisted with the support of the Air Force. General Fernando Sattori Rivera resigned to the triumvirate and joined the resisting forces. When Air Force planes zoomed over La Paz, the coup plotters were terrified.

On October 7, the figure of Juan José Torres emerged victorious. Plans by the CIA and the US Embassy failed for the time being.

The CIA destabilizes Juan José Torres' government

Arrival of Juan José Torres to power

At 10 a.m. on October 7, 1970, General Juan José Torres arrived at the Palace of Government. Ten minutes later he was sworn in as new President of Bolivia in the midst of a demonstration of workers, university students and people in general. Torres promised them that he would move forward in the revolutionary changes and those present cheered him and sang the National Anthem stressing the last stanza to reassert "To die before living as slaves", which was heard all over Murillo Square and its surroundings.

The Americans were concerned, for Torres' ascent to power had not been foreseen. The situation in Bolivia presented a serious scenario for imperialist interests. In Peru, Juan Velasco Alvarado was consolidating a revolution. General Omar Torrijos in Panama was becoming more radical. In Chile, socialist Salvador Allende had won the presidential election.

As soon as Torres was sworn in, the CIA began plotting to overthrow him, and with this objective in mind encouraged the rightist military to resist and not surrender their arms. At dawn on October 8, union leaders Juan Lechín Oquendo and Simón Reyes gave their full support to the new president. The rules of a co-government were discussed at the Palace itself.

Meanwhile, the Workers' Central and the University Federation of Bolivia met and drafted a popular mandate with the following points: the formation and acknowledgement of a political command that included leaders of the working class, university students, popular parties and the people; the ouster of fascist groups —whether military or civilian—, of missions and agencies of US imperialism; a full amnesty for all anti-imperialist prisoners; repeal of the decree of compensation for the Bolivian Gulf Oil Company; the establishment of workers' control in private companies; the validity of workers' and people's militias side by side with the patriotic armed forces; the transfer of the Bolivian-American Center to the university; radicalization of the agrarian reform; an independent foreign policy; and diplomatic relations with the rest of the socialist countries.

According to Oiga magazine (No. 394, October 8, 1970) Ovando "had everything at his disposal: military power, civilian support, the opportunity of the moment (but) he froze at the start and after a prolonged agony he went out in an undistinguished manner". The article assured that of the Ovando that on September 26, 1969 "pretended to wear the attributes of a leftist nationalism that did not fit him, of the chief of the revolution that on his first day asked for a formation of an 'ideological axis La Paz-Lima', of the leader that at Murillo Square signed the decree of expulsion of Gulf Oil, there is nothing left, barely the shadow of a man [...] that is not strong enough to define his wishes, perhaps because the revolution did not reach the bottom of his soul, as antimony reaches the utmost folds of his people's lungs [...]"

In relation to Juan José Torres and the process sparked by him, the magazine said:

"But since the heart of the Trans Andean Indian is as large as the shaft that swallows him at the mine, after Ovando's fall there is a new possibility incarnate in another military officer, olive colored skin and a mustache like the legendary Mexican revolutionaries: General Juan José Torres, the victor in a struggle for power."

And it ended saying that of "Juan José Torres Bolivians know that it was the impatient military officer that occupied on October 17 the Bolivian Gulf Oil Company's facilities in Santa Cruz, hours before General Ovando had signed the decree of expropriation at Quemado Palace. They also know that in his post as Commander

275

in Chief of the Bolivian Armed Forces he gave shelter to the leftist nationalist civilians in Ovando's first cabinet and that later were detached like kernels from a ripe corn cob when the rightist military entrenched in the regime grew strong. And lastly, they know that under his leftist revolutionary uniform beats a nationalist heart."

The ELN executes Dr. Hebert Miranda Pereira and Lieut. Col. Roberto *Toto* Quintanilla

Dr. Hebert Miranda Pereira had been sentenced to death by the ELN for murdering Inti Peredo, torturing political prisoners and administering drugs to make them confess their revolutionary activities. The sentence was carried out on October 9, 1970.

Sometime later another ELN commando executed Toto Quintanilla in Europe. The media at the time reported: "Spectacular execution of Toto Quintanilla. He was killed when a guerrilla commando hunted him down at the other side of the Atlantic. He was a cruel torturer. In Hamburg, Federal Republic of Germany, a pretty woman took his life."

Other news dispatches reported from Hamburg that the event took place in broad daylight at the Bolivian consulate on November 25, 1970.

Toto Quintanilla, one of the most notorious chiefs of Bolivia's political police since Barrientos took power, was a CIA agent. He was known for his brutal repression, his violent character and the use of barbaric and extremely cruel methods of torture.

Together with CIA agents Félix Ramos, Eduardo González and Julio Gabriel García he participated against Che's guerrilla. He also ordered to cut off the hands from Che's corpse. Quintanilla murdered Inti Peredo and many other Bolivian revolutionaries. For all these crimes the ELN of Bolivia sentenced him to death.

Quintanilla asked to be relieved, on condition that he be sent to the Bolivian Consulate in Hamburg. His petition was accepted and he left Bolivia convinced that he would live a quiet life in that European city. Press reports claim that shortly after he had moved to Hamburg a guerrilla command headed by a beautiful woman named Monica Earlt arrived in town. A slender and good looking blonde, she was a frequent visitor to the Consulate, posing as a

German student that wanted to visit Bolivia. The story goes that Ms Earlt's cleverness and her apparent naiveté convinced Quintanilla that she could be trusted. When he decided to grant her a visa, he invited her into his office. She entered in a calm manner, greeted the Consul, and when he stretched out his hand, she reached into her purse, pulled out a gun and shot him twice in the chest. When Quintanilla's wife heard the shots she ran to the office in time to see a beautiful woman leaving the premises. She tried to stop her grabbing the woman by the hair, but only a wig remained in her hands. Meanwhile, the young woman left the Consulate and got into an automobile that was waiting with the engine running.

The National Liberation Army of Bolivia assumed the responsibility for the killing and declared that Colonel Roberto *Toto* Quintanilla had brutally repressed leftist groups and had had disastrous participation in the 1967 guerrilla events.

On April 9, Colonel Toto Quintanilla's remains were flown to Bolivia on Lufthansa Flight 490, escorted by Klaus Georg Altmann, the son of Nazi war criminal Klaus Barbie.

Monica Earlt was the daughter of Hans Earlt, a German researcher and anthropologist residing in Bolivia, where she was born. The young woman escaped from the German police, the CIA and the Bolivian secrete services, and returned to Bolivia to continue the struggle.

The people back Juan José Torres and the rightwing military and the CIA plot

The Workers' Central and the University Confederation agreed to create a commission to negotiate with the Teoponte guerrilla about Torres' promise to respect their lives and allowing them to leave the country in exchange for putting down their arms. A spokesman from Torres' private secretaryship assured that guarantees would be given on the guerrillas' personal safety in the interest of national unity and the validity of the patriotic process that had been initiated. The government authorized the Peace Commission to go to the guerrilla zone. When the Commission arrived they were horrified to find out that all prisoners had been murdered by order of the military chiefs in the area. However, with the help of miners and farmers from Teoponte and Tipuani they were able to contact the survivors, arrive to an agreements and transport them to La Paz. Several days later the young guerrillas left for Chile accompanied by Bolivian Red Cross president Celso Rosell, Tipuani parish priest Father Ricardo Sanalde and the University of La Paz's rector Oscar Prudencio Cossío.

The CUB denounced to public opinion that guerrillas Ricardo Justiniano, Moisés Rueda Peña, Clemente Fernández, Carlos Rueda Cortés, Francisco Irakaki Vera, Julio Zambrano and Fredy Soria Galvarro had been murdered by the army. The news caused great indignation in the country. The burial of the first victims was truly impressive. A tribute was paid also at the School of Medicine to Raúl Ibarguen, José Paravicini and Horacio Rueda Peña. Father José Bassiana, a Jesuit, spoke about young Néstor Paz Zamora and stressed that to be a Christian is to struggle for revolution.

The local press reported the funeral in the following manner: the first fallen in the guerrilla —Adolfo Quiroga Bonadona, Juan José Saavedra, Antonio Figueroa and Adolfo Huici— caused a great demonstration of grief that took to through the main streets of La Paz in an uncommon funeral procession.

The coffins were taken to the Pérez Velasco Square on the shoulders of relatives, university students and friends. Famous popular artists and folk groups were in attendance, among them Los Caminantes, José Zapata, Pocho Novel, Gerardo Amézaga, Los Sin Nombres, Los Caballeros del Folclore, Hortica Gutiérrez, and many others.

Ana Harvey, who attended the funeral, told that the crowd cried while the remains were buried in their respective crypts to the sound of drums, guitars, *quenas* and *charangos* playing *La samba del adiós* (Goodbye Samba) and *No te dejaremos morir* (We Won't Let You Die). A mountain of flowers and wreaths covered their graves.

On November 17 Torres signed the decree that reversed Barrientos' 1965 order reducing miners' salaries. Ten days later he visited the Huanuni mines, where miners assured him that if he stayed on the revolutionary course they would follow him to final victory. The miners requested that he expel from the country the US military missions, the Peace Corps and all instruments of US imperialism, and asked for guns to defend the revolutionary process.

Previously Juan Lechín Oquendo had addressed the miners to tell them that the Americans wanted to (agarrar) the Bolivian government with the military missions, which are charged with shaping a mentality in the army turn the military into true representatives of the Pentagon. He also said that in order to be independent it was necessary that Torres kick those missions and the Peace Corps out of the country, because under that cover they did espionage. The ILO, another form of imperialist penetration in labor unions, should also be dealt with.

On November 30 the bodies of guerrillas Hugo Rodríguez, Carlos Navarro Lara, Arturo Callapiña, Enrique Farfán, Javier Landívar and Emilio Quiroga Bonadona were released. Quiroga's parents discovered that the remains were not their son's. Meanwhile, the government promised to release the remaining 43 in the following days.

After workers took over the newspapers *Los Tiempos* (Cochabamba), and *El Diario* and *Hoy* (La Paz), they decided to organize them into cooperatives. At Santa Cruz de la Sierra, a group of 150 armed peasants occupied barren lands. While the nationalist process was becoming more radical, the US Embassy in La Paz, the CIA Station and rightist sectors continued plotting. On December 9 it was discovered that a terrorist attempt was being prepared to murder Juan José Torres when the President would attend a graduation of cadets at the Military College in La Paz.

Groups of students occupied the Bolivian-American Center and subordinated it to the University of La Paz.

On December 24, Torres decreed the freedom of Regis Debray, Ciro Roberto Bustos and others imprisoned for their relation to Che's guerrilla. The measure angered rightist sectors who accused General Torres of being a prisoner of the left.

On January 10 there was a military uprising that was immediately crushed when great demonstrations against the coup took to the street. Sixteen top officers were dismissed from the army and several of them requested asylum in diplomatic facilities in La Paz. It was revealed that the US and Brazilian missions were implicated in the coup attempt.

Torres announced the creation of the Popular Assembly that would have legislative duties and would oversee the revolutionary process. He also promised a new Constitution for the country.

Demonstrators once more asked for arms to guarantee the revolution.

Contradictions between rightists and leftists among the military were increasing. Torres' advisors proposed a large demonstration of all leftist and nationalist forces, patriotic officers and people in general. Since there was a plan to transfer the remains of Bolivian patriot Colonel Gualberto Villarroel to the square named after him, the act could serve to exalt his figure, very much respected for his patriotism and for his defense of the interests of the most humble people.

Torres paid a visit to Elena López, Colonel Villarroel's widow, to get her consent. All was ready and a large demonstration of support for the revolutionary process and the leftist military was expected. It would be an anti US, anti-imperialist and nationalist act.

While preparations were on course and the process advancing, a German citizen resident of Bolivia, Richard Hebert, made sensational revelations to the press. He declared that Ovando and his main collaborators had masterminded the murders of General Barrientos, Senator Jorge Soliz Román, journalist Jaime Otero Calderón, Alfredo Alexander Jordán and his wife Marta Dupleych; that Ovando's political ambitions and the interest to silence other crimes committed during his government were the motives for those murders. This caused a scandal that made Torres create an investigative commission. Torres ordered Ovando back from Madrid, where he had been appointed Ambassador, so that he could clarify his position in relation to the serious charges. Ovando refused to comply and the fact increased the discredit of the Armed Forces.

Subsequently it was known that Richard Hebert was a CIA agent and that the agency had supplied him the information with the purpose of tarnishing the image of nationalist officers, particularly General Torres' —who had shared power with Ovando—, but especially to discredit the civic acts and the demonstration in honor of Colonel Villarroel.

The prestige of the Bolivian Armed Forces was so seriously affected that Villaroel's widow sent Torres a letter that read as follows:

"General Torres, I must refer to our conversation at the visit with which Your Excellency honored my house. Together with my

280

children I have reflected on the project of transferring the remains of my husband to the monument on Villaroel Square in a solemn act of tribute to his memory next July 21.

"The events of the past months of unease and anarchy in the very heart of the Armed Forces, and even more serious still, the tremendous revelations that shocked the country about massacres, crimes and murders in which generals and main exponents of officialdom are involved, have created an unpropitious atmosphere for the dignified objective of that purpose or when the press continually expresses the loss of prestige suffered by the Armed Forces and reflects the uneasiness of peasants and of labor unions, university and professional associations in view of the moral relaxation that prevents the action of justice.

"For this reasons and being in the public conscience the sacrifice of Colonel Gualberto Villarroel for the Bolivianist (sic) ideals that he defended with immaculate honesty, keeping high the decorum and honor of the Armed Forces of the Nation, my children and I feel obliged to inform you that it is not prudent nor appropriate at this moment to remove the remains of my husband from the humble grave where the destitute classes maintain the perpetual tribute of their flowers.

"I take advantage of the occasion to greet the General with my highest and most distinguished consideration."

The conspiracy gained strength. US Ambassador Siracusa made an angered claim that his correspondence had been violated and that several US officials had been raided. However, he was publicly accused of masterminding the conspiracy and that his protests were a part of it.

The University Confederation and the Workers' Central revealed that the CIA had a plan to murder Juan Lechín Oquendo, and that agent William Schwank Hagenbeck had been appointed to commit the crime.

In the midst of US attempts to overthrow Juan José Torres' government May Day was celebrated. Journalist Lupe Cajías describes it in the following manner:

"The demonstration was tremendous. The column headed by the COB vindicated Che and the fallen guerrillas. In Cochabamba, workers supported socialism as the only way out and university students occupied the seat of the Bolivian-American Center. In

Oruro, for the first time the ELN marched in public in one of the largest workers' demonstrations in the history of that mining district. University students took over the Oruro Tin Foundry. In Santa Cruz the ELN flag was raised and in Sucre the great march with enormous images of Che and Inti demonstrated amid dynamite explosions."

Juan Lechín declared that as long as the CIA and the Pentagon existed, General Juan José Torres could not sleep in peace, neither at his home nor at the Palace, and workers even less. He also called for the expulsion of the US military mission.

Lupe Cajías wrote that when COB columns marched in La Paz in front of the Palace of Government, Juan José Torres announced the expulsion of the US military mission in Bolivia. The miners shouted, "Socialism! Socialism! Socialism!"

The decapitated body of representative Zacarías Plaza is found

Representative Zacarías Plaza, who had been wounded in an attack on August 20, 1970, was found decapitated in the La Paz-Oruro highway on June 11, 1971.

The letters ELN were carved on the head and there was a sign in which a group of miners called The Eye of the Eagle took responsibility for the execution.

Zacarías Plaza committed multiple crimes and led the most repudiated massacre ever made in Bolivia, known as the "Massacre of the Night of San Juan", on June 24, 1967.

Bolivian researcher and journalist Lupe Cajías wrote about some of these crimes in her book *The History of a Legend*: soldiers ripped open a pregnant mining woman's abdomen; other soldiers raided a miner's house and when they only found his wife with her little children hiding under the bed, they fired their machine guns killing the mother and the boys. The oldest of the children, a daughter, was the only survivor, but her legs had to be amputated.

Uruguayan writer Eduardo Galeano, in his book *Memories of the Fire*, included the testimonial of Domitila Chungara, also published by Brazilian writer Moema Viezzer, who included it in her book *If I Am Allowed to Speak: The Testimonial of Domitila, a Woman in the Mines of Bolivia.*

On this woman, writes Moema Viezzer: "She lives in two rooms, no latrine and no water, with her miner husband and seven children. Child number eight wants to emerge from her belly. Every day Domitila cooks, washes, sweeps, weaves, sews, teaches what she knows and heals what she can, and also prepares one hundred turnovers and roams the streets looking for buyers."

Domitila, was accused of being a guerrilla liaison and interrogated by a soldier during the massacre of San Juan. She told the Brazilian journalist:

"He spat in my face. Then he kicked me. I didn't hold back and slapped his face. He punched me. I scratched his face. And he kept hitting me, hitting me... He kneeled on my stomach. He squeezed my throat and was about to choke me. It looked as if he wanted to make my belly explode. He was squeezing harder and harder. Then with my two hands, with all my strength I lowered his hands. And I don't remember how, but I was grabbing him by a fist and was biting him, biting... I was terribly revolted when I felt his blood in my mouth... Then, with all my anger, tcha, I spat his own blood in his face. There was a terrible shout. He was kicking me and shouting... He called other soldiers and made four of them grab me...

"When I woke up like from a dream I was choking on a piece of tooth. I felt it here in my throat. Then I noticed that the guy had broken six of my teeth. Blood was running and I could not open my eyes or my nose...

"And as it was my fate, I began my labor. I started to feel pain, pain, pain and sometimes the child overcame me to be born... I could resist no more. I went to kneel in a corner. I leaned and covered my face, because I had no strength at all. My face hurt terribly. And in one of those moments I was overcome. I noticed that the head of my little child was coming out... And I passed out.

"I don't know after how much time:

"Where am I? Where am I?

"I was all wet. Both blood and the liquid from childbirth had made me all wet. So then I made an effort and found my child's cord. And by the cord, pulling the cord, I found my little child, totally cold, ice cold, there on the floor."

Zacarías Plaza, besides leading the Massacre of the Nigh of San Juan and tortures to many miners, was directly responsible for many crimes in the mines of Catavi, Huanuni, Llallagua and Siglo XX.

His death was never solved. Some believe it was the miners who took revenge for so many crimes committed; others claim the CIA paid members of Zacarías Plaza's gang with the purpose of shifting the blame on the ELN and the miners. That is why they carved the ELN initials on the cut head. They also chose a date close to June 24 to link it to the massacre at the mines on the Night of St. John.

The Bolivian people call for a popular assembly and the reestablishing of diplomatic relations with Cuba

The COB called for the creation of a Popular Assembly, which was formally inaugurated on June 22, 1971, chaired by Juan Lechín Oquendo, and the participation of political leaders Oscar Eid Franco, president of the Bolivian University Confederation; Antonio Aranibar, for the Revolutionary Christian Democratic Party; Pablo Ramos, for the Spartacus Movement; Jorge Ríos Dalence and Adalberto Kuajara, for the Christian Democrats; and René Zavaleta Mercado, for the Revolutionary Nationalist Movement.

The Popular Assembly voted to be established in each of the nine departments of the Bolivian nation: La Paz, Santa Cruz, Tarija, Pando, Beni, Oruro, Cochabamba, Chuquisaca and Potosí. Likewise, at every work center, university and peasant association the political commandos were created. They also decided to create militias and popular courts, people's jails and the immediate expulsion of the CIA, the FBI and the Peace Corps.

In a massive act at Vallegrande, the authorities and the townspeople voted to name an important street as Commander Ernesto Che Guevara Avenue, while the Popular Assembly, echoing the will of ample sectors of the country, demanded the reestablishment of diplomatic relations with Cuba.

For the festivities of July 26, 1971, a delegation of miners, workers, peasants and students went to Cuba on behalf of the Popular Assembly and the people of Bolivia, with the mission of asking the Revolutionary Government of Cuba the reestablishment of diplomatic relations.

Coup d'etat against Juan José Torres

On August 19, 1971, the newspaper *Jornada* reported that Barrientos' followers, led by the US Embassy, tried to silence it and Altiplano Radio Station because they were disseminating an important meeting of a group called People's Military Vanguard, where they declared that they would only follow the people's orders. On Saturday, the 21, the coup d'etat organized by the CIA and the US Embassy was launched. The people resisted from the beginning, which resulted in several dead and wounded. Radio stations asked for urgent aid in bandages, cotton, different types of blood and reported a great deal of dead and wounded. Airplanes bombed the main points of resistance.

On Sunday, the 22, there was a truce to remove the dead from the streets. Conservative estimates considered the casualties at over 100 dead and 600 wounded, but months later it was known that they were more than 1,500.

There was an announcement that a new triumvirate would rule the country, formed by General Jaime Mendieta and Colonels Hugo Banzer Suárez and Andrés Sélich Shop.

Tanks surrounded the university and opened fire against that institution. Eye witnesses claim that soldiers threw students out of their classrooms, and kicked and beat them. The universities of Tarija, Sucre, Potosí, Oruro, Cochabamba, Trinidad and Santa Cruz were violently repressed, peasants and miners were massacred and radio stations occupied by the military.

The resistance in several points in the capital was brutally silenced. Many students and workers were executed, or simply shot dead, as in the cases of Vladimir, the son of Modesto Reinaga, brother of guerrilla Aniceto Reinaga; and of Rubén Sánchez, the son of army Major Sánchez Valdivia, who had fallen prisoner to Che at the ambush of April 10, 1967.

Special repression groups, put together and trained by the American, took to the streets to finish off the subversion. Andrés Sélich, Rafael Loayza and Guido Benavides personally led all the repression.

Mauricio Lefebre, a Canadian priest of the Order of the Oblates, and a professor of Sociology at the Greater University of San Andrés, died from a shot to the head. Lefebvre was close to the poor and most humble in Bolivia. Together with the students he participated in the protest marches against the visit of Assistant Secretary of State for Inter-American Affairs Charles Meyer. On another occasion he addressed the students that had gathered in front of the house where Inti Peredo had fallen shouting "We will avenge you!"

Father Lefebre joined the hunger strike that claimed the bodies of the Teoponte guerrillas. He was the keynote speaker at the memorial services on the first anniversary of Che's assassination.

Once the resistance was crushed and the Palace of Government had been taken, the triumvirate distributed the posts: President, Colonel Hugo Banzer; Minister of Defense, General Jaime Mendieta; and Minister of the Interior, Colonel Andrés Sélich Shop.

From that moment on in Bolivia began the practice of missing persons and one of the most ferocious repressions that the country had seen. Sélich declared to the press that his goal was to finish off the Reds first, and then move on against crooks.

The university was closed. Radio stations and newspaper occupied by the army. The daily *Presencia,* Bolivia's most influential newspaper, practically lost all its reporters. Of 17 before the coup only 3 remained. Religious institutions were violated to such a point that priests and nuns that defended the humble people were harassed. Union leaders, professionals, peasants, intellectuals, politicians and students were concentrated in special prisons, for which more than 200 of them had to be transferred to an army regiment. Members of the Armed Forces that were linked to progressive, nationalist and anti-US positions were eliminated in different ways. Some were arrested, others were discharged from the army or were forced into exile.

The lists of prisoners and exiled in the country included hundreds of names, and later thousands. The number of those murdered and disappeared was never determined.

Special torture houses were set up, and new concentration camps were opened, such as Achocalla, Chonchocoro, DOP, Pari and the island of Cuati.

The CIA began restructuring the Bolivian intelligence services in such a cynical fashion that Nazi criminal Klaus Barbie was reinstated in the post that he had occupied during the Barrientos government. Barbie right away began to form a special repressive group that years later was known as the "Fiancés of Death".

The peace and tranquility that the Americans had always asked for was being imposed.

On the same day of the coup the Revolutionary Left Movement (MIR) made its public appearance and through radio broadcasts called on its leaders and members to confront the fascist coup and defeat it. The movement went underground. On September 7 its first national underground direction was formally constituted by Jaime Paz Zamora, Antonio Aranibar, Oscar Eid Franco and others.

Contradictions in the new Bolivian government

The new Bolivian government, lacking any unity, rapidly deteriorated. Rivalries and ambitions of power among the military became public. In this sense there was a special virulence between Andrés Sélich and Hugo Banzer. In his book *Power and Armed Forces,* Gary Prado wrote:

"The next problem for President Banzer's government is generated by his own Minister of the Interior. Col. Andrés Sélich, surrounded by a group of collaborators that goaded him constantly, hoped to become the government's key figure. An intense advertising campaign was launched to present him as the true leader of the revolution and a representative of nationalism. Competing with the President he travels to the country's main cities where he is greeted by popular demonstrations organized by his followers that proclaim him a hero.

"The Minister of the Interior is permanently surrounded by a showy security display that included a motorcycle escort, several patrol cars and a large number of aides. He went with this entourage to public events, also arriving after the President, causing interruptions, commentaries and disruption of protocol that began to annoy Col. Banzer, who finally, to put order in his administration and reinforce his authority, decided to surprisingly reshuffle the cabinet on December 29, 1971, excluding the controversial former Rangers commander who was thus deprived of his power and influence.

"Considering he received no institutional backing, after a few days he decided to accept the post of ambassador to Paraguay, where he went without hiding his displeasure and his opposition to President Banzer."

Bolivian sources said that Sélich entourage arrived in advance to towns he was going to visit and hired music bands, distributed lots of *chicha* and *salteñas*. They paid a fee to those who attended, and also put up billboards, advertisings, posters, and painted signs with welcome phrases. After the act, they collected everything in a hurry and went to the next town to organize the same circus.

After his departure from the Ministry of the Interior, it was found that he had spent over $100,000 dollars from the budget to pay people for attending the demonstrations that received him as a hero.

Colonel Andrés Sélich dies from a beating and General Joaquín Zenteno Anaya is shot to death

From the Paraguayan capital Colonel Andrés Sélich continued with his plotting, now increased by resent and hate toward the Bolivian president. He prepared an assassination attempt against General Banzer on the occasion of a visit he would make to that country, but the Bolivian secret services knew of the plan and took measures to disrupt it. For this matter, Sélich was dismissed as ambassador.

In early May, 1973, he went back clandestinely to Bolivia with a false passport supplied by the Paraguayan secret services. The purpose of the trip was to put the finishing touches to a new coup and an assassination attempt against Banzer.

Minister of the Interior Alfredo Arce Carpio was duly informed and ordered Sélich arrested. An operative group of the Ministry detained him and held him at the home of the Minister himself. While he was being interrogated and violently beaten, a karate blow shattered his liver. He died minutes later at the Minister's own house. The event caused a political scandal of great proportions that forced Dr. Arce Carpio to resign and acknowledge his responsibility in the crime.

The official report of Sélich's death, released to the press by Minister of Information Jaime Caballero Tamayo, reads as follows:

"Sélich and other comrades were arrested without any bloodshed. But when he was taken to the Ministry of the Interior, on Arce Avenue, neighborhood of Sopocachi, Sélich tried to escape, losing his balance and falling down the steps from the second floor. An impact to the head proved fatal for the former Minister of the Interior, as later was confirmed by the medical examination."

Important military circles friendly to Sélich did not believe the report and began to pressure for an investigation. Meanwhile the scandal reached great proportions.

The Bolivian press gave the fact great coverage. On May 18, 1973 the daily *Última Hora* reported:

"Minister Arce adopts unprecedented attitude.

"The Truth: a New Style in Bolivian politics.

"Around midnight and before some thirty journalists from local media and foreign agencies, Minister Alfredo Arce, accompanied by Minister of Information Jaime Caballero Tamayo, revealed in an unprecedented act in our political history the truth about the death of Colonel Andrés Sélich. Journalists were summoned at 10:30 to the Minister's office and a few minutes before editors from the main papers had been summoned to Banzer's residence, where they conversed with the President, who asked them to treat with seriousness and meditation the information that some time later would be given by the Minister of the Interior.

"On entering Minister Arce's office, the reporters saw on his face the traces of fatigue and the strain under which he has been living the past few days. However, with a calm and sure voice, Minister Arce gave the final version of the facts.

"According to this new official version, former Minister Sélich died as a consequence of 'a single punch' to his right side by one of the three agents that had been charged with his interrogation.

"Visibly contrite, Dr. Arce recalled his previous appearance before the press the previous Tuesday, when he claimed that Colonel Sélich's death had been caused by an accidental fall down the stairs of a house in Calacoto, where apparently there is a facility of the Ministry of the Interior that up to the moment no one knew of its existence. On that opportunity the Minister assumed the responsibility for the unfortunate accident that cost Colonel Sélich his life and underscored the purpose of the government of governing under the rule of law and the truth.

"At last night's meeting with La Paz journalists, he told how when he was informed of Sélich's arrest he had ordered three agents

—Mario Zambrano Morales, Carlos Betancourt Pacelly and Juan Cassis Quiroga—to take him to his own home and that after a reasonable length of time transfer him to the Calacoto facility. This last order was never carried out.

"Underscoring the accidental character of the unfortunate event, the Minister said: 'Gentlemen, as you must be aware of, no one, much less a Minister of the Interior, would send a person to his home to be mistreated, or worse still, killed.'

"He revealed how after having given instructions for the transfer and interrogation of the detainee, he went to his office, where he was informed by telephone that 'due to an act caused by the state of nervous crisis in which Colonel Sélich was, he had lost consciousness.'

However, considering the Minister himself, who is also a man of the law, that the truth that his subordinates had given him was far from satisfactory, he decided to widen the investigation, having obtained from the three agents the confession that the Colonel's death was caused by blows dealt him by his interrogators.

"The Minister declared that he was not totally satisfied with this version, for it does not explain fractures of the ribs, adding that it is necessary to specify that the real cause of death must have been in the liver's fragility due to an advanced state of cirrhosis (…)

"He announced then that the three responsible agents, together with the obrados in the case would be delivered to the ordinary justice, which according to our judicial procedures is the one that must establish responsibilities and sanctions."

Andrés Sélich, besides his bloodthirsty attitude during the events at La Higuera and the violent treatment he gave to the Heroic Guerrilla, and being one of the architects of repressive policies in Bolivia after the coup against General Juan José Torres, had as Minister of the Interior direct responsibility in the Massacre at the University of Santa Cruz and of the death of peasants in that department. Together with CIA agents and US advisors, the Colonel organized a true criminal machinery that finally ended up swallowing him too.

Among the military who protested with energy for the form and circumstances of the crime was Joaquín Zenteno Anaya, who because of discrepancies with the upper echelons of government had been taken out of Bolivia by appointing him ambassador to

France. There were assurances that Zenteno Anaya, together with Andrés Sélich and other officers were implicated in the coup attempt. On May 11, 1976, Zenteno was shot to death in Paris.

The Bolivian press reported the assassination in the following manner:

"The tragic attempt that took the life of one of the most distinguished and outstanding military officers of the Bolivian army was perpetrated when the midday sun lit the banks of the Seine River that flows through the City of Lights. Who would have thought that in broad daylight an illustrious life would be mowed down with the ease that an insect is killed?"

And the report goes on: "The Bolivian Embassy in Paris is located at Klebert Avenue, very close to the Arch of Triumph (L'Etoile). It is one of the great avenues adorned with large gardens and beautiful parks. Traffic is heavy all day long. In its surroundings there are numerous accesses to the underground railway network that runs in all directions, transporting thousands and thousands of passengers.

"Among the crowd a young man was waiting, wearing a black beret, with a light step and a thick beard, according to some eye witnesses [...]

"Gen. Zenteno Anaya was watched at all times [...] Everything was planned to perfection, without the loss of a single detail [...]

"At the exact moment in which he came out of his office and went to his automobile taking out his car keys, a man with the characteristics described above took out a gun and acting with lightning speed emptied the homicidal weapon on the ambassador's body [...]

"The Paris police acted immediately and under the pressure of the energetic claims of the Bolivian authorities began an exhaustive investigation of the crime. Experts declared that the perpetrator(s) acted as professionals, without leaving any clues that could be used as a lead for the investigation. Another detail that said experts stressed was the instant disappearance of the aggressors, even if they did not use a vehicle, for they vanished into the subway station [...]"

The only element that the Paris police could obtain was a telephone call from a man that spoke perfect French and declared to the police stenographic service that the execution had been carried out by the Che Guevara International Brigades. According to French police sources, the man had said that they had killed the Bolivian Ambassador in Paris for being responsible for Che Guevara's murder, a tank attack on the University of La Paz in 1971 and for defending before French authorities the reasons why Nazi-Fascist hangman Klaus Barbie, chief of the Gestapo in Lyon, France, enjoyed freedom in Bolivia.

Nevertheless, in Bolivia it was claimed that the reason for his death were due to internal struggles in the Bolivian army caused by rivalries and ambitions of power, and that the military themselves ordered his elimination. These sources indicated that Zenteno Anaya had sent a private letter criticizing the top rulers of Bolivia, whom he accused of several crimes. At the same time he declared he was willing to travel to Bolivia and present in person the evidence he possessed.

The truth was never known. The perpetrators were never found, but his shooting death in a downtown Paris street increased the elements on the legend known as Che's Curse, and in particular the belief that it was God's punishment for the participation of Andrés Sélich and Joaquín Zenteno Anaya in the assassination of Che.

Former president Juan José Torres shot to death in Buenos Aires

When General Juan José Torres was overthrown in 1971 by a bloody military coup, he requested political asylum in Peru, and then went to Chile, where there was a terrorist attempt on his life. He escaped unharmed.

Two years later he moved to Argentina and lived in an apartment in downtown Buenos Aires. On June 3, 1976, when he was leaving his home, four individuals that had been posted a few meters away with their car's engine running, grabbed him and forced him into the automobile. The car sped away. Next day his corpse was found under a highway bridge in the town of Giles, about 100 kilometers away from Buenos Aires. His body was riddled by bullets, face down, with his hands tied and blindfolded.

A peasant that was some distance away saw when four men took him out of a car parked to the side of the road, led him under the bridge and shot him thee times in the head. Then, they slowly returned to the car and went back to Buenos Aires.

The assassins were never found. Some time later, the press at the time said in relation to the possible perpetrators: "The assassins are hired killers paid by repressive organisms like the American CIA, who have total impunity, for up to the moment none have been caught by the police [...]"

Union leader Juan Lechín Oquendo's claim that as long as the CIA and the Pentagon existed, Juan José Torres could not sleep in peace neither at his home nor at the Palace of government had been confirmed.

A press comment expressed that the tragic death of former President Torres was decided without doubt by the CIA's shadowy men due to the radical leftist positions he had adopted when he was president of Bolivia, expelling the US Peace Corps and leading a leftist movement that left an imprint in the Bolivian people.

The assassination caused deep grief in the Bolivian people. The University of La Paz and the Miners' Federation asked that the body be brought to Bolivia to hold a funeral in both of their buildings.

On June 6, when the population was getting ready to pay massive homage to Torres, the Press and Information Secretary of the Presidency of the Republic announced that the cabinet had met at 23:30 hours on Saturday, June 5 to release a communiqué that the transfer of General Torres' remains would not be authorized. A part of the communiqué said: "The Council of Ministers, after a detailed analysis of the situation, and considering the reports circulating in the Ministry of Interior, decided to suspend the repatriation of the deceased President of the Republic's remains."

Student protests increased, so the government decided to close the University of La Paz and others in the rest of the country. They were also forced to cancel the traditional August 7 parade.

The Armed Forces were confined to their barracks for fear of popular condemnations because of the crime.

The miners decreed an indefinite general strike.

Due to the denial of the Bolivian government, Mexican President Luis Echeverría Álvarez offered Torres' widow Emma Obleas to take General Torres' remains to Mexico City and bury him there.

Because of students' and workers' demonstrations the Bolivian government declared a state of siege, placed under military control

Bolivia's most important mines and several union and student leaders were arrested; many others had to go into exile.

Repression continued for almost seven years until, due to popular and international pressure, the Popular Democratic Union formed by the Leftist Revolutionary Nationalist Movement led by Dr. Hernán Siles Zuazo, Jaime Paz Zamora's Revolutionary Leftist Movement, and the Bolivian Communist Party with Jorge Kolle Cueto, ascended to power in 1982 and inaugurated a democratic government.

La Higuera rises against the CIA

Homage in La Higuera

For the CIA and the representatives of the exploiting interests of the US government, for Barrientos and all those who thought like him, the guerrilla had reached its end. They believed that they had heard the last of Che; that the epic would fall into oblivion. They tried to ignore that just ideas can not be killed and that Bolivians descended from common stock that joins all Latin Americans at their very roots.

In their own land fought the Bolivians who founded the National Liberation Army of Bolivia. They were young men and women from different sectors of society –teachers, doctors, peasants, writers, economists, engineers, miners, bakers—, all members of honorable families with a patriotic tradition, some of them descendants of heroes of the Chaco War or of beneméritos of the Motherland. These youngsters explained in their farewell letters to their relatives the reason for joining the liberation movement and their yearnings for social justice.

It was in the vicinity of La Higuera, on October 9, 1967, when the survivors of the guerrilla —Inti, Darío, Ñato, Pombo, Benigno and Urbano— on hearing of Che's fall, swore to continue the struggle. One year later Guido Peredo reorganized the National Liberation Army of Bolivia and called again to the struggle for definite independence.

The ELN reemerged, and its action transcended when in July, 1970, multiplied in 75 young men –most of them university students and professionals from different religious beliefs, but identical ideals of freedom— went into the jungle with ideas brimming of social justice. Of those Teoponte guerrillas, 61 were Bolivians, 4 Argentineans, 6 Chileans, 2 Peruvians and 2 Brazilians.

In a message sent to the media in La Paz, young university students claimed that they had renounced the leadership in order to join as simple soldiers of the glorious army founded by Che: "What is happening now is but a mere example of what will happen in the future, and that makes us trade study for action, the book for the gun and comfortable life for the revolutionary pilgrimage in the geography of our country, fighting the supporters of imperialist exploitation to the death."

Che's enemies wanted to make his body disappear. They officially declared that his ashes had been scattered in the foothills of the Andes. They believed that no one would pay tribute to him, that there would never be a pilgrimage to that piece of forgotten land of Our America where he was murdered and in whose entrails he rested. However, his presence lives on; his serene face of a commander is increasingly loved by all who are humble; his struggle understood and admired; his ideal respected and followed by millions of young people all over the world.

On the 20th anniversary of his assassination, the march to La Higuera was the most outstanding evidence that nothing could stop the course of history nor the veneration that new generations feel and will feel for him wherever his cry for justice was heard.

On October 1, 1987, a representation of the Latin American Generation of the 20th Anniversary of his fall was in Buenos Aires to pay tribute to Commander Che Guevara, most of them Latin American students summoned by the Latin American Continental Organization of Students (OCLAE).

The delegation left an indelible imprint on every town it went through. They traveled in a caravan of buses with the flags of all the Latin American countries, like a rainbow of sister nations that fluttered in the wind of the same pampas that years before a young Ernesto Guevara traveled in a motorcycle.

In the anecdotes about those days, in history evoked, Che was present. His image journeyed through the University of Buenos

Aires' School of Medicine; in Rosario, his hometown: and in Cordoba at the Dean Funes School, in Chile St. and parks and avenues. On passing through, several popular acts greeted it.

In Bolivia they set off from Yacuiba, on the border with Argentina. Through the entire journey they were joined by their Bolivian comrades: workers, miners, students, peasant, religious people, intellectuals and the general public that marched with the visitors until they reached La Higuera. And there, among steep rocks and high hills, remained the legend of the train, the buses and other vehicles that on that October, 1987 came with its load of young voices singing to the Heroic Guerrilla.

Through Vallegrande, Pucará, and Jagüey, "the children of Che", as the townspeople called them, planted seeds and harvested the yield. And the story goes that at La Higuera, the landscape quickened the beat of their hearts, that all gazed anxiously on the trees, the sown fields, the houses, the roads, the heights, the arid land, the stones, the poverty, until they arrived to the little school were Che was murdered.

The mission had been accomplished. In the midst of actions that attempted to intimidate the visitors, a bust made by Bolivian sculptor Pablo Paz was installed. A large cloth with his image was displayed to the sun. Children held in their hands books, pencils and copybooks that Che's heirs had brought to them, and also the small toys, probably the first ones of their lives.

Among the speakers was Rodolfo Saldaña, a member of the urban support network of the guerrilla, and Ramiro Barrenechea, the young university leader who had spoken at the University of Cochabamba meeting in 1967, when the proposition was made that Che should be declared a Bolivian citizen for having fought for the country's liberation. Lastly, Father Miguel Bopp said mass.

On that October 8 the sons of those who fought against the guerrilla were paying homage to Che: present in the march was the first born of then Captain Gary Prado. Admiration and respect aroused the peaks that surrounded La Higuera

Present at the act were the guerrillas: Vitalio Acuña, David Adriazola, Apolinar Aquino, Serapio Aquino, Jaime Arana, Walter Arencibia, Tamara Bunke, Restituto Cabrera, Carlos Coello, Octavio de la Concepción, Casildo Condori, Benjamín Coronado, Simeón Cuba, Pablo Chang Navarro, Alberto Fernández Montes de Oca, Lucio Galván, Moisés Guevara, Mario Gutiérrez, Manuel Hernández, Francisco Huanca, Antonio Jiménez, Gustavo Machín, José María Martínez, René Martínez, Freddy Maymura, Julio Méndez, Orlando Pantoja, Álvaro Peredo, Roberto Peredo, Raúl Quispaya, Aniceto Reinaga, Eliseo Reyes, Israel Reyes, Antonio Sánchez, Jesús Suárez Gayol, Lorgio Vaca, Jorge Vázquez and Ernesto Che Guevara.

They were present in the fervent words of the speakers that echoed in the ravines and in the revolutionary slogans painted on the walls of La Higuera's humble houses.

The generation of the 20th Anniversary spoke through them and with passion announced its Declaration of La Higuera. The second cry for justice launched at La Higuera, which is a call to those who try to ignore the existence of the large dispossessed masses, their needs, their penury, the hunger and the abject poverty that lacerates the soul, shortens life and wears down patience.

Declaration of La Higuera

"Twenty years have passed since Ernesto Che Guevara's blood exploded in the school of La Higuera, where we meet today.

"It was not the first blood nor will it be the last that humanity must shed to defend its dignity, to conquer its right to joy.

"And nevertheless, it is not any offering for the redemption of men. Bolivia has covered twenty years of anguish, of struggle, of sacrifice, of great falls, of intense hopes. The life of the people can not be otherwise as long as it does not achieve its definite emancipation. And on each step, each difficulty, in each dream was present –and will never cease to be— the deed of the consistent and pure, heroically human, generously universal, authentically revolutionary man.

"No one will be able to tear him from our chests, from our conscience shaken since then. No one will be able to surpass neither the astonishment of his death nor the open luminosity of his life. In order to be free, we men and peoples must ascend to that stature, which is the exact level in which history stops being an episode to become the sign of an era.

"Ernesto Che Guevara and the heroes that fought with him, that died with him, are not a myth, because myths demand the bronze to perpetuate themselves in the unconsciousness, stimulated only by the gesture, by the symbol that awakens feeling, passions and epic reflections, but nothing more.

"Che and the men that shared their heroic attempt of 'assaulting heaven' to hand it over to women and children, to men, to the elderly, to the living and those to come are part of our blood, of our bones, of our muscles and brain, but also of the earth, of the tree, the light and the road that will not be closed again to our feet, to our hands, as long as we conserve the authentic human purity of their sacrifice, of their generous dedication. That is the meaning of our commitment; that is the dimension of our homage.

"As Amaru and Bolívar, as Katari, Azurduy, Lira, Villca and Barzola the men that planted their blood in Ñancahuazú come from our history. A new generation of the new man that also opened new routes to the struggle of the Latin American peoples.

That is the reason why they are more ours that those that barely have a judicial relation to the country, but that alienate it, humiliate it, mock it. The Motherland is in its roots, nailed to this land forever. In the miners that are being mowed down by the scythe of oligarchic insensitivity; in the peasants that still are unable to reap the grain of freedom; in the men and women that suffer exploitation. In all of them, in all those who struggle, in all those who feel the need to change Bolivia in order to conquer collective happiness, without limits nor boundaries, without selfishness nor jails. In all of them lives the Motherland, because it is built with their hands, with their sweat, with their blood,

That is why, here at La Higuera, twenty years after the crime, we women and men, young and old, believers and unbelievers, declare:

"—Our boundless admiration for Ernesto Che Guevara and his brave ones, who fought a battle to defeat death and were successful.

"—Our deepest adherence to the human aspiration to freedom, to dignity and abundance for all.

"—Our unitary decision of preserving and multiplying the values of consequence, of human authenticity that from La Higuera sheds their light for all men.

"—Our irrevocable decision to fight, above all things, for the emancipation and the happiness of our Motherland, independently of creeds, of the temporary differences, of slight disputes.

"Here, with the emotion of sharing the epic of the life and death of Guevara and his heroes, with the maturity demanded by history, we sow our commitment of incorruptible consequence with the aspirations of our people.

"Here at La Higuera, twenty years after his death, we proclaim his heroic life as the good tidings exemplarily displayed at all the courses of struggle, of collective construction.

"Such will be our homage. It is not a simple episodic offering, but the definition of an unrenounceable principle: the human consequence that has neither time nor space, which must be the way of existence of all men.

"La Higuera, October 8, 1987."

The CIA still against Che

The CIA fears Che's body

The CIA and the Bolivian military high command maintained the secret of the events during and after the combat on October 8, 1967 at Quebrada del Yuro: the capture of Commander Ernesto Che Guevara, the source of the order to assassinate him, his murder at the La Higuera school, the moving of the corpse to Vallegrande and his burial in a common grave by the side of the airport's runway. In the course of thirty years, secrets were revealed little by little. One of the most guarded was the one related to the burial place of Commander Ernesto Che Guevara and his comrades.

Since 1967, the official version was that Che had died from his wounds in combat. The military forged the death certificate and lied when they declared that the body had been cremated and its ashes scattered in the jungle. They feared that his grave could become a place of pilgrimage and veneration for revolutionaries and, because of Bolivian customs, a sanctuary.

In the course of time, numberless witnesses denounced the crime, the perpetrators, the CIA's participation and the possible location of the burial site. Even without knowing the exactl place where his remains were, the Bolivian people turned Vallegrande and La Higuera into centers of veneration and pilgrimage where they continually paid silent homage and believers transformed the place into a sanctuary.

New revelations about the place where Che was buried

During our stay in Bolivia from 1983 to 1987 we collected documents, photographs, objects, and the testimonials of several of participants in the events, among them Generals Gary Prado Salmón, Mario Vargas Salinas and Arnaldo Saucedo Parada, and Colonels Miguel Ayoroa and Rubén Sánchez. We also collected data supplied by Dr. Walter Guevara Arce, Minister of Foreign Relations under Barrientos; by Dr. Mario Agramont, one of the chiefs of Intelligence of the 4th Division at Camiri; by war correspondents; by Dr. Moisés Abraham, a Vallegrande physician; and by former CIA agents. We also had access to several archives, among them General Joaquín Zenteno Anaya's.

In late 1986, General Arnaldo Saucedo Parada, then chief of Intelligence of the Army's 8th Division stationed at Vallegrande, published the book *Don't Shoot, I'm Che.* On pages 140-141 he wrote:

"At Vallegrande the body remained all night on the 9th and all day on the 10th, waiting mostly for an Argentinean commission that was coming to identify it. On the afternoon of the 9th, Lieutenant Colonel of the Police Roberto Quintanilla took several set of fingerprints (...) On the evening of the 10th, seeing that the Argentinean identifying commission had not arrived, it was decided that the seven bodies would be buried, for decomposition was setting in. The aforementioned Lieut. Col. Quintanilla brought some dentists plaster and made a death mask of Che that came out perfect, to which all hairs from the beard were stuck. Che's face was devoid of any hair and eyebrows. Immediately he said that he had orders from Minister of the Interior Arguedas to cut off the corpse's head and hands and take them to La Paz. At that moment I strictly forbid that the body be desecrated any more, which to me as a Catholic I considered sacred. He insisted that probably Arguedas was following orders from General Barrientos. I still refused and went to Colonel Zenteno, who was in his hotel. We went with Quintanilla and there it was agreed that only the hands would be cut off, for the purpose of identification, which was done by Dr. Moisés Abraham.

"Dr. José Martínez Caso did not want to perform the autopsy, saying that it was useless, but Quintanilla insisted until he convinced him (...)

"Since I wanted to go to bed because I did not feel well and was tired, at 2:00 a.m. on October 11, I warned the doctors that I would hold them responsible if the head was cut off. They asked me to say it in the presence of Quintanilla, which I did and later went to my quarters.

"The next day the corpses were gone. I asked about them and I was told that Lieutenant Colonel Sélich had taken them during the night for burying. It did not call my attention, for he was in charge of that funereal task, as he had been with those at Vado del Yeso and Abra del Picacho. Neither did I ask about the site, because Sélich had told me that they were at the cemetery. The exact reports were made by Colonel Zenteno to the Army Command."

In early 1987, General Gary Prado Salmón published his book *The Sacrificed Guerrilla*. On pages 203-204 he wrote: "The forces of the left, overwhelmed and depleted due to the failure of the guerrilla, say nothing and some attempts at paying homage Che do not prosper, so they look for other means to tarnish the image attained by the Armed Forces, and paradoxically the authorities themselves clear the way to this campaign with their improvisations, divergences and lack of seriousness.

"The first criticism appears when it is not clearly said what was done with the body of the guerrilla chief. While the rest of the bodies were buried at the Vallegrande Cemetery, the corpse of the guerrilla chief is taken to an isolated place of the city in the early morning hours on the 11th, and an officer is appointed to cremate the remains until nothing is left of the guerrilla. The mission is accomplished and the process took two days, but the division commander, questioned by the press, simply indicates that it has been buried in a secure place, thus leaving the event open to speculations that range from the transportation of the body to the United States for more identification tests, to the version that it has been made to disappear because the remains were not Che Guevara's. Confusion increases when the commander in chief admits to the press that the body has been cremated, which sparks off new commentaries, for neither in Vallegrande nor in the rest of the country there was an appropriate facility for cremating bodies, a reason to doubt the claim and the procedure."

All information gave different data and in some, like the latter, in which there were contradictory declarations where on one hand it was claimed that the body had been cremated, and on the other that in Vallegrande and in the whole country there were no appropriate facilities to cremate a body. Also it was said that the rest of the guerrillas were buried in the cemetery, which obviously was not true.

On May, 1987, General Mario Vargas Salinas published the book *Che, Myth and Reality*. On page 18 he wrote: "Dr. Ernesto Guevara La Serna lies interred on Bolivian soil. This is an unquestionable truth and we will not linger on details."

In 1989 we published our book *De Ñacahuasú a La Higuera* (From Ñacahuasú to La Higuera). The broadening of data obtained and collection of others from several private and public sources, documents, military reports and the testimonials of the townspeople where the guerrilla operated, allowed us to write about different places where there was evidence that some of the comrades that fought with Che had been buried. In relation to *Tuma*, on page 281 we wrote: "The peasants from those places remember every detail, every fact, every word. They know Tuma as 'Che's son', and they speak of him as someone still present. They told us that after the guerrilla left for Samaipata, the *tatús* dug Tuma out, and the first that saw him were Román González and Andrés Yépez. Then the 'Army came to see' and then in a helicopter to identify him. The military said that it was a Brazilian guerrilla.

"Several peasants buried him right there by the Dry Lake, no more than twenty meters away from where the guerrillas had buried him, deep enough, so the *tatús* could not dig him out. All are respectful of the area, because Tuma was Che's son."

In 1989 CIA agent Félix Rodríguez Mendigutía, together with John Weisman, published *Warrior in the Shadow* in the United States, a book that received wide press coverage.

The main ideas of the CIA agent that was present when Che was murdered were widely spread by several news agencies. The book was published in several languages.

In the part related to the assassination and disappearance of Che's body, Félix Rodríguez claims that on October 9, 1967, at 7 a.m. he flew from the Vallegrande airport to La Higuera in a small helicopter with Colonel Zenteno Anaya and pilot Jaime Niño de

Guzmán. The flight took some thirty minutes. He says that at seven thirty they landed on a piece of open ground near La Higuera and he and Colonel Zenteno went to the place was Che was held isolated at the school. Rodriguez stood face to face with one of his greatest enemies.

He said that around ten in the morning he was able to make radio contact and send a coded message to the CIA. Later on he received a telephone call from Vallegrande and he was instructed to eliminate Che. Rodríguez writes that he spoke to Zenteno Anaya and informed him of the telephone call and the serious consequences that it could have. He claims in his book: "I insisted that the instructions that I had received from the United States government was to try to keep the guerrilla leader alive under any circumstances. I knew that the United States had helicopters and planes ready to evacuate Che to Panama, where he would be interrogated, and keeping him alive was of prime importance."

The CIA agent expressed that after the order given by telephone was carried out, he took the body to Vallegrande and narrates an episode that he classified as "curious":

"In the case that followed the death, it emerged from the decision by General Ovando Candia of preserving concrete proof and evidence of Che's death, in case Fidel Castro denied the whole episode. What the Chief of the Bolivian General staff wanted was to cut off Che's head and keep it, after a conservation treatment. Fortunately they were able to convince him that the act was improper and it was suggested to him that perhaps a surgically removed finger would be evidence enough.

"Ovando's answer was instantaneous: he ordered that both of Che's hands be cut and preserved. He also ordered that the body be destroyed.

"I returned to Santa Cruz the same night where Jim, my CIA contact, was waiting for me, and I told him my story again [...]"

On the first edition of our book *The CIA against Che* we revealed the results of the historical investigation carried out in Bolivia, when we interviewed over 300 people: military officers and government officials, as well as Carlos Cortez, Colonel Andrés Sélich's driver, people closely linked to the main characters of these events. We had access to recorded tapes of the CIA Station in La Paz and interviewed several of the townspeople and authorities at Vallegrande.

In relation to the place where Che and his comrades were buried—Alberto Fernández Montes de Oca, Orlando Pantoja Tamayo, René Martínez Tamayo, Simeón Cuba Sanabria, Aniceto Reinaga Gordillo and Juan Pablo Chang Navarro Lévano, we wrote the following on page 153:

"The body was taken in a jeep to the Pando Regiment barracks in Vallegrande. It was 2 a.m., October 11.

"The military had four gasoline tanks for the cremation, but they were unable to do it because it was close to daybreak. They also were concerned about the reaction of the townspeople of Vallegrande and about the presence of foreign correspondents. These two factors were decisive and the body was buried in the same ditch made with a tractor for the rest of the guerrillas. Che's body was carried by Andrés Sélich and Major Walter Flores.

"Information collected gave two probable burial sites for the guerrillas, one in a plot behind the dormitory at the Pando Regiment barracks, and the other besides the runway at Vallegrande's airport, a few meters from the head of the landing strip. Both sites are 200 meters apart. Nevertheless, the Bolivian Army maintained the official version that Che had been cremated and his ashes scattered in the jungle."

On page 158 it can be read that guerrillas who died in combat (Bolivians Jaime Arana –Chapaco—, and Francisco Huanca – Pablito—, Cuban Octavio de la Concepción –Moro—, and Peruvian Lucio Galván) were taken to Vallegrande by helicopter.

"At six o'clock a dump truck picked up the bodies and left en route to Guadalupe, to Vicente Zavala's hacienda, where they were secretly buried."

There are also references to possible places where other guerrillas were buried. Both in this book and in From Ñacahuasú to La Higuera, we claim that the group of the rearguard, of which Coco Peredo and Tania were part, was buried in Vallegrande.

In August 1993 the book Che in Bolivia, by Bolivian writer and journalist Carlos Soria Galvarro, was presented in La Paz. It discussed the different versions published about Che's murder and the possible destinations of the corpse. Among the versions mentioned is the one that we published in The CIA against Che.

In October of that same year, as part of the tributes to Che on the occasion of the 26th anniversary of his assassination, an important debate on the issue was held at the Greater University of San Andrés in La Paz. On October 8 General Luis Antonio Reque Terán, the former commander of the 4th Army Division at Camiri, assured that Che was buried in Vallegrande. The press published his declaration. Reuters news agency reported from La Paz:

"A member of the Bolivian military high command, that on this date twenty six years ago ordered Ernesto Che Guevara's execution, assured that the remains of the revolutionary physician will never be found [...]

"[...] Che was executed on October 9, 1967 by order of the military high command and of Bolivian president General René Barrientos [...]

"Reque Terán thus became the first member of the Bolivian military leaders that confirms the execution of the Argentinean medical doctor `[...]

"The Bolivian army had officially maintained since 1967 that Ernesto Guevara had died in combat [...]

"Reque Terán denied versions about the destination of Che's body, exhibited on October 10. He said that the remains of the Argentinean-Cuban revolutionary were not cremated, as it was thought for some time, nor thrown from a helicopter into the jungle, as it also was said at the time. 'I know, from several indications, that Che was buried at a place that nobody knows at present, for all that knew are dead'.

"The elderly general recalled some names that knew of Che's place of burial and mentioned, among others, General Barrientos, who died in 1969 in a helicopter accident while still president; General Juan José Torres, then Chief of Staff of the Armed forces and murdered in his Buenos Aires exile in 1976; General Joaquín Zenteno Anaya, former commander, 8th Division, that fought Che, murdered in Paris in 1976 when he was the Bolivian ambassador in France; and Colonel Andrés Sélich, former commander of the Vallegrande Engineers Battalion, who was killed in 1973 by torturers while undergoing interrogation at the Ministry of Interior."

General Reque Terán revelations caused different commentaries and contradictions. Bolivian Minister of Foreign Relations Guillermo Bedregal said that the body should be disinterred and delivered to his family. The military high command sent an energetic answer to Minister Bedregal that the body had been cremated. With these declarations, once again the different contradictory versions were closed for the Bolivian press.

Old and new information on the place where it is said the Heroic Guerrilla was buried

As it can be seen, many countered versions and real or false testimonials have been disseminated through different means, creating confusion and hindering the objective analysis of the events. The Bolivian press has reported close to seventy versions, among them that Che was buried in ten different sites of the Lord of Malta Hospital at Vallegrande; at the cemetery together with Tania; that the body had been taken to La Paz, to the Panama Canal, and even to the United States, where it had been frozen; and the most insistent one, that it had been cremated.

From November, 1995, several old conjectures and some new ones flooded the news media and created great expectations, given the possibility that Che's remains could be found. Considering those precedents we believe to be useful the inclusion in this book of a chronology of the most important elements, published by the press, and related to the search of the remains and its results.

On November 15, 1995, Bolivian journalist Ted Córdova Claure wrote for the newspaper *La Razón* an article in which he claimed that General Mario Vargas Salinas had revealed to him that the body of Ernesto Che Guevara was buried in a common grave at Vallegrande. The information says in one of its parts:

"LA PAZ.— Che Guevara is still at Vallegrande; his remains are buried in a place known by a former top army officer. In a conversation at his Florida home in the outskirts of Santa Cruz, retired General Mario Vargas Salinas said clearly and sincerely to me: it is time to end this mystery. Time has passed. We live in other times.

"On August 31, 1967 Vargas Salinas was the protagonist of the ambush at Vado del Yeso, on the Masicuri River [...]

"The time has come to reveal where Che is buried, and I know it, of course, because another officer who has already died and I were commissioned for that task. Of course, there is also the driver of the dump truck and those who helped to cover the common grave.

"A common grave?" I asked, somewhat incredulous.

"Yes, there were six bodies that we took in the dump truck and that we buried. One of them was Che.

"Vargas idea is that the government, and of course, the Armed Forces, should be the ones to decide what must be done. But he believes that there is no sense in letting speculations or versions about where he is buried run rampant, or that the body was cremated or that it was stolen.

"We spoke about the possibility of going public, and even of the consequences. For example, that it could provoke the creation of a sanctuary and even the licit exploitation of promoting a place for historical tourism, which in a certain manner already exists.

"But Vargas' main argument is that there is no sense in keeping so much mystery, a situation already overcome that has healed with time and that will serve better to explain the epic of the Bolivian army and the one of the famous guerrilla, who is definitely buried in Vallegrande."

The information, revealed in La Paz had slight repercussion in other capitals of the world.

On November 21 US journalist Jon Lee Anderson wrote in *The New York Times* a piece presenting as previously unknown the claims that General Mario Vargas Salinas had revealed to Ted Córdova Claure, although Anderson added that he knew the exact place where Che was buried.

In this manner he was advancing one of the chapters of a book he was writing on Che and that later on was published in Spanish by the same publishing house that had released the book by CIA agent Félix Rodríguez.

On November 22, 1995, *The New York Times'* piece was picked up by all news media in Bolivia and other capitals of the world. The newspaper *Presencia* pointed out that Anderson had claimed that "Speaking the truth will help closing the episode of Che."

The news was turned into a veritable information explosion covered by all international news media. In Bolivia it caused different reactions.

President Gonzalo Sánchez de Lozada declared to the press that there was a possibility of a search and of delivering Che's remains to his relatives.

General Gary Prado Salmón said that Che's body had been partially burned and "what was left of it must have been buried with the other four guerrillas."

On November 23, 1995, Vice Minister of Interior Hugo San Martín announced that the government would ask Vargas Salinas to make an official declaration to the press, so that Che's remains could be found, dug out and delivered to his family.

Loyola Guzmán, a member of the urban support network for the guerrilla, arrived in Vallegrande on November 29, 1995 as president of the Association of Relatives of Martyrs and the Disappeared for National Liberation, and as representative of relatives of those fallen in Ñacahuasú. Guzmán told the press that during the different dictatorial regimes in Bolivia there had been around 400 missing persons and announced the arrival of Alejandro Incháurregui, head of the Argentinean team of Forensic Anthropology that would lead the excavation and exhumation.

A Special Commission created by President Sánchez de Lozada left for the city of Santa Cruz to interview Generals Mario Vargas Salinas and Gary Prado Salmón. Vargas Salinas denied he had said that he knew the exact location of the burial site, but ratified that Che had been buried at some place near the Vallegrande landing strip. He added that together with Officer Guido Flores, already deceased, he had signed the certificate of burial and that Che had not been cremated. Vargas refuted Jon Lee Anderson's claims and promised to go with the Commission to Vallegrande to establish the site.

General Gary Prado Salmón declared that on October 19, 1967, Vargas Salinas had told him that Che's body had been cremated on October 10 and the remains buried.

The Commission left for Vallegrande on November 30 and were accompanied by General Mario Vargas Salinas and a tractor driver who identified himself as Sabino Álvarez. Vargas Salinas made a tour through all the places where he had been on that 1967 night, and finally said that he did not know the exact place.

Searching for the site of Che's burial

General Vargas' claims were disallowed, which caused harsh commentaries. He was so questioned that he was dubbed a liar, that his words were for propaganda purposes and personal prominence, and that he had received a sum of money for the data he had given to the US journalist. There even was speculation that Anderson had previously gotten him drunk with whisky, to which General Vargas was very partial.

On December 1, 1995, the morning program on Bolivian Channel 2, hosted by popular Cristina Corrales, presented journalist Ted Córdova, who referred to the news that he had published on November 15, 1995, pointing out that it attained national credibility only when it was published in the US by *The New York Times*. Córdova valued that fact as evidence of the existence of a small town mentality. In several countries of Latin America it is identified with a colonized mind, a lack of self-esteem, inferiority complex and subjection, giving more credit to versions from abroad, particularly from the United States.

On December 5 the first news was published about the finding of human bones five kilometers away from the airport, at a place known as Cañada de Arroyo, on the farm of Vicente Zavala. The press reported that the farmer himself had been the source of the news.

On December 13 two graves were dug out and the remains of three guerrillas were found.

On December 15 Dr. Jorge González, Head of the Cuban Institute of Forensic Medicine, arrived in Vallegrande in representation of the families of Cuban guerrillas and of Tamara *Tania* Bunker's parents. On the same day the finding of three bodies at Cañada de Arroyo was confirmed.

In late December a lawyer named Ricardo Rojo, author of a slanderous book titled *My Friend Che*, declared to France Press in Buenos Aires that Guevara's body had been discarded at a practically inaccessible place.

On Friday, December 29, the daily *Granma* published the full details of the search for the remains of Che and his comrades.

After the New Year holidays, on January 8, 1996, the search for the bodies at the Vallegrande landing strip restarted. On January 12 the remains of Jaime Arana Campero, *Chapaco,* were delivered to his sister Marta. It was announced that DNA analysis would be made in order to identify the other two skeletons found at Cañada de Arroyo. On March 15 a fourth one was found.

On June 21, 1996, the body of guerrilla Carlos Coello (Tuma) was found and taken to the Japanese Hospital at Santa Cruz de la Sierra.

311

Granma printed an article on the front page of its Wednesday, June 26, 1996 edition with the title: "IN CUBA THE REMAINS OF CHE'S GUERRILLA CARLOS COELLO (TUMA)."

"The mortal remains of the Cuban combatant of Che's guerrilla Carlos Coello (Tuma) arrived from Bolivia by airplane to our country.

"The finding and exhumation of Carlos Coello's remains took place at Tejeria, 135 kilometers away from the Bolivian department of Santa Cruz, where he was located last week at a place known as Laguna Seca."

The remains of Che and six of his comrades are found in a common grave

On Thursday, July 3, 1997, *Granma* gave wide coverage on its front page to the search and finding of the remains of the guerrillas:

"The sequence of the recent findings has been the following:

"—On June 28 at 9:00 hours the remains of the first cadaver were found. From that moment on work was intense on the part of Cuban experts and Bolivian workers, who were joined by three members of the Argentinean team of forensic anthropology that had worked in 1995 and 1996 in the exhumation and identification of remains of guerrillas fallen in Bolivia.

"—At noon, June 29, after tracing a piece of cloth, apparently a fragment of a green nylon cape, a second body is found.

"On June 30, around 15:00 hours, the excavation is deepened and a third body appears.

"—At 9:30 hours, July 1, indications of a fourth one are located and discovered.

"—Working at the same site, at 15:15 hours new remains appear, and given its position it is believed to be a fifth guerrilla.

"—Around 15:35 hours the presence of a sixth one is established.

"—Almost at finishing time a cloth fragment is detected. After digging at the site a long bone, darker than the previous ones, is found at some distance of the piece of fabric.

"—With much difficulty digging is done around it using dentistry tools, and around 17:00 hours of July 1, the conclusion is reached that the remains belong to a seventh guerrilla.

"—Now it is imperative to finish in the next few days the complete excavation of the burial site to exhume all the remains, which must be done with extreme care.

"—Subsequently the anthropological identification will be done.

"The research team that is taking part in the search, exhumation and identification includes Argentinean forensic anthropologists Patricia Bernardi, Alejandro Incháurregui and Carlos Somigliana, Cuban forensic scientists Jorge González and Héctor Soto, and Cuban archeologist Roberto Rodríguez.

"As soon as new elements are available they will be reported in timely fashion, conscious of the deep sensitiveness with which our people has received always, since 1967, any information linked to Che and his comrades in arms."

On Saturday, July 12, 1997, *Granma* headlined the news in its front page:

"INFORMATION TO THE PEOPLE. COMMANDER ERNESTO CHE GUEVARA'S REMAINS IDENTIFIED. COMRADES WHO FELL WITH HIM ALSO IDENTIFIED. SOON THE MORTAL REMAINS OF THE HEROIC COMBATANTS WILL BE BROUGHT TO CUBA."

New elements of CIA Operations against Che are made public

After thirty years, the remains of Che and of his comrades emerged as phoenixes from the entrails of the earth of Vallegrande to continue their battle on behalf of the dispossessed of the world.

Meanwhile, new elements about the role of the CIA against the Heroic Guerrilla were made public and new disinformation campaigns were launched against him. But as Cuba's National Hero José Martí said, "Truth, once awakened, does not sleep again."

On July 20, 1997, former CIA officer Phillip Agee made declarations published by journalist Héctor Igarza in the London monthly *Noticias, Latin America*. On its front page of its August, 1997 was a large headline: "FORMER OFFICER CLAIMS: THE CIA KILLED CHE."-

Phillip Agee worked for the Central Intelligence Agency for twelve years, all of them against Cuba, under diplomatic cover in Quito, Montevideo and Mexico City.

His first book —*Inside the Company: CIA Diary* (1975)— caused a huge scandal. It was a conclusive, detailed and sensational exposé of many of the undercover operations of that espionage agency in Latin America.

A great campaign was organized against Agee. Richard Helms, CIA Director at the time, ordered his intimidation. His successor, William Colby, tried to have him indicted for revealing secrets related to national security. George Bush, Sr., when he was the agency's Director, tried to frame him for the death of Richard Welch, Head of the CIA Station in Athens.

In his declarations, the former CIA officer said that the agency ordered Che Guevara's assassination, and that since 1959 it had been planning the destruction of the Cuban revolution because of its example.

Agee said that CIA stations in the region had as its number one mission to obtain information of the actions that Che was preparing, due to his influence on Latin American guerrillas, a reason for having him always pinpointed, and claimed: "The CIA opened a file on Che in 1953 in Guatemala, where the young medical doctor had arrived in search of a job, months before Jacobo Árbenz government's overthrow. There he was related to the popular militias that demanded weapons to fight against US intervention. When he later traveled to Mexico and joined Fidel and Raúl Castro, their concern was sickening."

In Havana, journalist Heriberto Rosabal published in the *Juventud Rebelde* daily an interview with Phillip Agee. Rosabal reminded Agee of a recent declaration in which he had expressed that for the CIA Che Guevara was the most feared person, and that the Agency had assassinated him.

"According to my experience and memory", Agee answered, "I remember very well that the CIA as an institution feared Che, and the reason was that the agency understood very well objective conditions in Latin America and also knew Che's beliefs in relation to armed struggle. The Vietnam War was raging and the US wanted to avoid another insurgency in Latin America at all costs. And that was exactly what Che was promoting, organizing these guerrillas.

"That is why the CIA feared Che so much, because of his ideas and practice, aside from his example, and that makes me believe that the CIA knew that if there was someone who could carry out the creation of a continental struggle, that person was Che.

314

"In Montevideo the CIA Station set a trap, as it also did in all of Latin America, in case that he came to the continent through there. In 1965, I believe it was that year, Che disappeared and the chief of operations against Cuba in the CIA toured Latin America, insisting on control of all travelers, because he did not know where Che was and it was thought that he might return to Latin America.

"The problem was that there was no photograph of a beardless Che. So a CIA artist drew a picture of him without a beard. When we received it, it was exactly as a photograph. The CIA Station in Uruguay gave a copy to every member of the team that it had at the Montevideo airport. They were told to brand that image in their brains and not to forget it. Actually they were more motivated by smuggling than with such a mission. In my case, I never knew how Che got to Bolivia, whether it was through Montevideo, Sao Paulo or some other place. As we now know, he was not detected, and the CIA took months to find out that Che was in Bolivia.

"In relation to the CIA killing Che, I don't mean they pulled the trigger, because it is common knowledge that Sergeant Mario Terán was the perpetrator, but it is known that the CIA had a central role in surrounding him, tracking him and detecting him with airplanes, infrared photographic cameras, coordinating with Special Forces in the training of Bolivian Rangers. Also there was the participation of individuals such as Cuban born Félix Rodríguez, among others."

The former CIA officer added that on the morning of October 9, after Che spent the night guarded by Bolivian soldiers, Félix Rodríguez arrived as CIA representative together with Bolivian officers. He was one of many that were working with the military and the Ministry of the Interior with the order to eliminate Che; that Rodríguez had been there, had photographed the diary, tried unsuccessfully to question him and was witness to the assassination.

Additionally Agee said: "There is a controversy about the source of the order to assassinate Che, because everybody wants to blame someone else. There are many indications that the order came from Washington, and that means a decision in which the CIA participated."

A new disinformation campaign was beginning to brew when on July 20, 1997 CIA agent Félix Rodríguez claimed in Miami that the Cuban government had replaced Che's body with another with the same anatomical characteristics and with its hands cut. This preposterous declaration was picked up by the Spanish newspaper

ABC, and on reporting it on July 24, 1997, said that former CIA agent Félix Rodríguez had questioned that the remains found in a landing strip in Vallegrande were those of the Cuban-Argentinean guerrilla. The newspaper claimed that according to Rodríguez Che's body, as well as those of the other guerrillas, had been buried in a common grave in the middle of the landing strip, some 500 meters away from the place they had been found, and that those remains had been substituted by the Cuban government for political reasons.

The former CIA agent's declarations had an immediate repercussion in the media, especially in the reactimary press. It found particular fertile ground in Argentina.

However, on August 17, 1997, the Buenos Aires daily *El Clarín* published an article by journalist Rogelio García Lupo under the title "Intrigue in Miami", as well as an interview with Argentinean forensic anthropologist Alejandro Incháurregui, who identified Che's remains.

García Lupo mentioned a letter sent from Miami, Florida to different addressees, signed by Gustavo Villoldo Sampera, another former CIA agent that participated in operations at Vallegrande against Che. The letters, dated on April, 1997, allegedly revealed where Che's remains were, but actually it was trying to impede the success of the mission or cast doubts in case Che's body were found

In relation to the letters, Garcìa Lupo wrote:

"This documentation agreed on the Vallegrande landing strip, although it pinpointed the exact location where to dig some 200 meters away from the site where they were actually found. It added another wrong detail: Che's remains had been buried besides another two bodies, and not with six of his comrades, as he was finally found. In any case, the person volunteering the information had participated in the guerrilla events and was offering details. It was not an involuntary mistake.

"The source turned out to be a Cuban born CIA agent, Gustavo Villoldo, who indeed was a member of the team that the US intelligence agency had sent to Bolivia at the time Che's guerrilla began operations. Villoldo used the cover name of 'Eduardo González' and was in charge of interrogating Jorge Vázquez Viaña [...]

"Now Villoldo was spontaneously offering tips about the place where Che's body had been buried, with a gross error margin that looks unexplainable in view of his record thirty years ago. But it is reasonable to think that his discrepancy with the place and number of bodies in the burial site was for creating doubt among the public on whether the remains were Che's or not."

"The CIA's battle against Che is still on, even after his death", concluded García Lupo."

In relation to the interview with the Argentinean forensic scientist, he said that for Incháurregui there were no doubts about the identification of Che's remains. He pointed out that the only person that had questioned it was the CIA agent that took part in the persecution and death of Ernesto Guevara.

"The bulk of the verifications that you made", García Lupo asked Incháurregui, are they enough to be completely certain that they are Che's remains?

"Absolutely," answered Incháurregui

"This former CIA agent that says that the remains could have been substituted...

"In the first place, we use scientific methods that anyone may verify. The identification of Che's remains was possible due to the abundance of pre-mortem data. We had X-rays of all his remaining teeth; we had craniometrical measurements, we had photographs. He had a tropometric and odontological file made before leaving Cuba, so that his remains could be identified in case he died. That was invaluable data."

"An exceptional data bank."

"Exceptional. We also had some of his features, such as the protuberance of his superciliary ridges. Also an autopsy. An autopsy was performed on Che thirty years ago, and the lesions match those in the bone remains. We even found the wear of the upper and lower right incisors from biting the pipestem, and it was the only skeleton whose hands had been amputated.

"About DNA testing. How can it affect the credibility of the report?

"DNA testing would have been an exaggeration. The condemnation comes from a CIA agent, not from a scientist.

"Do you think there is a campaign in that sense?

"I wish it were, because it would be very easy to refute it."

The reactionary mainstream media continued to spread different slanderous elements about Commander Guevara, fabricated by

CIA agents or writers and journalists in the service of the agency, attempting to deteriorate Che's image and prestige, and make the world believe that the agency and the US government had nothing to do with the crime, that they wanted to keep him alive to take him to a base in Panama to interrogate him, and that the assassins who planned and perpetrated the killing were Bolivians. Some of those writers traveled to Cuba several times or lived in the country, in order to legitimate their slanders and disinformation.

On September 28, 1997, *Juventud Rebelde* published an interview by René Tamayo León, translated by Víctor Pineda, with jurists Michael Ratner and Michael Steven Smith, active members of the US National Lawyers' Guild. Both had access to FBI secret files and found that in the 1950s that agency compiled a list of people suspicious of being communists. The list reached 450,000 names, and one of them was Ernesto Guevara de la Serna. By law, the FBI should not be involved in intelligence work, a role pertaining to the CIA. The FBI compiled the list from its own data, but particularly from the CIA and from other twenty espionage agencies of the US government.

Together with the CIA, the FBI was very active in the organization of the plot against Che, as evidenced by part of the agency's declassified documents and included in the book *Che Guevara and the FBI*. The documents compiled by the two US lawyers prove how thousands of Latin Americans that are opposed in any manner to Washington policies are under unscrupulous surveillance. Assassination is not ruled out.

Michael Ratner pointed out that after a legal suit for declassification they finally forced the FBI to send them two boxes with documents –about a thousand— that ranged from 1954 to 1968, but he assured it was not everything, that it was probably a minimum, and most of the lines were crossed out. Additionally, there are other unreleased documents that go beyond Che's death. Ratner wants to obtain those too, especially documents that prove that US intelligence was trying to assassinate Che. He said that the CIA was extremely interested in any physical weakness Che might have, allegedly to exploit it in an eventual plot. For that reason the agency focused its attention on Che's asthma and his need of inhalators, and tried to find ways to block his supply of medicine or to administer poison through it. Ratner pointed out

318

that in 1964 the FBI requested a set of Che's fingerprints and he wondered if the petition was related to a plot for killing him and be certain that they had the right person.

Michael Steven Smith said that when Guevara was assassinated, two Cuban born CIA agents were present. Both Eduardo González and Félix Rodríguez had been in the CIA's payroll since the 1950s. Rodríguez served the agency in Cuba, El Salvador and Iran, and on retiring received a plaque from the CIA for his service. According to Smith, on the following day of Che's assassination, the Bolivian Ministry of Foreign Relations reported the event to the CIA.

He added that Bolivian troops that had captured and assassinated Che were trained and overseen by US soldiers brought from Vietnam for that purpose. Although the perpetrators of Che's assassination were the Bolivian military, the order, came from the CIA. The agency also paid for the electronic equipment installed on planes to track and locate the guerrillas.

He also said that the CIA and the FBI plus other twenty sources— Army, Navy, Air Force, Treasury Department, practically all government agencies—were spying on him. Many were of the Radio Transmission Service, a special radio monitoring operation. They had files of his speeches, interviews, trips. All kept constant monitoring since 1954, more intense after 1959, and only lost track of him when he left for Africa. Smith says that the first signal appears in 1952, when he wanted to go to Miami, but the real tracking began in 1954 in Guatemala, during the military coup against Árbenz.

Michael Ratner claimed that the CIA supplied information to the FBI, that it had agents all over Latin America –in labor unions, in cultural associations—and since Che went to work in Guatemala at the time, the CIA immediately tracked him, and one of the notes on him is about an Argentinean medical doctor on whom a file should be opened. It was pointed out that he tried to create a resistance against the coup, and when the agency found out it was said: "The best we can do is make war against this man."

Michael Steven Smith commented that in time the file on Che became one of the biggest in history. US espionage against Latin Americans was and still is massive. Many US agencies share information and plot to assure that only leaders acceptable to Washington ascend to power. And in that task they have as main allies the intelligence services of the region.

Ratner added that Che was also spied on during the Cuban struggle against the Batista dictatorship, although he had no evidence of who the informers were. They knew that among them were people from the press, and that many of the cards about the time that the FBI declassified had many parts crossed out, so maybe the names of the informers are there; that another method was the use of US journalists that went to Sierra Maestra to interview Fidel and also talked to Che. When the journalist returned to Havana they went to the US Embassy and were debriefed. Not all journalists had such a negative role, and he cited the case of Herbert Matthews, who after writing an objective report almost lost his job.

One of the documents made by the CIA, said Ratner, included Che's physical description, his upbringing, his political beliefs, his relation to Fidel, his reading habits and a discussion whether he was a communist or not. His favorite readings are also noted and he was described as "quite intellectual for a Latino." He was considered another regular Latin American that did not agree with the United States because he was young and came form a poor backward country.

Michael Smith added that according to the documents Che's hostility had no base, because it was a rather common attitude among young people to have the emotional hostility of a nationalist from a small, backward and weak country toward a big, rich and powerful country.

There was the view on declassified documents that Che had no personal interests, that he fought for the liberation of peoples in an unconditional manner, and that he had no ambitions of personal power. Additionally he was thought to be an extraordinarily brave and fearless man who had the loyalty of his subordinates, and an intellectual who read on many subjects besides politics.

Smith claimed that the CIA had a spy, probably a US journalist who slept besides Che for a week while waiting for an interview with Fidel. The agent wrote that in the evenings Che smoked a big fat cigar and read to soldiers. This person was so interested in every detail that he even reported Che's bathing habits.

According to Ratner, one of the strategies of the intelligence service was the use of the press to disseminate adverse opinions against Cuba. Subsequently the United States would express its intention to have better relations with the island, but that conditions there would not allow it.

One of the last documents obtained by Ratner and Smith included a summary of eleven pages of a private meeting in July, 1968 between the *New York Times* editor and Richard Goodwin, President Lyndon B. Johnson's advisor and speechwriter. Goodwin wanted the newspaper to print an article on the possibility of driving a wedge between Moscow and Havana, and cited several examples of Fidel Castro's opposition to Soviet style of communism.

Smith pointed out that with the exception of small progressive magazines, in the US, Che is presented as a puritanical murderer. His ideology was rejected and he was feared, and through the press the government tried to plant in the minds of readers that revolutions were obsolete. It wanted to bury Che's thoughts with his body, but a change was taking place that although slowly it pointed to the future.

He said that present day teenagers are rethinking their thoughts, they are not prejudiced by the ghosts of the Cold War, and it is possible that they might know Che better. Lincoln said that a nation that enslaves another one can not be free itself, Smith concluded.

He predicted that although Che had been dead for thirty years, and almost fifty years had passed since US espionage began to follow Che's footsteps, with this rebirth of his ideals they will reopen his file, if it ever was closed.

Ratner said that a few weeks before, he had obtained a document sent to the Agency that tried to tell who Che really was.

Due to the growing interest for his life, particularly among young people all over the world, US espionage services may have been backpedaling and if they deem it necessary they would reopen the case; that *Che Guevara and the FBI* discovers to the world the manner in which his image was so insidiously persecuted. But its transcendence is based on the fact that these FBI documents say much about how the United States act and how they see Latin America.

Ratner agrees with Uruguayan journalist and writer Eduardo Galeano, on the issue of declassified documents, when he says: "Very eloquent about Washington's prejudice, its disdain and ignorance."

On the occasion of the thirty anniversary of Che's assassination in Bolivia, important political, cultural, scientific, labor, and student figures, as well as the public in general in the entire world pay homage to him. The enemies of Che and of the Cuban revolution intensified a manipulated and distorted marathon campaign of slanders that included documentaries, articles and several biographies that repeated the same CIA interests.

Most probably in a few years more documents will be declassified and we will know again how these campaigns were orchestrated, just as it happened on 1977. On December of that year *The New York Times* published a series of documents about the CIA and the media under the banner headline "A worldwide propaganda network set up and consolidated by the CIA"

UPI reported on December 28 that the newspaper "finished today the publication of a series of three articles about the penetration of the Central Intelligence Agency (CIA) in the US press, coincidentally with the beginning of hearings by a Congressional subcommittee on the subject."

In one of the articles, the *Times* claims that in past decades, during the tense period of the Cold War between the United States and the Soviet Union, the CIA had launched a huge world propaganda network using US journalists and foreign correspondents, financing newspapers and publishing books.

"The majority of the cited publications and organizations," pointed out the newspaper, "said they had no knowledge of those links. As a source of its claims, the *Times* supplies confidential information by former CIA agents or journalists that in most of the cases it does not identify.

"Among subsidiary foreign news organizations," according to the *Times*, "there were renowned publications such as *Paris Match*. Additionally, the CIA had financed newspapers, most of them English speaking ones in foreign capitals, and mentions *The Daily America,* in Rome; the *Times,* in Brussels; the *Times,* in Manila; the *World* in Bangkok; and the *Evening News,* in Tokyo. It also says the CIA had placed agents in Santiago de Chile's *South Pacific Mail,* Guyana's *Chronicle;* Haiti's *Sun*; and Caracas' *Daily Journal*.

"The CIA", continues the article, "had agents in a number of foreign news services, including Latin, the Latin American news agency operated by Reuter, and the Scandinavian organization Rithaus (...).

"Although there were CIA agents in foreign bureaus of Associated Press and United Press International, it is said that the CIA did not have one at Reuters because it is a

British agency and as such a potential target of the British Intelligence Service. But sources familiar with the situation say that occasionally the CIA borrowed British "assets" (sympathizing journalists) in Reuters in order to plant information [...]

"According to the newspaper, the CIA had also penetrated in different ways other large news organization in the US, such as television networks ABC and CBS, *Times* and *Newsweek* magazines and newspaper such as *The New Times, The Christian Science Monitor* and others, sometimes with the consent of its editors.

"The newspaper also says that the CIA had channeled propaganda through special features agencies such as Editors Press Service, whose owner was Joshua B. Powers. Powers said that it was not the case, although he had friends in the CIA, that he only remembered one occasional link with the CIA in which organization funds were paid to fund a trip of columnist Guillermo Martínez Márquez through Latin America in the 60s [...]

"According to the *Times*, the CIA had likewise funded US publications in the past, most of them related to Cuban exiled journalists through a company called Foreign Publications Inc. [...]

"In its final article published today, the *Times* refers to the connections of several US correspondents with the CIA, many times unbeknownst to their editors. It points out two kinds of connections, one based on the payment of fees and another one based on the unpaid cooperation of journalists who were partial to the agency. Among the latter it mentions the late Jules Dubois, of *The Chicago Tribune,* who was a prominent reporter on Latin American issues, and Sam Poper Brewers, a correspondent of *The New York Times* itself in the Middle East."

The New York Times articles caused a great scandal, although its revelations were no more than a confirmation of what was well known by many political analysts and observers. It is common knowledge that for certain periods and even years the CIA funded journalists, writers and social scientists so that they would write or research subjects in which the US espionage agency was interested in, or that under the cover of academic or journalistic research they would carry out specific missions.

Top bolivian military officer acknowledges motives for hiding Che's body

At Cochabamba General Luis Antonio Reque Terán was interviewed by his daughter Jeanine for the *Los Tiempos* newspaper. The piece was published on July 13, 1997. The following are excerpts from that interview:

"In your opinion, what was the reason for which the secret of Che's body has been so zealously guarded, so much so that it has given rise to a thousand speculations?

"At the time that Che was eliminated the order was to bury him in secret and that it was not to be told to anyone. So much so that only three professional Army men know the exact site of the burial.

"Who were those people?

"The Chief of Intelligence, Chief of Personnel and the Chief of Staff, 8th Division (Major Arnaldo Saucedo Parada and Coroneles Ricardo González Lock and Joaquín Zenteno Anaya, respectively.)

"Besides them, the High Command did not know it?

"Not the burying site.

"There was speculation that Che was cremated, but ongoing research does not verify it.

"We could say that empirically there was a kind of psychological war diverting information to different sources and forms of interment and disappearance of the cadaver. It was said that it was cremated, buried in one site or another, precisely to dilute the source.

"How did General Mario Salinas know and divulged the first clues that Che was buried at Vallegrande?"

"The fact that he was buried in Vallegrande was never denied. Yes, somewhere in Vallegrande. Mario Vargas said that it was at the hospital and at the landing strip, but he did not say where, because he did not know the exact place for, as I said, only three people knew of the burial site."

"Why was it necessary to hide Che's burial place?"

"To avoid what is happening now, the influx of people of the left that are attempting to turn him into the country's greatest hero."

In the interview General Reque Terán revealed the true purpose that the Bolivian military and the CIA had for lying in relation to the whereabouts of Che's remains. The confession was nothing else than the acceptance of the evaluations made by Commander in Chief Fidel Castro when he spoke on Cuban TV on October 15, 1967 about the reasons why the Bolivian military hid the Heroic Guerrillas burial site.

In that speech Fidel claimed that the assassins, knowing they were to be condemned by History, feared that the site where Che was buried would become a place of pilgrimage. They also wanted to deprive the revolutionary movement of a symbol, a site, a place. In short, they feared Che even after he was dead. Those who thought that assassinating Che and making his body disappear would end his ideas and his example were wrong: History and peoples do not forget.

On the same day that General Reque Terán's interview was published, *Presencia* reported that once the guerrillas' remains were exhumed and taken to Santa Cruz, the Vallegrande townspeople visited the grave en masse to leave lit candles and flowers, and took some earth as a memento of Che.

Che in Santa Clara, a place fit to battle for socialism

On October 17, 9997, the remains of Che and his comrades were placed in the memorial built at the city of Santa Clara. In a speech on that day Fidel said:

"Relatives of the comrades fallen in combat, guests, citizens of Villa Clara, fellow countrymen,

"It is with deeply felt emotion that we live one of those moments that are not frequent. We come not to say farewell to Che and his heroic comrades. We come to welcome them.

"I see Che and his men as reinforcements, as a detachment of invincible combatants that this time includes not only Cubans, but also Latin Americans that come to fight at our side and to write new pages of history and glory.

"Additionally I see Che as a moral giant increasingly growing, whose image, whose strength, whose influence have multiplied all over the planet.

"How can he fit under a gravestone?

"How could he fit in this whole square?

"How could he fit only in our dear but small island?

"Only in the world he dreamed about and for which he fought there is enough space for him.

"His figure will be greater as long as greater injustice, exploitation, inequality, unemployment, poverty, hunger, and destitution prevail in human society.

"The values he defended will keep rising as long as the powers of imperialism, hegemonism and interventionism keep growing at the expense of the most sacred rights of the peoples, especially of the weak, backward, and poor people that for centuries were the colonies of the West and sources of slaves.

"As long as more abuse, selfishness, alienation, discrimination of Indians, of ethnic minorities, of women immigrants exist, as long as more children are the object of sexual trade or forced to work in figures that reach the hundreds of millions, as long as more ignorance, insalubrity, insecurity, and neglect subsist, more will outshine his profound sense of humanism.

"As long as more corrupted demagogical and hypocritical politicians exist anywhere, more his example of a pure, revolutionary and consistent man will stand out.

"His personal bravery and revolutionary integrity will be more admired as long as more cowards, opportunists and traitors exist on the face of the earth; more his will of steel as long as there are others weaker in the fulfillment of their duties; more his sense of honor and dignity while more persons lack a minimum of human pride; more his faith in men while more skeptics there are; more his optimism while more pessimists exist; more his audacity while more indecisive people; more his austerity, his spirit for study and work while more lazy people squander in luxury and leisure the work of others.

"Che was a true communist and today he is an example and paradigm of revolutionaries and communists.

"Che was a teacher and a builder of men like himself. Consistent with his acts, he did what he preached and demanded of himself more than he demanded of others.

"Every time someone was needed for an official mission, he was the first to volunteer, in war or in peace. His great dreams were always subordinate to the willingness to generously give his life. Nothing was impossible for him, and what was impossible he was able to make it possible.

326

"The invasion from the Sierra Maestra through the vast and unprotected plains, and the battle of the city of Santa Clara with a few men are witnesses, among other actions, of the feats that he was capable.

"His ideas about the revolution in his native land and in the rest of South America, in spite of enormous difficulties, were possible. If he had attained them, perhaps the world would have been different today. Vietnam proved that it was possible to battle the interventionist forces of imperialism and defeat them. The Sandinistas vanquished one of the most powerful puppets of the United States. Salvadoran revolutionaries almost attained victory. In Africa apartheid was defeated, although it had nuclear weapons. China, thanks to the heroic struggle of its workers and peasants, is today one of the countries with the greatest future in the world. Hong Kong had to be returned after 150 years of occupation, undertaken to impose the drug trade to an immense country.

"Not all periods or all circumstances demand the same methods and the same tactics. But nothing will be able to halt the course of history; its objective laws have perennial validity. Che used those laws; he had an absolute faith in men. Many times the great transformers and revolutionaries of humanity did not have the privilege of seeing their dreams come true as soon as they expected or wished, but sooner or later they triumphed.

"A combatant may die, but not his ideas. What was a man of the United States government doing at the place where Che was wounded and a prisoner? Why did they believe that after killing him he would cease to exist as a combatant? He is not in La Higuera now, but he is everywhere, wherever there is a just cause to be defended. Those who wanted to eliminate or disappear him were not capable of understanding that his indelible imprint was already in History, and that his luminous gaze of a prophet would become a symbol for the poor of this world that are billions. Youngsters, children, the elderly, men and women who knew about him, the honest people of the Earth, no matter their social extraction, admire him.

"Che is waging and winning more battles than ever.

"Thank you, Che, for your history, your life and your example!

"Thank you for coming as a reinforcement in this difficult struggle that we are waging today to save the ideas for which you battled so much, to save the revolution, the Motherland and the conquests of socialism, which is a part fulfilled of the great dreams that you harbored!

"In order to accomplish this enormous feat, in order to defeat imperialist plans against Cuba, in order to resist the blockade, in order to achieve victory, we are counting on you.

"As you may see, this land that is your land, this people that is your people, this revolution that is your revolution, still raises with honor the banners of socialism.

"Welcome, heroic comrades of the reinforcement detachment! The trenches of ideas and justice that you will defend with your people, the enemy will never be able to conquer! And together we will keep on struggling for a better world!

"Onward to victory forever"

Santa Clara, October 17, 1997.